PARENTS AND CHILDREN IN HISTORY

PARENTS AND CHILDREN IN HISTORY

The Psychology of Family Life in Early Modern France

BY

DAVID HUNT

Basic Books, Inc., Publishers

NEW YORK   LONDON

© 1970 by Basic Books, Inc.
Library of Congress Catalog Card Number: 70-110772
SBN 465-05449-8
Manufactured in the United States of America
DESIGNED BY VINCENT TORRE

Sh695/347/10/29/70

To My Mother and Father

Our jealousy in seeing children appear and enjoy life when we are about to part with it makes us more grudging and strict with them. We resent it when they step on our heels as if to urge us to be gone. And if we are afraid because, to tell the truth, it is in the order of things that they can exist and live only at the expense of our existence and our life, then we should not get mixed up in the business of being fathers.

—MONTAIGNE

ACKNOWLEDGMENTS

I spent the summer of 1965 working at the Residential Treatment Center for disturbed children in Rochester, New York. From Olive Williams, Roger Lowe, Dorothy Jones, Sydney Koret, Armin Klein, and the other members of the staff, I learned a great deal about child psychology, and about myself. I also remember the children with fondness and admiration. Perhaps they were the best teachers of all; I am persuaded that in their maladaptation we find a telling and eloquent indictment of the world as it is.

This book owes a lot to the works of Erik Erikson and Philippe Ariès. During the academic year 1965–1966, I had the opportunity first to teach in Professor Erikson's undergraduate course at Harvard and then to take part in his seminar on life histories. The experience meant a great deal to me, and it has very much shaped my thinking about psychology and history. The next year was spent in Paris on a Fulbright scholarship. Two conversations with Philippe Ariès were among the more agreeable aspects of this sojourn. With uncommon patience, M. Ariès listened to my many questions (stammered in French) and provided me with numerous useful suggestions and references. I much appreciate his thoughtful assistance.

Acknowledgments

Many friends and colleagues helped with the subsequent stages of the project. In the midst of research, I had the privilege of reading part of Nancy Roelker's biography of Jeanne d'Albret, as well as Pierre Maranda's dissertation on French kinship, before these works appeared in published form. My thanks to both authors, and also to Jane Amsler for sharing with me her very interesting essay on methods of childrearing in a contemporary French community.

I should also like to thank Elizabeth Fox, Irene Brown, Robert Wheaton, and Gerald Soliday for suggestions and criticism from the perspective of their own researches on seventeenth-century Europe. In addition, I received valuable guidance from Bruce Mazlish and John Demos, who have led the way in attempts to fuse psychology and history. Virginia Demos, Lynn Lees, and Tamara Hareven all took time off from their own work to review and comment on substantial parts of the manuscript. The text further benefited from a careful reading by Mary Louise Charles.

Thanks are also due to David Maybury-Lewis, who guided my first encounters with some of the anthropological literature on kinship, and Edward Shorter, who offered a critique of parts of the manuscript, as well as advice on ways in which the issues I was raising might be related to debates within the sociological community. That my understanding in these areas remains incomplete is not the fault of my able informants.

Before the book was completed, a grant from the Social Science Research Council enabled me to study for a year (1968–1969) in the Social Relations Department at Harvard. The friends I made there taught me much about clinical psychology. I would especially like to thank Lane Conn for his pertinent criticisms of the chapters I had written on childhood development, and Richard Segal, who gave the whole manuscript an exhaustive reading and whose trenchant observations helped me to clarify a wide range of problems, from points of style to the intricacies of psychoanalytic theory.

Only people who have been through this kind of thing before can know how hard it is to offer a truly helpful criticism of someone else's manuscript, and how invaluable such assistance can be. Peter Weiler went through the whole text with me just before the publisher's deadline, and his unfailingly lucid analysis of what I was, and was not, doing added substantially to my own sense of what the book was all about. I also wish to thank Paul Robinson who at various points in the course of the project contributed a characteristically subtle critique of what I was thinking and writing. In general, I have learned more from him than from anyone I can think of, and I look back with great pleasure on the talks we have had concerning Freud, Erikson, and many other things as well. I owe a similarly important debt to William Beik. What I know about France and French history, and about my role as a student of such matters, has been worked out gradually in the course of many long and fondly remembered conversations with him.

In retrospect, I can see that this work really got off the ground not in the Widener Library or the Bibliothèque Nationale, but rather on the day I got married. The most heartfelt acknowledgment is to my wife, Persis.

DH

Cambridge, Mass.
December, 1969

CONTENTS

Contents

PART THREE
Children

PART FOUR
Conclusion

xiv

PARENTS AND
CHILDREN IN
HISTORY

INTRODUCTION

This is a study in history and psychology. To some extent, the project grows out of trends already at work among social scientists. The French historian, Philippe Ariès, has recently argued that the evolution of old regime society was significantly related to changes in family structure and in the treatment of children. By demonstrating that "private" transactions, like those between parents and infants, are linked to the "public" events on which historians have tended to focus their attention, Ariès has broadened our notion of history to include specifically psychological themes. Concurrently, in his book *Young Man Luther*, Erik Erikson has shown that psychoanalytic thinking, although developed in clinical work with individual patients during the last century, can be usefully applied to personal and social problems drawn from the history of early modern Europe. From very different starting points, Ariès and Erikson move toward a fusion of history and psychology. In Chapters 1 and 2, I explain how their work serves as the foundation for my own research.[1]

The major part of this study has to do with childhood and family life in seventeenth-century France. My objectives are, on the one hand, to add to our understanding of the social history of the period and, on the other, to demonstrate some of the strengths and the limitations of psychology as an instrument of historical analysis. In Chapters 3 to 5, I describe certain features of conjugal relations: why people decided to get married and how they got along once the step had been taken, what factors influenced conception and the birth of children, how responsibility for care of the very young was distributed among different members of the household. Then, in Chapters 6 to 9, I discuss methods of childrearing by following the course of infantile development through its various stages from birth up to the age of about seven.

Two difficulties inherent in this kind of research deserve special mention. In the first place, each of the intellectual traditions I am trying to bring together has its own peculiar methods and values. These differences are in part what makes the prospect of interdisciplinary study seem so intriguing. At the same time, if spokesmen for each field cling too jealously to their own style and point of view, historians and psychologists can be driven into positions which are mutually exclusive and which no longer allow for the possibility of collaborative work. Psychoanalysis has always been a reductionist science, attempting to find the laws of personality, the uniformities in human behavior beneath the façade of individual and cultural differences. If I were to stress this aspect of psychoanalytic thought in my own work, the family life I am studying would serve merely to illustrate a universal theory of domesticity and would lose all the special characteristics which it derived from its position in the distinctive social order of the old regime. Following this line of attack would greatly diminish the historical interest of the project.

On the other hand, historians often tend to be cultural relativists. As scholars, they are committed to the notion that each historical society has its autonomy and integrity and should not be judged in terms of the values of other social worlds. All customs and beliefs, including our own, make sense only for the people who have articulated them and put them into practice. Seventeenth-century France did indeed have a distinctive culture and mentality, but if, in my research, I were to concentrate too closely on the unique features of this way of life, I would be in a poor position to relate what I was discovering to the very modern, and very alien, theories of the psychoanalysts. If the analysts are correct, history is meaningless; but if I sided with the historians, psychoanalysis would be stripped of its pretensions as a comprehensive theory of personality and could no longer be regarded as a legitimate guide for interpretation of seventeenth-century society.

I do not attempt to settle the dispute between these two points of view. My own approach is something of a compromise. I am interested in the way people felt about the family, the importance they attached to relationships with their close relatives, the attitudes they seemed to hold with regard to the duties of parenthood. In discussing the phases of infancy, I concentrate on those aspects of childrearing which psychoanalysis has always regarded as most significant: feeding, cleanliness training, discipline, the management of infantile sexuality. Throughout these investigations, I am guided very much by a set of expectations, borrowed from psychoanalysis, about the nature of family life and the role of childhood in shaping human personality. I realize that this conceptual framework does not precisely fit the circumstances of seventeenth-century France, a milieu different in important respects from the world in which psychoanalysis has been conceived and practiced. I try to carry this line of reasoning as far as possible without doing violence to a historical reality which obviously cannot be expected to correspond too closely to our "modern" ways of thinking. My own experience has been that there is much to learn from the not always harmonious encounter of these two intellectual traditions. Having resolved to respect the basic rights of each side, I hope that the method of inquiry employed in this study will seem to lie somewhere between the poles of an arrogantly ahistorical retrospection and a timid relativism.

The second of the two major problems has to do with the availability of evidence: psychological history has been neglected in part because it is so difficult to find reliable sources of information on the matter. My research has been designed first of all to elucidate the family background of Cardinal Richelieu, politician and minister in the royal court of France from 1624 to 1642.

Archival materials pertaining to this topic convey some sense of the relations among siblings, parents, and in-laws in the Richelieu family and thus serve as a convenient point of departure for study of domesticity in the old regime.[2] Another major source comes from the pen of Jean Héroard, the doctor appointed by Henri IV to look after his son and heir, the future Louis XIII. Héroard kept a *Journal* on the upbringing of the dauphin, and this detailed and candid account of the day-to-day experience of an infant, albeit a very special one, in the seventeenth century is an indispensable resource for scholars interested in the history of childhood.[3]

I also found the medical literature on childrearing very helpful. Doctors who took as their task the criticism of prevailing customs and the dissemination of a more enlightened understanding of children provide us with considerable information on this aspect of family life. Further, I have consulted some of the published *livres de raison*, the account books kept by urban notables, in which household finances were recorded, with an occasional mention of domestic events (births, the hiring of a nurse, the date of weaning) thrown in for good measure. Finally, I looked through the standard sources of the period. Philosophical treatises, letters, books on etiquette or on methods of educating the young, and the memoirs and personal reminiscences which make reference to the writer's own experience as a child or parent—all these materials helped to fill out a picture which tends in the major sources to be either idiosyncratic (the childhood of Louis XIII) or markedly didactic (the medical literature).

The book covers the years 1550–1700. Starting with the documents on the Richelieu family and Héroard's *Journal*, I have used 1600 as a point of reference (the Cardinal was born in 1585, Louis XIII in 1601). Speaking generally, I was interested in the fathers and the children of this generation. Richelieu's father was born in 1548, Henri IV in 1542, Héroard in 1551. Stretching a bit, I included people like Montaigne (born 1533) and Estienne Pasquier (1529). In the other direction, I concentrated on writers reaching maturity in the early and middle parts of the century. Eventually I included figures as late as Fénelon and Jean-Baptiste de la Salle (both dead in 1715). The medical literature falls in the same time span. The earliest treatise on childrearing in my bibliography was published by Simon de Vallambert in 1565. Pierre Dionis, the last of the doctors consulted, died in 1718. Eighteenth-century *philosophes* are cited almost entirely for contrast and historical perspective. Stopping around 1700 also makes sense in terms of the existing literature on the subject; Roger Mercier's book on children in eighteenth-century society carries forward the story from that date.[7]

This list of sources has one obvious weakness: it tells us about only a limited segment of seventeenth-century society. Even in the years of comparative obscurity before the Cardinal's rise to power, the Richelieu family was still unusual in its noble status, its estates, and its ties to the royal court. The childhood of Louis XIII also provides a dubious base for generalization to the whole society (although I think that in some instances this difficulty can be overcome). Furthermore, the doctors speak from a relatively narrow social experience. Most were affiliated with the court and were clearly directing their advice to a privileged clientele. *Livres de raison* and memoirs broaden the base somewhat, but the fundamental problem remains. Relying on written sources, I am confined to a discussion of family life among nobles and urban patricians. I try whenever possible to draw inferences about childrearing in peasant society, but in general this remains a neglected element, and a very important one, in our picture of the old regime family.

This limitation should not, however, obscure the more basic point: that there is available a substantial body of material on childhood and the family in seventeenth-century France. My next task is to outline the specific questions I have attempted to answer in connection with this subject.

PART ONE

Points of Departure

1

THE
PSYCHOLOGICAL BACKGROUND:
ERIK ERIKSON'S THEORY OF
PSYCHO-SOCIAL DEVELOPMENT

I

In this chapter, on Erik Erikson, and in the next, on Philippe Ariès, I offer an analytic summary of theories which have guided the present research. The two chapters form a unit. I am attempting to show how each point of view has resources which help us to understand some of the shortcomings of the other. The arguments of the two thinkers should be regarded as provisional hypotheses. I present them as forcefully as I can, but with the expectation that I will also be able to demonstrate that they are incomplete in certain important respects. This exercise suggests a set of problems, to be considered in more detail, and makes clear how my investigations (discussed in Parts II and III) are to be understood.

I approach psychoanalysis and the Freudian tradition primarily through the work of Erik Erikson, who can be placed alongside theorists like Heinz Hartmann, Anna Freud, and Ernst Kris in the school of psychoanalytic ego psychology.[1] These clinicians have been innovative in a number of respects. First, they have shifted the emphasis within psychoanalysis from a study of pathology to a consideration of healthy psychic functioning. Whereas Freud was primarily interested in the *id*—the storehouse of sexual and aggressive drives—and in psychic phenomena closely related to it (repression, symptom formation, neurosis, and so on), many of his successors have placed more stress on the *ego* and its capacity for integrating internal and external demands (which Freud generally saw to be in perennial conflict) and for adaptation and growth (while by contrast Freud was preoccupied with the danger of breakdown and regression).

Another way of formulating these differences has to do with the autonomy of the ego. Freud believed that sexual and aggressive instincts were the most natural of human endowments and that there were no "genetic ego roots independent of the instinctual drives."[2] In spite of the sympathy which a "civilized" man might feel for its plight, the ego (along with the principles of order and culture which it represents) was conceived as a relatively feeble, extraneous segment of the personality. For Erikson, Hartmann, and their associates, however, the ego is just as basic as the id and operates on a level of parity with it. Growth and adjustment are prompted by forces which emerge from the same matrix as those of the id and which, like the latter, are operative from the beginning of life. In the sense that they too are expressions of man's basic inner disposition, health and normal development are given a certain legitimacy which they had at least by implication lacked in Freud's drive-oriented analysis.

Another aspect of the contrast between these two positions is how the "environment" or "society" is regarded. Freud assumed a conflict of interest between the individual and the social world around him. He believed that the suffering which comes "from our relations to other men . . . is perhaps more painful to us than any other."[3] By contrast, ego psychologists have called attention to the way in which the individual, and most notably the child, needs the support and the encouragement of the people around him. For Freud

it was important to establish the fact that moralistic and hypocritical social demands are apt to crush the adult and to exploit the child. It was important to conceptualize certain intrinsic antagonisms between the individual's and society's energy households. However, the implicit conclusion that an individual ego could exist against or without a specifically human "environment," i.e., social organization, is senseless.[4]

In place of this natural antagonism between the individual and society, ego psychologists assume that, as Hartman has put it, the infant brings to his relations with the world an inborn "state of adaptedness" which can be expected to unfold in the process of interacting with "average expectable environmental situations."[5] Ego psychologists, then, are much more interested than Freud had been in the social influences which shape personality, and more inclined to see such influences as benign.

Erikson's most distinctive contribution to ego psychology has been the formulation of a developmental scheme for the growth of the ego. One of Freud's accomplishments was to establish a timetable for the maturation of man's sexual constitution (the libido), which, he believed, passed through oral, anal, and phallic stages, as well as a period of latency, before adult genitality might be achieved. However, he said nothing about a schedule for the ego, which, we are left to assume, simply improvised as well as possible in reaction to the changing demands of the id. Erikson has suggested that, on the contrary, individual resources and skills (or that in one context he has called "virtues")[6] proceed through a corresponding set of stages and that just as the growth of the child exposes him to problems and instinctual dangers, it also releases potentials for coping and for positive advancement.[7] Thus, in the first stage of life, the infant's orality can lead to different kinds of pathological attachments and anxieties. At the same time, Erikson would add, a sense of basic trust can be established, a sense which, if not undermined by exceptionally trying circumstances later in life, will provide the foundations of a stable personality.

For each of the succeeding stages of life, Erikson has tried to show how different strengths may develop in the process of grappling with inner and outer difficulties which, according to Freud, threatened to overwhelm the individual, leaving him inevitably sick and unhappy. Erikson is aware of these dangers. If, for example, conditions are not favorable in the first stage of infancy, the child will be burdened with a sense of mistrust rather than of trust and hope. Still, I think his basically optimistic attitude contrasts with Freud's skepticism about human development in the face of a contradictory and antisocial instinctual nature. Erikson affirms

that in the sequence of significant experiences the healthy child, if halfway properly guided, merely obeys and on the whole can be trusted to obey inner laws of development, namely those laws which in his prenatal period had formed one organ after another and which now create a succession of potentialities for significant interaction with those around him.[8]

By indicating specifically in the form of a schedule of ego strengths how and when this "succession of potentialities" emerges, Erikson has built convincingly on the general contention of Freud's successors that the ego as well as the id has an impetus and an autonomy of its own.

It should also be noted that Erikson extends this schedule throughout life in an attempt to show that adolescence, adulthood, and old age have their own particular crises and possibilities. He has thus counteracted the tendency among psychoanalysts to reduce all experience to its infantile origins and to argue that the behavior of the adult simply recapitulates the decisive events of childhood. While not denying the powerful influence of early life, Erikson has tried to show that personality continues to unfold after the completion of biological maturation: people work out some distinctive identity, learn how to be intimate with others, conceive and bring up children, and ultimately try to make some sense out of their lives. They approach these tasks with options limited by what has already happened to them, but at the same time such crises always involve hitherto unexplored and untested areas of potential development and are therefore to some extent open-ended.

Thinking about postinfantile experience significantly extends the scope of psychoanalysis. Erikson has explored the implications of this line of thought in connection with adolescence (in his many papers on problems of identity, as well as in the study of Martin Luther) and has now completed a similar venture for adulthood (a biography of Gandhi). However, I have decided to concentrate on childhood, where Erikson has established an especially promising theoretical foundation. He has done more than indicate what kinds of strengths can be expected to emerge under optimal conditions in the first three stages of life. In effect, he has superimposed a whole psycho-social dimension on Freud's psycho-sexual timetable for the growth of the libido. Erikson translates the biological facts Freud had represented in his oral-anal-phallic scheme into what he calls organ modes.[9] The infant's orality in the first stage of life, for example, is in fact the most typical manifestation of an incorporative mode which, while it is exercised primarily through the mouth, is actually characteristic of the body as a whole. This mode blends into a social modality, that of getting or taking in with the mouth, eyes, ears, and hands. Such activity is not blindly instinctual and does not find its fundamental expression in autoerotic pursuits. On the contrary, it is a kind of interpersonal activity—the only one of which the infant is capable—aimed at other individuals and requiring a response from them. This adult response to infantile modalities is institutionalized in particular methods of childrearing which are designed to shape the activity of the child in ways his culture finds appropriate. The effects are long-lasting. The manner of getting and taking established in the first stage of infancy will influence the way an individual "takes in" his social world even as his taking in becomes more complex and diversified later in life. For the second and third stages of infancy (Freud's anal and phallic stages), Erikson has again tried to show that a biological disposition, when it is molded by childrearing practices, will lead into a distinct form of social behavior.

In effect, Erikson is saying that group action is articulated in terms of modes of behavior, themselves formed during the first stages of life as a function of methods of childrearing peculiar to the society in question. An example, based on Erikson's work with the Sioux Indians, will clarify how an analysis along these lines might work. He detailed the liberal way in which Indian mothers breastfed their children and speculated that very frequent feedings, along with late weaning, had something to do with the way Indians regarded property and with the high value they attached to the virtue of generosity: "The cultural demand for generosity received its early foundation from the privilege of enjoying the nourishment and the reassurance emanating from unlimited breast feeding." Further, Erikson wondered if the fact that after teething the infant had to learn not to bite when feeding (at the risk of a blow on the head from his mother) might not have helped generate the cruel belligerence of the Sioux warrior: "Did the necessity of suppressing early biting wishes contribute to the tribe's always ready ferocity?" Erikson continued in this vein, trying to show how collective traits and activities might be related to distinctive childrearing practices in this particular culture.[10]

To the schedule of modes and modalities, Erikson adds a timetable for the evolution of *parental* conduct. If childhood behavior is predominantly a kind of interaction which develops through a predictable set of stages, then it stands to reason that the other partners in this interaction must change too, and with equal predictability. To give an example, the infant's getting in the early period of infancy must be met by a corresponding desire and ability on the part of the adults to give.[11] In fact, Erikson argues that generativity, which includes the adult need to care for small children, is one of the essential strengths individuals are given the opportunity to develop in the course of a normal life. In the best of circumstances, parental generativity complements the infantile modes; life cycles interlock to assure that parents will be equipped with the specific skills needed to care for their children.

Pushing the exercise even further, Erikson has tried to project this process of fitting together onto the sociological level by suggesting that stages of infancy are linked to specific institutions:

Each successive stage and crisis has a special relation to one of the basic elements of society, and this for the simple reason that the human life cycle and man's institutions have evolved together. . . . This relation is twofold: man brings to these institutions the remnants of his infantile mentality and his youthful fervor, and he receives from them—as long as they manage to maintain their actuality—a reinforcement of his infantile gains.[12]

To illustrate, Erikson posits that the aspirations of the first stage will find in adult life their most characteristic expression in religion. The infant, with his own needs and fears, converses not only with parents (whose corresponding inclination for care equips them to complete the dialogue in a beneficial way) but also with the institutions of his society, which, in some cases at least, are designed to provide continuing reassurance for human anxieties rooted in the very earliest period of life.

These speculations perform an essential function in provisionally linking the psychoanalytic point of view to an area of inquiry which historians and sociologists have thought of as their own. There have been experiments with this kind of thinking in the past—attempts to connect the Protestant ethic with some form of anality, for example—but Erikson has gone further. He has added to the Freudian notion of libido development a plan for the growth of the ego as well as a schedule indicating how adults and children interact during the first stages of life; he has also suggested that these stages can be linked with "related elements of social order."[13] By postulating that organ modes are simultaneously social modalities, associated with specific kinds of adult behavior and ultimately related to social institutions, he has bridged in theory the gap separating biology from society, a gap which was intrinsic to Freud's way of thinking and which, it should be added, has made it hard for historians and sociologists to reconcile themselves to psychoanalysis.

Another way of putting it would be to say that Erikson has made two basic additions to the Freudian point of view. Freud had succeeded in linking aspects of individual infantile experience to the appearance of symptoms in later life. Erikson wants first to create connections of an equal plausibility between infancy and a wider spectrum of normal adult activities. Second, he hopes to expand the area of discourse so that collective behavior can be traced to the first years of life. For historians, these efforts are of the first importance since it is precisely nonpathological activity on a collective level which supplies them with the bulk of their subject matter. Erikson's speculations thus serve as an essential point of reference for anyone attempting to fuse history and psychology.

II

So much for the virtues of Erikson's system; our task now is to consider some of its possible shortcomings. In this section, I describe how my research has been organized from an Eriksonian perspective, but one in which some of the more conspicuous elements have been played down and a subsidiary point in the argument given special emphasis. In addition, I attempt to show that historical work can supplement ego psychology in an area where Erikson and his colleagues have made only preliminary investigations.

The theory of modes and modalities is Erikson's major attempt to correlate childrearing and socio-historical issues. I see this theory as the most sophisticated version of an approach which many anthropologists and psychologists of the last generation (Ruth Benedict, Margaret Mead, Geoffrey Gorer, and others) have followed in their efforts to demonstrate the cultural importance of childrearing.[14] At first, I assumed that my own research on seventeenth-century childhood would be organized along these lines. I posited that the way infants were handled in that period encouraged them to develop certain needs and aspirations; as they grew up, these traits proved to be functional in the social world of old regime France. The child's early experience endowed him with a set of predispositions, to be carried through life and eventually expressed in adult behavior: the acts of peasants, magistrates, intendants, and kings, as they are recorded in the sources. Put another way, historical scholarship has given us some sense of the patterns of conduct (the "social modalities") characteristic of the period. My task was to show how grownups first shaped these patterns, by the way they responded to the demands (the "organ modes") of their children. Childhood and society would thus be linked through the medium of individual life history.

However, the more I tried to think along these lines, the less comfortable I felt about the theory of modes and modalities. For example, I would like to believe that the indulgent breastfeeding provided by Indian mothers helped to encourage the propensity for generosity which is so highly valued in Sioux society. Granted that Erikson is not making a narrowly causal argument, a particular style of breastfeeding does not unilaterally cause the child to grow up into a generous adult. He is saying that the mother belongs to a society in which generosity is a prized and useful virtue. Something in the way she handles the infant conveys this understanding to him. He learns first to value generosity at his mother's breast, but the lesson is reiterated in a variety of social situations as he matures and takes an adult role.

Still, given these refinements, Erikson has to maintain that there is some functional connection between the individual's experience as a child sucking at the breast and his attitudes toward his property and that of others. What is this connection? If generosity is related to the first, or oral, stage, why is its opposite, stinginess, usually linked in psychoanalytic literature to anality? Similar questions occur to me when I read that Sioux ferocity was shaped by the blow on the head the infant received when he bit his mother's breast. I am not averse to this kind of reasoning in principle, but over the course of my work I have reluctantly concluded that it usually does not produce very plausible results. In most cases, we simply do not yet have the theoretical resources to make this kind of functional connection between infantile experience and mature styles of behavior.[15]

Under the circumstances, my efforts to apply the theory of modes and modalities have been very cautious. There is, however, another way of approaching the problem. Let us imagine child-rearing customs and cultural configurations related in a circle of cause and effect. For example, according to Erikson, generosity is a valued trait in Sioux society, a fact well understood by Indian mothers, who feed children in such a way that the infantile mode of incorporation is shaped to establish the groundwork for a generous temperament. The child grows into an adult who is inclined to deal generously with property, and who in turn is ready to raise his own children so that they too will share this propensity. Thus cultural characteristics are transmitted from one generation to the next.

As we have seen, the links of the circle connecting the child to his parents, and to the social life in which he will participate as an adult, are difficult to explain conclusively. As an alternative, I propose to concentrate on the first step in the process, that is, on the meaning of parental conduct. In the terms of our illustration, what specific factors prompt the Indian mother to breast-feed her child so liberally? In other words, let us set aside for the moment the question of the effects of childrearing methods and focus instead on their causes. The theory of modes and modalities involves a time lag. Childrearing prepares infants so that, after a period of maturation, they can function in the social world of grown men. We simplify the task of relating child-rearing to socio-historical issues by studying parental behavior, where psychological and cultural factors are simultaneously at work in the same person. Whatever their putative consequences for the young, and for the society infants will form after having grown up, methods of childrearing tell us first of all a good deal about the world of the adults who put them into practice.

This way of formulating the problem should be of interest to psychoanalysts as well as to historians. I think it is fair to say that with respect to childrearing, analysts have been primarily concerned with the infant, who is supposed to pass rapidly through a series of dramatic, highly differentiated phases of growth which profoundly affect the whole of personality organization. By contrast, parents are usually pictured as influential, but also as relatively unchanging, one-dimensional figures. Analysts have not sufficiently recognized the fact that parental responses to the evolving demands of the infant vary with the nature of these demands; that parents are influenced by their offspring even as they influence them; finally, that possibilities for the constructive care of children are hedged in by the social and historical circumstances in which family life takes place.[16]

Erikson has been one of the few analysts to consider these questions. By going more deeply into his thoughts on the matter, we can gain a better understanding of how psychoanalysis, even in revised form, still has not adequately explored the dynamics of parenthood. Erikson's major contribution in this area is the notion of a timetable for parental conduct. If the three stages of infancy are distinctive, each with its unique characteristics and problems, then it stands to reason that parents will have to deal with each phase in an equally distinctive manner, calling upon particular resources to meet the specific demands of the child. Earlier, I gave an example of this correspondence: the new-born infant's need to get must be met by an appropriate readiness on the part of adults to give. For the second and third stages, Erikson has again attempted to outline how parental behavior must be organized to "fit" emerging modes of infantile activity.[17] It is therefore possible that some aspects of childrearing will be easier for parents than others, and that their experience may equip them to meet certain kinds of infantile demands, but leave them helpless in the fact of the other developmental problems. Put another way, parental care should be as many-sided and as plastic as the childhood growth it is designed to oversee.

We should be clear about the fact that infantile and parental schedules are qualitatively different in one very significant respect. Childhood growth is tied to changes in the organism (hence "organ modes"). It is true that these modes are not entirely biological in that they do not dictate to the infant a complete sequence of activity. The modes are open-ended predispositions or tendencies, to be shaped by the particular reception they receive from their culture.[18] On the other hand, the child "incorporates" during the first stage, for example, because the mode is innate and comes to prominence naturally at this time without any prompting from the environment. Although cultural conditioning may determine the form of expression for infantile modes, no amount of conditioning could prevent the child in the first months of life from trying to "get." And the succeeding modes emerge, not because of something the child has learned or because they are invited in any way by the culture, but automatically because the infant's body is changing in response to laws of its own.

The situation is quite different for adults. Significant biological change (except for decline and death) has been completed by the time they undertake the obligations of parenthood. As the infant is born, grows, and makes a rapid series of demands on its parents, the latter get very little inner instruction in trying to formulate an appropriate response. What Erikson has called "generativity" is not a biological stage. It may be that something innate prompts the mother to "give" in a way which fits with the infant's innate need to "get." But her biological impulse is much more diffuse, much less specific, than that of her offspring. For the most part, what she does will be culturally determined:

This is far from being a merely instinctive, or a merely instinctual matter. Biological motherhood needs at least three links with social experience: the mother's past experience of being mothered; a conception of motherhood shared with trustworthy contemporary surroundings; and an all-enveloping world-image tying past, present, and future into a convincing pattern of providence. Only thus can mothers provide.[19]

For the second and third stages of infancy, the innate or biological element in the behavior of parents is even more amorphous and difficult to pin down. The child's body presses him to reach out toward the adult world in a variety of complicated ways. His parents must respond without getting anything like the same amount of guidance from nature.

In the light of these arguments, we might be tempted to conclude that Erikson's analysis of parenthood rests on a clear distinction between cultural and biological realities. However, as I attempted to demonstrate earlier in the chapter, Erikson and the other ego psychologists are uncomfortable with sharp dichotomies between culture and biology, the ego and the id. In actual discussion of the matter, he argues that these two spheres are substantially interrelated. Erikson does believe that adult care for infants is shaped by cultural considerations. However, the fact that parents are interested in this task, that there is energy available (however it might be mobilized) for the job of raising children, is taken for granted. In this respect, generativity, whatever its particular manifestations may be, is considered an innate human potential.[20] Although this potential is not triggered by any specific biological change, Erikson includes it among the other phases of human growth, which in almost every case are linked to obvious physical developments. Theoretically, generativity is exactly equivalent to the infantile stages, when maturation of the body plays an important role in motivating the child; to adolescence, when the search for identity is prompted, among other things, by the arrival of puberty; to old age, when man's sense of his own physical decline impels him to strive for integrity. This line of argument leaves us with the impression that generativity, the desire to care for the very young, is built right into human nature.

Erikson's conception of the sociology of childrearing also works to minimize the differences between biology and culture. He tends to see "culture" as a unit, an integrated system, one of whose principal functions is the training of small children. This system instills in parents a sense of the kinds of energies and potentials their offspring will need as they grow up, along with some notion of how, in their handling of infants, they can encourage these desired traits to emerge. Erikson is not a positivist; he does not believe that cultural conditioning operates like a machine, processing children so that they will come off the assembly line of infancy shaped to the specifications of society. However, he does seem to believe that childhood and society combine to form a closed, self-sustaining system. The concordance of social patterns, childrearing customs, and infantile growth is described not with mechanical terms, but in intuitive, almost mystical, language:

There seems to be an intrinsic wisdom, or at any rate an unconscious planfulness, in the seemingly arbitrary varieties of cultural conditioning: in fact, homogeneous cultures provide certain balances in later life for the very desires, fears, and rages which they provoked in childhood.[21]

For Erikson, culture becomes a kind of overarching presence, assuring that social, parental, and infantile needs are all harmoniously coordinated.

These views, which are very much in the spirit of post-Freudian ego psychology, depart from early psychoanalytic orthodoxy. For Freud, the child was ruled by instinctual drives, and the task of his parents was to domesticate him, train him out of his primitive ways, prepare him for the kinds of self-discipline which all civilized life requires. In this endeavor, parents simply acted as the agents of a culture which was inalterably opposed to the childishness in children, and indeed to all forms of unbridled instinctual expression. Men could function in such a world only by renouncing an important part of themselves.

Erikson has obviously brought about a change of emphasis within Freudian theory. Children are no longer seen as little animals, but as fully functioning human beings, with their own emerging skills and capacities for self-regulation. In turn, parents are not the enemies but the partners of their infants. Mothers and fathers need children, in order to satisfy their urge to care for others, just as the infant needs his parents to guide him through the first years of life. Further, the culture which parents represent is no longer seen as the implacable opponent of the instincts and of children. On the contrary, because infants are themselves basically social, cultural conditioning simply helps them to give form to their propensity for communal life. In Eriksonian theory, forces which Freud thought incompatible are apparently reconciled. Culture synthesizes the biological drives of small children with the imperatives of its own survival.

This debate raises a number of significant questions. The ego psychologists make advances in theoretical sophistication, but at the same time they seem to lose touch with certain hard-won Freudian insights. I can see that Erikson's revision of psychoanalysis has important strengths. He appreciates how man's bodily needs and his relations with his fellows can be coordinated, how social life is a natural expression of human aspirations instead of an extraneous and alien threat to the happiness of the individual. With respect to the more specific question of interest to us in this study, he is right in calling our attention to the fact that childrearing is a mutual process, that parents as well as children have something to gain in the communication between generations; and he adds to our understanding when he demonstrates that the culture which adults represent can support as well as frustrate the child's natural predisposition toward growth and self-realization.

On the other hand, we should also consider the possibility that Erikson may have gone too far in endeavoring to correct what he regarded as an extreme bias in Freudian theory. I find plausible

the suggestion that there is an innate generative impulse account-
ing for the fact that in all cultures adults do get involved with the
problems of caring for infants. Further, I recognize that in this
case, as with all the stages of life, Erikson acknowledges the dark
side of individual development: attempts to be generative may
miscarry, leaving the adult with a sense of stagnation. Still, I have
the impression that he overestimates the degree to which life
cycles interlock. The "fit" between parents and children is not
at all inevitable. We must keep in mind the qualitative differences
between the child's needs and the parents' willingness to be caring. The infant must ask for certain things, which he will get
only if his parents want to give them. Freud's picture of childrearing is tragic; parents and children stand for principles which
cannot be reconciled, and conflict is unavoidable. In attempting
to modify this interpretation, Erikson may have stressed too much
the reciprocal quality of the relationship between adults and their
offspring.

Along similar lines, we must ask if, in reacting against the
naively antisocial quality of Freud's thought, Erikson has adopted
an equally naive belief in the benign potential of culture to
satisfy individual needs. Admittedly, he recognizes that cultures
vary in "homogeneity." Nonetheless, in developing his argument, Erikson leaves us with the impression that, more often
than not, collective life promotes, rather than discourages, the
prospect of human contentment. Although his treatment of
socio-historical issues is often heavy-handed, Freud's basic assumption that individual happiness and the cultural enterprise are
always at odds may be fundamentally correct with reference to
many specific societies. At the same time, Erikson's considerably
more discriminating and conscientious consideration of such
questions can ultimately mislead the reader because it is based
on an unsound premise: that, in the social worlds we know well,
biological and cultural imperatives can be, and often are, brought
into a harmonious relationship.[22]

Choosing between Erikson and Freud on this point presents
me with a dilemma. In its details, Erikson's discussion of parenthood is much more authoritative, and yet intuitively I feel that
his optimistic view of generativity is no more convincing than

the pessimism of his mentor. The historical research in this study is designed to explore some of the ramifications of the controversy. My investigation of parents and their children in seventeenth-century France is conducted along the lines of Eriksonian theory as it has been spelled out in this chapter. At the same time, I reserve judgment on the question of generativity. In fact, the historical situation to be considered sharply challenges such a notion. Insofar as seventeenth-century culture was a unit with a set of goals and priorities, the welfare of children was not a matter of particular concern. As we shall see, in this period, being a good parent did not add to a person's standing, and being a bad one brought no discredit. Adults had scant respect for children and neither the ability nor the inclination to make many sacrifices on their behalf. Parents understood little of infantile experience and did not especially care to know more. Children were treated with considerable callousness. Some historians have gone so far as to affirm that parents were completely indifferent to children and barely took notice of their existence.

I discuss these historical questions more fully in the following chapter. For the time being, I wish to point out that the situation described above is totally at variance with our own. The Freudian tradition has unfolded in, and indeed has helped to create, a relatively child-centered world. Adults often abuse their offspring, but such mistreatment takes place within a milieu where the obligations of parenthood are generally recognized and respected. One might well wonder what happens to the delicate transaction of childrearing when cultural factors do not encourage a conscientious parental effort. In fact, "generativity" is a cultural artifact, and a very fragile one at that. Societies certainly do influence the way adults treat their infants, as Erikson has argued, but seldom with the "unconscious planfulness" or the "intrinsic wisdom" which he has tried to document. One of my aims in studying a milieu where these traits were conspicuously absent is to extend our understanding of the dynamics of parenthood.

26

2

THE
HISTORICAL BACKGROUND:
PHILIPPE ARIÈS AND THE
EVOLUTION OF THE FAMILY

I

Until recently, most historians interested in the old regime have not paid much attention to the family. Believing that what went on in the household was either irrelevant or inaccessible, they have preferred to study other institutions. There are, however, some exceptions to this rule. A small group of scholars, whose ideas I review in the first part of this chapter, have kept alive a tradition of historical research on family life. Writing within this tradition, Philippe Ariès has managed, through the force and originality of his contribution, to move domesticity into the center of our picture of society in early modern France. I describe his findings, and attempt to measure their significance, in sections II and III of the chapter. These tasks completed, I bring together some of the psychological and historical themes which have been considered in this introduction as a way of leading into my discussion of parents and children in the seventeenth century.

For a long time, family history in France was the special preserve of monarchist and corporatist scholars. Mention of the topic was almost equivalent to a confession of conservative political allegiance. According to these historians, family life was once carried on in an atmosphere of piety and security. Each member recognized and accepted a role which had been sanctified by tradition and which in everyday life was reinforced by a satisfying interchange of services and duties. One of the charms of this family arrangement was that it seemed to exemplify the principle of hierarchy without resentment. As Gaxotte phrased it, the family was free from

social envy, jealousy and bitterness. The principle of paternal authority made of each man "a sovereign who stands erect in his own rights by the virtue of the hereditary value which he represents and which he transmits. He has neither inferior nor superior. He is what he is, and he is proud of it."[1]

In this sense, and in many others, the virtues of the family are made to stand for those of a vanished order, in which the cohesiveness and stability of collective life provided a kind of security whose impact we of a more modern era can only dimly understand. Well might Funck-Brentano end his idyllic discussion of the traditional family with the rhetorical question: "Where are the dances and the songs of the old France? But where are the snows of yesteryear?"[2]

For these historians, the modern family is an entirely different institution. Torn apart by the centralizing tendencies of modern society, undermined by the general attack on principles of religion, authority, and tradition, this family can no longer provide the kind of emotional ballast which at one time had been among its major contributions to social life. On the contrary, domesticity has been brought into disrepute, husbands and wives neglect each other, and children lose their old habits of reverence and obedience. The modern family, like its ancient counterpart, thus comes to symbolize a whole era for conservatives. It represents all the evils of a modernity without a moral center of gravity or a workable network of authority.

Debate about the family has, for the most part, gone on within this conservative framework. There has been, for example, considerable disagreement about when the old family gave way to the new and about who was responsible for the disaster. Some historians, in the tradition of de Tocqueville, have singled out the absolutist monarchy as the promoter of revolutionary, damaging change in French history. For them, the position of the father was undermined in the seventeenth century: "Paternal authority is of little weight, its arms are feeble and its situation precarious in presence of the absolutism of civil power." The classic illustration of this relationship was the law enabling the state to remove "converted" children from the control of their Protestant fathers.[3]

On the other hand, in documenting the collapse of domesticity, Taine turned all the powers of a malicious wit against the insouciance of eighteenth-century society. At that time, love of luxury, disdain for domestic virtues, and the shameful evasion of the obligations of childrearing all contrived to reduce family life to a low ebb.[4] This critique has called forth a number of rejoinders from other conservatives. Of the eighteenth century, Gaxotte has written: "As soon as one leaves the restricted circle of the Parisian salons, it is very clear that France was not corrupted. The family remained so respected and so solid that the family virtues injected a certain greatness into the most insignificant lives."[5] But while rejecting Taine's chronology, these scholars would not quarrel with his categories. The evils he documented were, and are, real enough, but they belong to a somewhat later period of French history.

The common theme running throughout this literature is that the family is no longer what it used to be, that it does not easily accommodate itself to the conditions of modern life. Many scholars will be tempted to dismiss such arguments, and indeed the whole topic of family history, because they seem to be so closely associated with reactionary nostalgia. However, I think that there are at least two good reasons why historians should continue with their investigations of family life along the lines suggested by Gaxotte and his colleagues.

In the first place, while these conservatives have focused on the moral decay of the family, the theme of decline is also strongly supported by the institutional historians. The traditional family's multiple roles have been well documented. In the form of the vendetta, it handled certain kinds of judicial problems. It was also at the center of property relations. Until 1789, the law guaranteed the right of the relatives of anyone selling a piece of property to buy back that property from the new owner at the original price. In addition, a portion of family holdings was often entailed, because people still tended to think that goods belonged to the "line" (*lignage*) rather than to its individual members. Furthermore, the household was an economic as well as a conjugal unit; the master of a craft, for example, presided over a "family" in which children and journeymen were indiscriminately mixed together, just as his own functions as parent and chief of the enterprise tended to be confused. Relatives also played a peace-keeping role. In the absence of organized police forces, family discipline was the only insurance against disorder. Finally, kinship was important in political affairs, in the dynastic quarrels of princely houses, but also as centers of organization for competing factions and interest groups.[6]

Anyone reflecting for a moment on the role of kinship ties in contemporary society can see that they no longer hold together a network of judicial, economic, and political affairs. In fact, for a generation this "loss of function" has been taken for granted by many sociologists interested in the family.[7] When considered in the light of the institutional evidence, the decline theories of the conservative historians have a certain plausibility.

There is a second reason for pursuing the matter. While conservative historical research on the family was dedicated to narrow political ends, the general point of view which informed this work has been taken up in a much more sophisticated form by a major school of social thought. The contrast between the traditional community, based on associations (church, guild, family), and the atomized society of the contemporary industrial world, in which institutions like the family no longer have a viable role, has served as a point of reference for scholars like Durkheim, Weber, and Simmel, as well as for Gaxotte and Funck-Brentano.

Recently, even radical thinkers have picked up the theme. Thus Herbert Marcuse takes for granted "the decline of the social function of the family." He believes that in modern industrial society methods of domination have been refined to the point where the father is no longer needed as the middleman between authority and the individual. The head of the household is still to some extent responsible for "the basic regimentation of the instincts which prepares the child for the surplus-repression on the part of society during his adult life." But in terms of broader questions of control, "the father, restrained in the family, and in his individual biological authority, is resurrected, far more powerful, in the administration which preserves the life of society, and in the laws which preserve the administration." In the light of Marcuse's analysis of modernization, the displacement of the traditional father, which had distressed Gaxotte and Funck-Brentano, takes on its full significance.[8]

To sum up, conservatives have staked out the history of the family in France and have agreed that this history is one of decline and decadence. These conclusions are often a special pleading for the old regime. At the same time, the interpretation can be squared with the findings of perfectly apolitical institutional historians interested in the family's "loss of function." Even in political terms, a number of possibilities grow out of the assertion that the family is on the decline. Such notions can be adapted to radical as well as to reactionary perspectives. I want to stress the fact that the ideological situation in connection with family history is in a fluid state. The example of Marcuse shows that those who agree with disappointed corporatists and monarchists that the family lacks the vitality it once possessed are not themselves to be identified with corporatism and monarchism. A somewhat less obvious but equally important conclusion to be drawn from the same example is that criticisms of the traditional family do not necessarily rest on the belief that the institution is in a healthy state today.[9] I hope that these points can be taken for granted as I embark on my own, often hostile, analysis of domesticity in the old regime, and that this discussion has succeeded in freeing the subject, at least in theory, from the restricted setting in which it was originally introduced by Gaxotte and his friends.

II

Interest in the history of the family was strikingly revitalized by the publication in 1960 of Philippe Ariès' *L'enfant et la vie familiale sous l'ancien régime.* This analysis of domestic life is much more ambitious than anything attempted by the earlier, conservative historians and must serve as the foundation for any further study of the subject. At the same time, there are some problems in Ariès' work, especially when it is measured against the psychological standards established in the last chapter. In this section I provisionally summarize what Ariès has had to say. Later on, there will be time for a critical evaluation of his conclusions.

Ariès bases his interpretation on a particular view of medieval society, which he sees in clear contrast to the social world of today. According to him, in modern society class and age units are sharply defined, and isolated one from another. Class boundaries are unambiguous; a wide physical and moral gulf separates the rich from the poor. Familiar relations are no less easy between the generations, with young and old divided into mutually suspicious camps. But in the "polymorphous" society of the Middle Ages, one "unique social body embraced the greatest possible variety of ages and classes." Differences in rank and in maturity did exist, but they did not stand in the way of a constant, familiar interaction between rich and poor, young and old.

The idea of service had not yet been degraded. . . . There still remained between masters and servants something which went beyond respect for a contract or exploitation by an employer: an existential bond which did not exclude brutality on the one hand and cunning on the other, but which resulted from an almost perpetual community of life.[10]

And a similar "existential bond" united parents and children.

"Sociability" was the most representative characteristic of medieval life, which was lived in the street and in other public places much more than in the private home. Privacy itself was unknown. So was the "work ethic."

Work did not take up so much time during the day and did not have so much importance in the public mind; it did not have the existential value which we have given it. . . . On the other hand, games and amusements extended far beyond the furtive moments we allow them.[11]

Ariès pictures "a primitive way of life, . . . a wild population . . . given up to riotous amusements." In this unruly atmosphere, violence was common, but also a rough kind of freedom; for example, "the roughness of schoolchildren," who were not subject to any effective authority, was a direct consequence of their independence.[12]

For Ariès, medieval society was free from the regulatory pressures determining to a large extent the character of modern life, in which "all sorts of public authorities and police controls" play such a prominent part. The state as we know it hardly existed. "A boorish rural population" lived as it pleased, free even from the constraint which we might expect in a Catholic society. In a departure from the traditional view of the medieval period as an "Age of Faith," Ariès sees Catholic moralists and prelates as an embattled minority unable to curb the tumultuousness of medieval people. "The growing influence of Christianity on life and manners" was still to come.[13]

This interpretation centers on the family and, more specifically, on the child within the family. As I have indicated, one of the characteristics of medieval "sociability" was the mixing of the ages:

Transmission from one generation to the next was ensured by the everyday participation of children in adult life. . . . Wherever people worked, and also wherever they amused themselves, even in taverns of ill-repute, children were mingled with adults. In this way they learnt the art of living from everyday contact.[14]

Ariès is anxious to emphasize the precocious quality of this "participation in adult life," finding in it the most characteristic feature of medieval childrearing. "As soon as the child could live without the constant solicitude of his mother, his nanny or his cradle-rocker, he belonged to adult society." On the other hand, the infant still requiring this attention—the new-born baby who had not yet mastered the physical and intellectual skills needed to stand by himself—was treated by grownups with "indifference." Too fragile as yet to take part in the life of adults, the infant simply "did not count." Ariès maintains that this indifference was not incompatible with parental love and did not necessarily lead to neglect or bad feeling toward children. Even so, his basic point is that parents in the Middle Ages had no "awareness of the particular nature of childhood" and, apart from "participation in adult life," no detailed program for the raising of children.[15]

However, throughout the Middle Ages, this situation was gradually changing. A concept of childhood began to emerge. For the first time, there was "a tendency to express in art, iconography and religion (in the cult of the dead) the personality which children were seen to possess, and the poetic, familiar significance attributed to their special nature."[16] This "special nature" was emphasized with particular force in the sixteenth and seventeenth centuries when infants were given clothes distinct from those of their elders, began to have their own toys and games, and were singled out for special attention more often (for example, by portrait painters).[17] After centuries of neglect, adults were developing a marked interest in small children.

Ariès seems to be saying that attitudes toward the early years of life were changing in two ways. First, adults began to take an interest in children, expressed in "coddling" and then more seriously in a concern for the child's moral welfare and development. In place of the old careless indifference, parents now tried to keep their offspring under a constant surveillance, to subject them to a thoughtful and rigorous regime designed to help inculcate self-control, to shield them from the immodesties of adult life, and to treat them with seriousness and respect.[18]

Second, the notion of childhood was expanded beyond infancy through school age and even into adolescence. To guide this newly created group of "children," the institution of the *collège* was reformed specifically for their care. In the Middle Ages, schools were simply places where Latin was taught. There was no established enrollment, no logical progression of studies, no notion that certain subjects were appropriate to certain ages. The schoolboy was regarded as an adult who came and went as he pleased. Pupils banded together in *corps*, made their own rules and chose their own leaders. The *corps* of students was simply one among many self-determining, independent units in adult society.[19]

However, with the lengthening of childhood, the *collège* became an instrument of discipline. The *corps* were stripped of their independence and students placed under the control of authoritarian masters. The new regime, exemplified by the Jesuit *ratio studiorum* at the end of the sixteenth century, stressed corporal punishment, institutionalized informing, and constant surveillance. These reforms were not accepted without a struggle, but "in France, the great school mutinies would stop at the end of the seventeenth century. One has the impression that a disciplinary system already over a century old succeeded then, but only then, in curbing the turbulence of youth." No longer an adult among his peers, the student was now considered a child and as such was deprived of his autonomy.[20]

These developments were paralleled by changes in the nature of the family. During the Middle Ages, the nuclear family was a relatively insignificant institution. For work or play, its members spent more of their time in other groups, and thought these groups were more significant than the one centering around the hearth. Blood ties were important, but it was the line, or extended kinship group, rather than the conjugal family, which counted in people's minds.

One has the impression that only the line was capable of exciting the forces of feeling and imagination. That is why so many romances of chivalry treat of it. The restricted family community, on the other hand, had an obscure life which has escaped the attention of the historians. But this obscurity is understandable. In the domain of feeling, the family did not count as much as the line. One might say that the concept of the line was the only concept of a family character known to the Middle Ages.[21]

Gradually, however, the family became more important. The sentimental bonds uniting its members grew tighter, and the family turned inward, slowly pulled people out of their old habits of sociability and created a private space inside the home where individuals now spent most of their time, regarding the outside world with suspicion or indifference and relying on their close relatives for the satisfactions and the entertainments which in an earlier day had been derived from a much richer variety of social contacts.

The increasing importance of children played a major role in this evolution. "The concept of the family, which thus emerges in the sixteenth and seventeenth centuries, is inseparable from the concept of childhood." In fact, it was precisely the desire to provide the child with a safe and well-regulated living space which led families to draw together into closely knit units posed over against the outside world.[22]

A dedicated elite was responsible for these changes in the character of childhood and the family. Ariès speaks of "magistrates, police officers and jurists, all enamoured of order and good administration, discipline and authority," who were determined to impose "social discipline" on fractious medieval populations. These men, "few in number before the sixteenth century, and a far greater number . . . in the seventeenth century," gradually accumulated the power needed to transform society. The establishment of the *collège* on a new basis was just one of their major achievements. Throughout, Ariès associates them with some more general moral and political reformation, leading to increasing institutional controls over individual behavior. The new status for children and "the establishment of monarchical absolutism" were parallel developments. Within the household, and outside as well, the forces of order and discipline gradually succeeded in putting their ideas into effect.[23]

These changes were related to the class structure of French society. The modern family organization was at first "limited to the well-to-do classes, those of the notabilities, rural or urban, aristocratic or middle-class, artisans or merchants." Ariès characterizes the eighteenth century, during which the modern family clearly emerged, as the period in which "the nobility disappeared as a class with a social function and was replaced by the bourgeoisie." In fact, it was this bourgeoisie which defined the new style of domesticity and then gradually imposed it on all of society.

The middle class could no longer bear the pressure of the multitude of the contact of the lower class. It seceded: it withdrew from the vast polymorphous society to organize itself separately, in a homogeneous environment, among its families, in homes designed for privacy, in new districts kept free from all lower class contamination.

By the middle of the twentieth century, what had once been true of the middle class was now characteristic of the society as a whole, and the modern, tightly-knit, child-centered family was firmly established.[24]

III

One of the charms of this very persuasive book is that it seems to break so cleanly with the conservative view of family history. Ariès gives a clear summary of the issues involved:

For a long time it was believed that the family constituted the ancient basis of our society, and that, starting in the eighteenth century, the progress of liberal individualism had shaken and weakened it. The history of the family in the nineteenth and twentieth centuries was supposed to be that of a decadence: the frequency of divorces and the weakening of marital and paternal authority were seen as so many signs of its decline. The study of modern demographic phenomena led me to a completely contrary conclusion. It seemed to me . . . that on the contrary the family occupied a tremendous place in our industrial societies, and that it had perhaps never exercised so much influence over the human condition.[25]

We should not, however, be too hasty in deciding on the polemical meaning of Ariès' book. In this section, I relate what he has said to other views on the history of the family in an effort to bring out the real implications of his argument.

The case Ariès makes against the conservatives has one major weakness. As I indicated earlier, their interpretation is buttressed by some substantial evidence on the family's "loss of function." Like his opponents, Ariès is primarily concerned with the moral and affective aspects of domestic life: he is not so much interested in the "reality" as in the "*sentiment*"—the "idea" or "concept"— of the family.[26] The last third of his book is devoted to an analysis of the organizational as well as the conceptual history of the household, but even in this section he does not discuss the problem of the institution's loss of function, the very considerable shrinking of its responsibilities and powers in economic, judicial, and political affairs.

His failure to deal with this question weakens Ariès' contention that "the family occupies a tremendous place in our industrial societies." However, having found support for the conservative position among institutional historians (whose conclusions are not explicitly acknowledged in the books of Gaxotte and Funck-Brentano), we can perform a similar service for Ariès by mobilizing on his behalf potential allies whose scholarly work he has not consulted. I am thinking of the model of structural differentiation suggested with reference to the family by Neil Smelser, Talcott Parsons, and other sociologists. Parsons grants that the movement from simple to complex societies involves a loss of function for the household. Anyone comparing the role of kinship systems in primitive and modern societies must take note of the contraction in the influence of such systems. But at the same time, in those areas where the family retains some responsibilities—and Parsons singles out socialization of children and stabilization of adult personalities—it is even more important than in the past.[27]

Conceived in this way, family development is characteristic of the process of modernization:

When one social role or organization becomes archaic under changing historical circumstances, it differentiates . . . into two or more roles or organizations which function more effectively in the new historical circumstances. The new social units are structurally distinct from each other, but taken togteher are functionally equivalent to the original unit.[28]

In premodern society, the family was the major institution. Today a whole roster of organizations—judicial courts, the industrial sector, political parties, schools—perform the functions which it once monopolized. In other words, structural differentiation involves the multiplication of institutions, a greater precision in defining the tasks which each has to perform, and a heightened specialization and efficiency in the execution of these tasks.

We must consider the possibility that Ariès' thesis can be reformulated according to the model of structural differentiation. In the Middle Ages, child care was one of the minor responsibilities of the extended family. But as the society modernized, and the family was stripped of its other functions, this domestic duty gradually became more important. Eventually, the process was carried a step further, and a new institution (or rather an old institution completely transformed), the *collège*, was organized to share with the family the obligation of looking after children. By a process of differentiation, the family and then the school were set apart with one specialized role. Ariès has described one thread in a general development; in his account, the family singled out certain tasks as its own and began to perform these tasks with an intensified single-mindedness. On the other hand, he has neglected the fact that other roles have gradually fallen away from the family, to be taken up by specialized judicial, political, and economic institutions. But his basic point remains unaffected: *at least in certain areas* (the upbringing of children), the family has indeed "never exercised so much influence over the human condition."

While others might disagree (maintaining that Smelser and Parsons offer a value-free interpretation of modernization), it seems obvious to me that these theorists are implicitly putting forward a justification of the trend they seek to conceptualize. In this respect, they are in opposition both to the critics of mass society and to the conservatives, who unite in their apprehensive and largely negative assessment of contemporary life. Where one side sees modern industrial society as a human disaster, the other interprets it as a progressive force. One group stresses the disappearance of autonomous institutions while the other emphasizes the proliferation of such institutions. Where conservatives and radicals tend to see rationalized methods of administration cutting into the sphere of individual freedom, thinkers like Smelser and Parsons translate historical processes themselves into administrative adventures, in which social systems (conceived as problem-solving machines) delineate work to be done with increasing precision and refine institutions to do this work more efficiently.

This scheme would seem to confirm our analysis of Ariès. Having tentatively placed him in the camp of the proponents of structural differentiation, we now find him confronting the conservatives—the very group which, according to his own statement, he had set out to refute. I think, however, that a more careful analysis will show that Ariès does not belong with the structural differentiation theorists. Convenient as the above interpretation may be, in the end it does not grasp the distinctive message he is trying to send his readers. Let us assume for a moment that Ariès is a champion of modern life and in particular of the modern family. In fact, when I first read *Centuries of Childhood*, I did think that he viewed reform in the treatment of children as a progressive trend. It will be remembered that I divided this reform into two parts: the development of solicitude for small infants, and the expansion of the notion of childhood to include schoolboys. The first reform seems to have been especially positive. Ariès describes the recognition of the special character of small children, tracing the evolution from medieval indifference to "coddling" to a more serious kind of attentiveness. We witness an increased ability to recognize and take pleasure in the "sweetness, simplicity and drollery" of children, a growing "psychological interest and moral solicitude," in short, "the beginning of a serious and realistic concept of childhood." It is true that the new attitude had its "grim" side, in the sense that children were treated more rigorously and that more was expected of them, but there was also "humor . . . and undisguised tenderness" in the new approach to children.[29]

However, with reform in the handling of children divided into two parts, the reader may have trouble keeping together the different features of Ariès' presentation. It might be argued that the second aspect of the change in attitudes (the lengthening of childhood) grew naturally out of the first (the greater tenderness toward infants) and that the *ratio studiorum* institutionalized for schoolboys the "moral solicitude" felt to a growing extent for younger children. In this light, both aspects could be regarded as positive achievements. But upon closer inspection, it will be seen that Ariès is far from favorably disposed to the schools. How can greater love for infants lead to the conclusion that their older brothers and sisters—who had before been regarded as part of the adult world—should henceforth be treated with a severe brutality, that they should be subjected to the discipline of the newly organized *collèges?* It is hard to understand how "a desire on the part of the parents to watch more closely over their children, to stay nearer to them, to avoid abandoning them even temporarily to the care of another family" should have been translated into a decision to send them off to school.[30]

The problem of consistency in Ariès' interpretation clearly arises in connection with one of his favorite analogies: that notions of childhood are linked to those of class. He feels that the process by which the lower and upper classes were separated physically and morally is paralleled by the separation of children from the adult world.[31] In each case, a familiar intimacy gave way to estrangement and exploitation. The change in the significance of the *collèges* fits this interpretation plausibly enough: the schoolboy was changed from a free individual among his peers into a "child," an incompetent creature subject to a special, humiliating discipline. But how does this analogy square with the first aspect of the reform in attitudes toward children? In the medieval period, the infant was already separated from the adult world. He "did not count." Presumably, he did not have much to lose in the society-wide process of differentiation which separated poor from rich, young from old. He was already isolated from the broader human community. In these terms, the change in attitudes toward children performed just the contrary service; it led to the recognition of the humanity of infants, helped to integrate them into the world of the living, and raised their importance and the degree of their rapport with adults.

I am not sure how we should resolve this problem. The simplest explanation is of course that we have stumbled on a weak spot in Ariès' argument. On the other hand, as I have thought about the matter, I have been unable to dismiss the possibility that the "inconsistency" was of my own making, that Ariès does in fact treat childhood as a single unit, in which infant and schoolboy are subsumed, and that he regards *all* aspects of the changing status of children as unfortunate—the development of a greater solicitude as well as the organization of the regimented *collèges*. There is no alternative, if we are to make any sense of his conclusion, where he speaks of the modern point of view about children imposing itself "tyrannically on people's consciousness."

The evolution of the last few centuries has often been presented as the triumph of individualism over social constraints, with the family counted among the latter. But where is the individualism in these modern lives, in which all the energy of the couple is directed to serving the interests of a deliberately restricted posterity? Was there not greater individualism in the gay indifference of the prolific fathers of the ancien regime?[32]

Clearly, Ariès prefers "gay indifference" to "serving the interests of a deliberately restricted posterity." So much for parental solicitude!

A look at Ariès' first major work, a demographic history of France, will help us to resolve this problem. In that book, written several years before *Centuries of Childhood*, he had already shown an interest in the contrast between medieval and modern world views. In fact, this contrast provided him with his central theme. He argued that for most of history "man has lived close to the instincts." On the other hand, today "human life in its spontaneity—the simple fact of living—is no longer distinguished from the vast domain of technics. . . . All is crystallized in a world made heavy by its conquests over nature and immobilized by the mechanization of its own humanity."[33]

The contrast is exemplified in differing family organizations. The medieval family, the *type fécond*, was "characterized by a demography close to instinctual nature" and was, as a consequence, so large that parents sometimes did not know how many children they had. By contrast, the family today, the *type malthusien*, is based on birth control: "One no longer allows conjugal life to be given over to the thrusts of the instincts, abandoned freely to the laws of nature."[34] The man of the medieval and early modern period was subject to his impulses, without self-consciousness or self-control, utterly unable even to conceive, let alone practice, the simple act of coitus interruptus which his more disciplined descendants in the nineteenth century would master, thereby changing decisively the nature of the family: "This power of objective, reasonable, calculation, at the heart even of sexual frenzy, had no place in the mental and physical structure of the populations [of earlier times], still close to the instincts. Such calculation was literally impossible."[35] For Ariès, Western rationalization has changed not only man's social and intellectual life; it has affected the most intimate aspects of domesticity as well. We are different from our medieval ancestors in inhabiting a transformed social world, and also, perhaps more profoundly, because we are in a changed relation to our own bodies.

Ariès tempered his interpretation in *Centuries of Childhood*, but its general outlines are still visible. The "primitive way of life," the "wild population," the "gay indifference of the prolific fathers" of the medieval period, all these phrases recall his notion of a life lived "close to the instincts," as it was described in the earlier book. Similarly, modernization for Ariès is not just a matter of improving methods of administration. The originality of his interpretation lies in the connections established between institutional and individual psychological changes in European society. The elite of reformers, whose activities Ariès tries to follow, worked not only to build monarchical absolutism but also to improve the quality of private morality, to make men more rational and self-controlled. The reformation which they sponsored had a moral as well as a political dimension.

The most significant insight of this elite was to appreciate the importance of the first years of life. Ariès sees medieval childhood as a great arena of free expression and spontaneity. The creation of the schools was a direct attack on this freedom, a characteristic manifestation of the modern impulse toward control, that spirit of calculation which men now wanted to cultivate in themselves and to encourage in their offspring. Parental "solicitude" should also be seen in this light. In the Middle Ages, people let the young grow up as they pleased. On the other hand, the

43

"power of objective, reasonable calculation" typical of modern man is manifested strikingly in the attention given to children, in the efforts made to analyze more exactly their needs and to design effective methods of controlling their development. This growing concentration on the infant and the interest taken in childrearing are signs of an increasing need to dissect reality, to reduce it to the contours of a sterile rationalism. Looking at the matter from this perspective, Ariès naturally tends to prefer the "gay indifference" of medieval fathers.[36]

We can see that Ariès is not being inconsistent in condemning the schools. On the contrary, his negative picture of this aspect of child care fits quite well into a generally critical view of modernization. The anomaly lies in his treatment of infancy. All his historical biases prompt Ariès to condemn modern "solicitude" and to praise medieval "indifference" toward the very young. But in actual practice, as he traces its historical development, his description of parental solicitude is characterized by a certain sympathy. I get the impression that Ariès is perplexed by the first years of life. Primarily interested in the schools, and in the somewhat older children who attended them, he leaves his argument on the earlier phase of childhood somewhat in disarray. I have more to say about this matter in the next section.

In any case, we are now in a better position to understand the distracting echo of conservative slogans which occur throughout Centuries of Childhood, a book ostensibly dedicated to the task of demolishing the corporate interpretation of family history. Ariès is a stringent critic of modernity. It is no accident that he evokes an era in which the lower classes accepted their inferior rank and that he mocks middle-class domesticity. His anticlerical and antiabsolutist slant (it was, after all, "an elite of thinkers and moralists who occupied high positions in Church and State" who were responsible for the segregation of schoolchildren)[37] should not throw us off the track. As I have tried to show, at least with respect to absolutism, there is a precedent within the conservative historical tradition for this bias. If we make a correction in the classical scheme, specifying that it was the extended kinship group, rather than the nuclear family, which stood alongside the guilds, communes, and estates in the Middle

Ages, and that, further, the leveling process in modern society has not completely isolated the individual, but rather has organized people into tiny, atomized groups—the conjugal families —Ariès takes his place within the tradition which he set out to refute. His message is that conservatives have misread history, mistaken the real enemy: "It is not individualism which has triumphed, but the family."[38] Here, as in the past, the history of the family marches forward under the banner of a certain nostalgia.

By a circuitous route, Ariès has apparently brought the problem back to its starting point; he has given us another conservative version of French history, with the family, as usual, playing a prominent part. On the other hand, all the elements of the argument have been juggled, and the way conjugal life and political and social developments influence one another has been completely reinterpreted. Earlier in this chapter, I suggested that on the theoretical plane the character of domesticity, as it had been outlined by Gaxotte and Funck-Brentano, was related to major historical debates whose implications transcended the limitations of any one political point of view. Ariès has exploited this theoretical potential and has transformed the family into a topic of ongoing research, one which is plausibly linked to our attempts at understanding the general transformation from a medieval to a modern society.

IV

We are now in a position to take stock of the psychological and historical theories which have been summarized in Part One and to set a course for the remainder of the study. As we have seen, in his discussion of psycho-social growth, Erik Erikson argues that attitudes toward children depend to some extent on the nature of the parents' social experience, and on the kind of cultural support they receive as they undertake the task of caring for infants. At the same time, he has not gone beyond some general remarks in this vein; the mechanisms by which cultural conditioning is itself culturally conditioned are not carefully explained. More important, Erikson suggests that we can take for granted an innate generativity, a desire to look after small children, which is a part of human nature, a constant, appearing across cultural and historical lines in all societies.

In one sense, Ariès complements Eriksonian theory. Childrearing is indeed influenced by sociological realities. In fact, the treatment of children is related to family organization and, beyond that, to fundamental social, ideological, and political changes in the character of European society. At the same time, this historical interpretation challenges a basic tenet of Erikson's system. The concern for children, which he seems to assume is a part of human nature, the generativity all adults manifest in some form, is for Ariès a historical phenomenon, what he calls solicitude for children, a singularly modern development. According to Ariès, in the Middle Ages, parents were indifferent to their offspring, and whatever generative impulses they may have felt were channeled in other directions. This lack of interest in children was part of a cultural synthesis, complementing the powerful spirit of community, the freedom from regimentation, the impulsive primitivism of medieval man. We care for children only because of the peculiar quality of our own, quite different, culture. For Ariès, Erikson's work, and indeed all psychoanalysis, with its exaggerated concern for the welfare of infants, is far from being a universal theory of personality, but is instead the product of our own particular, and transitory, way of looking at children.

If we look at the problem historically, psychoanalysis is clearly placed on the defensive. However, the matter should not be allowed to rest at this point. In presenting Ariès' views, I have stressed their provisional quality. We have already seen that, with respect to infancy, the preschool years of childhood, his analysis was marked by a certain confusion. Ariès did not know what to make of the care, whether negligent or attentive, given to very young children, and in general left this aspect of childhood relatively unexplored. We must now reverse our procedure and test the plausibility of his discussion of children in the premodern period against the standards which Freud and his successors have so carefully worked out.

To summarize again, according to Ariès, the very small infant in the Middle Ages did not arouse the interest of adults, who in fact had no real conception of infancy and no special ideas about the way in which such creatures should be cared for. The child's status, however, was soon changed. Very early in life, after mastering some of the necessary physical and intellectual tools, he was integrated in a relatively complete way into the adult world, where his "education" became a matter of direct emulation of the grownups around him.

When did this graduation take place? As Ariès indicates, the age of seven is often cited in the sources. At that time, the young boy passed "out of the hands of women," went to school, was apprenticed, or sent to serve in another household.[39] In the light of our present ideas about infancy, it seems astonishing that the child should so long rest in a kind of limbo, treated without any special care. In trying to evaluate this position, I was reminded of the ethnographic literature on children. Coming from a culture in which childrearing is discussed with a great deal of self-consciousness and where adults enter into parenthood with a burden of advice about handling their young, some of the first anthropologists naively mistook the more relaxed and unarticulated style of raising infants in primitive societies for no style at all and assumed that children in such circumstances survived the first years of life more or less by accident. However, more careful study has clearly demonstrated that primitive societies have coherent and well-conceived methods of childrearing which these earlier, more ethnocentric observers had overlooked.

Ariès may have made a similar error in dealing with the "primitive" society of the Middle Ages: perhaps he has not looked carefully enough for the pattern beneath medieval "indifference" to children. I think that Ariès himself senses that the first stage of life, when children supposedly "did not count," is the weak link in his interpretation. In order to reduce the conspicuousness of this perplexing state of infancy, he frequently attempts to lower the age when the very young "graduated" out of childhood: "Until the mid-seventeenth century, people tended to stop infancy at the age of five or six, when a boy would leave his mother, his nanny or the servant girls; at the age of seven he could go to school." In other passages, he carries this tactic even further; for example, children played the games of adults from the age of three or four. Even in retaining the age of seven years as the turning point between infancy and normal life, Ariès tries to anticipate, and to counteract, the reader's skepticism: "At the beginning of modern times . . . children were mixed with adults as soon as they were considered capable of doing without their mothers or nannies, not long after a tardy weaning (in other words, at about the age of seven)." Tardy indeed! Infants were weaned relatively late by our standards, as we shall see later on, but to suggest that weaning was postponed until the age of seven is a substantial exaggeration. It would be convenient if in fact the period of helpless dependence most characteristic of the newborn infant (and most consistent, I suppose, with the very low status of "not counting" in the eyes of adults) lasted seven years, but the reality of childhood stubbornly resists such juggling of figures.[40]

In his interpretation of premodern infancy, Ariès flies in the face of much that we take for granted about human development. It is now assumed that the small child passes through extremely complex and momentous stages of growth before he reaches the age of seven. The whole problem of childrearing is that the infant can communicate with adults, can sustain a complicated relationship with them, making demands, inspiring normal amounts of love and exasperation, well in advance of the time when he is capable of interacting with his elders in an adult way, that is, with the controls, the skills, and the reason which they expect in their dealings with one another. In short, the child "counts" long before he "belongs to adult society."

Ariès has nicely traced the growing awareness of infancy in Western culture. For example, he points out that the development of a sufficiently discriminating vocabulary was one of the keys to the historical "discovery" of childhood. In this evolution, a general term, *l'enfance*, was gradually broken down into more precise categories, with the word *bébé* eventually borrowed from

English to single out the "very little child." Similarly, in the iconography of the stages of life, artists gradually began to pay attention to the first period (ages one to seven) and to note its particular characteristics with a more sympathetic accuracy.[41] In our own day, these trends have proceeded much further. Erikson's scheme for the "stages of life" divides the first seven years into three phases. Infancy, which was once regarded as inconsequential, has become for us a highly differentiated, very distinctive process, in which growth and mastery proceed at a tremendous rate, much more rapidly than is the case later in life. Thinking in these terms, it seems clear to me that Ariès is much closer to the medieval than to the Eriksonian view. We find no sense for the uniquely infantile dimension of human growth in his book. Following in the footsteps of his medieval forebears, he demonstrates only a superficial interest in the first part of life. As a result, Ariès does not really understand the modern view of children which he is attempting to place in historical perspective.

These oversights are very damaging to Ariès' case. Psychoanalysts have at least taken into consideration the realities of biological growth. On the one hand, it is admittedly difficult to pinpoint the physical developments which trigger each of the first three Eriksonian phases, although Erikson tries his best to do so (and, in general, I find myself persuaded by these attempts). Even granting that these distinctions are hard to make, it still seems clear that the psychoanalytic view of infancy rests on a more general schedule of organic change. The fact is that children are weak and immature both physically and cognitively and must depend on the strength and experience of adults in order to survive. If parents are interested in preserving their offspring, they must recognize this situation and take steps to meet the needs of infants. "Indifference" is not enough. If parents were truly indifferent, their children would die. The argument in *Centuries of Childhood* is thus biologically almost inconceivable.

If Ariès were correct about premodern childrearing, the universality of psychoanalytic thought would be powerfully challenged. However, the shortcomings of his discussion on this point suggest to me that the question is still open. A genuine search for the relativity of Eriksonian theory will require a much more thorough and informed examination of the psychoanalytic picture of infantile experience. Just as Erikson's description of generativity lacks a historical dimension, Ariès, in his analysis of premodern indifference to children, does not deal authoritatively with the psychological issues involved in the controversy. My own discussion of parents and children in the seventeenth century situates itself between these two somewhat flawed concepts, not with the intention of taking sides, but in the hope that the common questions they attempt to elucidate can be more fully explored.

I should add a final word on Erikson and Ariès. My extended criticisms are not offered in the hope of discrediting these thinkers. In fact, I believe that the problems we encounter in reading their works are inseparable from the impressive intellectual ambitions of the two men. For example, the sweeping statements hazarded by Ariès on the character of medieval and modern society do not square well with the more cautious habits and rhetoric of academic historians, and there are many dubious and even reckless passages in *Centuries of Childhood*. At the same time, it seems to me that the distinguishing virtue of this book is its conceptual boldness. Ariès has succeeded in taking the most unlikely, the most "unhistorical," of topics—man's intimate familial and psychological existence—and demonstrated that it too is part of Western history. By attempting to pull together all the strands of human experience, he places himself in the unjustly neglected tradition of nineteenth-century system builders, who chose for themselves the project of explaining the history of our civilization as a meaningful whole.

If Ariès belongs to the tradition of metahistorians, Erikson is the one psychoanalyst who has most imaginatively carried on Freud's project of formulating a metapsychology, a comprehensive theory of human nature. Historians were impressed (and not all in a positive way) by the scope and audacity of *Young Man Luther*, but in fact this work is a relatively modest affair, with its well-defined biographical format. In his first book, *Childhood and Society*, Erikson not only presented a fully developed theory of infantile sexuality and a scheme for the stages of life, but also attempted to relate these theories to the plight of the Sioux Indians, the question of American national character, the origins of German fascism. Discursive and speculative as these efforts may have been, they nonetheless represented an unprecedented and very exciting development within the psychoanalytic tradition. Here Erikson directly confronted the challenge of relating the insights of his own field to the most pressing social and historical problems of his day.[42] Historians and psychologists together need look no further for an agenda. In the present, more modest, study, I try not to lose touch with the general concerns which Ariès and Erikson have placed at the center of their work.

PART TWO

Parents

3

CHARACTER OF THE SEVENTEENTH-CENTURY FAMILY

I

Before describing the way seventeenth-century parents handled their children, we ought to make some effort to ascertain how they felt about one another. The step is necessary because modern notions of childrearing are closely linked to a set of expectations concerning conjugal relations. Setting aside for the moment the reality of contemporary family life, our ideal is a situation where the depth of understanding between the marriage partners enables them to work together, presenting a common front to their offspring, sharing the obligations of child care. Without such a bond, we find it hard to imagine children being raised successfully. This ideal is embodied in the Eriksonian scheme for the stages of life. After the adolescent has decided who he is, confirming his identity, he is free to grow into the next stage: learning how to be close to another person. Managing intimacy is a complete phase in itself, with its own promise and difficulties. Only when these gains have been consolidated will individuals be ready to move to the next plateau, where generativity becomes the central issue.[1]

Looking at family life historically, we find immediately that these assumptions about marriage and childrearing are thrown into doubt. There is a general feeling among sociologists and historians that the modern family is special, that in earlier periods the institution was held together by political, economic, and social pressures rather than by individual choice and psychological affinity, as is the case today. According to these scholars, the association of intimacy and marriage is a modern invention. The contrasts implied in such a formulation are candidly spelled out by Ernest Burgess:

The family in historical times has been, and at present is, in transition from an institution to a companionship. In the past the important factors unifying the family have been external, formal, and authoritarian, such as the law, the mores, public opinion, tradition, the authority of the family head, rigid discipline, and elaborate ritual. In the new emerging form of the companionship family, its unity inheres less and less in community pressures and more and more in such interpersonal relations as the mutual affection, the sympathetic understanding, and the comradeship of its members.[2]

I have already had occasion to refer to the multiple functions of the traditional family and to the way in which these functions have gradually been dispersed throughout a more differentiated social system. Both Burgess and the proponents of the model of structural differentiation are interested in the fact that the modern family has managed to retain responsibility for certain psychological tasks. The household once performed a multitude of duties, among the least important of which were the care of children and the maintenance of the psychological balance of the marriage partners. But as a consequence of its loss of function, the family is now a specialized institution (or, as Burgess would put it, a "companionship"), to which the members look primarily for moral support and emotional security, rather than for economic, political, or social advantage.

These considerations also relate to what Ariès has had to say about domestic life. The development of what he calls the "concept" of the family corresponds to the emergence of companionship. Medieval "sociability," which brought the individual into familiar relationship with all age groups and classes and involved him in a variety of activities outside the home, has been gradually withdrawn from this broader social milieu and concentrated within the nuclear family. Domesticity, which was once regarded with a minimum of interest, is now closely linked to our notions of worth and happiness. I have argued that Ariès regards this evolution with a certain hostility. But the categories are the same: for Ariès, as well as for Burgess, the companionship family is a modern institution.

These theories suggest that individuals in the premodern world brought a different set of expectations to marriage, that they regarded it as a perfunctory and superficial relationship without the promise of any particular warmth or closeness. If this is the case, then obviously the whole tone and meaning of domesticity in that period would be so foreign to us that we might find it hard to think about the traditional family in the psychological language which seems so appropriate to our own day. I would question the accuracy of "companionship" as a description of contemporary conjugal relations. Burgess does not make clear whether he is referring to the aspirations people bring to marriage (which may, or may not, be realized), or to the actual state of married life. At the same time, it does seem to me that the term captures something of the mythology which we all share. Marriage is supposed to be a companionship. A whole string of consequences follow from this fact: concerning organization of the household, the manner in which parents regard one another, and, most important for our purposes, the way they feel about the coming of children. To orient ourselves, to measure the extent to which our presuppositions about marriage, the family, and childrearing practices make sense for a premodern milieu, we must look into this question of companionship with respect to the seventeenth-century family in France.

II

The obvious place to begin is with the problem of why couples in this period decided to get married and how the ceremony was carried out. In approaching the matter, we quickly encounter a large body of evidence supporting the view that traditionally marriage was an institution rather than a companionship. The principal factors determining the nature of the union were socioeconomic. In order to marry, the woman needed a dowry, and in order to get something for his investment, her father would try to find a son-in-law willing and able to lend him assistance in return. The groom himself could not marry without a certain economic power, at the very least a place for him and his bride to live. These economic realities worked to minimize the number of marriages. Providing a daughter with a dowry or a son with an independent situation put great strain on family financial resources, and as a result, children, especially the girls, who chose a celibate life, were making an important gesture of family loyalty. Hajnal believes that this and other factors created a unique demographic situation in Western Europe in the early modern period, one characterized by a high proportion of lay and clerical celibacy and by a relatively late age of first marriage.[3]

Considered in this light, marriage was more a contract, negotiated by two families, than an agreement between the bride and groom. When Jean de Beauvau wanted to marry a distant relative, Françoise du Plessis (a sister of Cardinal Richelieu), he penned ardent love letters—to her oldest brother, Henry: "I want so much to change my relationship to you, my good cousin." When the match had been made, Beauvau added: "It is no longer to my cousin that I write at this moment, my good fortune having changed this relationship, confirming by an even closer tie the vows of my service, which your merits have certainly acquired for you." He now styled himself Henri's "most affectionate brother" and begged the latter "to love me in this capacity."[4]

This way of thinking about marriage, that is, in terms of the men, and ultimately the families, which it would unite, was pervasive. Conjugal life began not with a proposal but with bargaining sessions designed to fix the terms of the marriage contract. The case of Robert Arnauld d'Andilly has often been cited as an exception because, on the occasion of his choosing a bride, the two families professed to be indifferent to the terms of the contract.[5] However, the significance of the gesture can be overrated. Even in this case, all participants realized that an important part of the transaction concerned the property which would change hands as a result of the union, a fact which Arnauld himself makes clear: "The articles of marriage were signed *en blanc* by each side, which I think is almost unprecedented, and they were filled in only when it was necessary to draw up the contract." In discussing the negotiations, the groom ruminated for several pages on the admirable qualities of his future in-laws. Almost as an afterthought, he commented: "With respect to Mademoiselle de la Boderie [his fiancée], who was then only fourteen, I will be content to say that she had all the qualities which can make someone of this age amiable and estimable." Looking back, Arnauld wrote: "No words can express the pleasure of life with M. de la Boderie."[6]

In these situations, the bride seems to go almost unnoticed. In fact, her role, along with the whole sentimental dimension of marriage, was treated deprecatingly by many observers. For example, Henri de Campion wrote:

I know that marriages are made for only two reasons: love and interest. . . . Those which are made for love are nearly always condemned with justice. . . . As for the others, people ordinarily approve of them, although the satisfactions derived from these unions are usually more apparent than real.[7]

Campion's analysis tends to confirm the theory advanced by Burgess and others. Marriages based on "interest," on institutional considerations, are regarded with approval, even though they are gratifying only in a superficial sense to the people involved. On the other hand, those motivated by "love," by companionship, are "condemned with justice." In following Burgess, these are the views we would expect to hear from Campion, or any other seventeenth-century authority. Along with the descriptions of actual marriage negotiations offered above, they indicate that the traditional notion of the family was firmly established in the period we are examining.

At the same time, the quote is interesting because it clearly states that marriages were made "for *two* considerations." While Campion prefers arranged matches, and assumes that most people would agree with him, he does acknowledge the existence of another school of opinion—those who marry for love. These couples, who defied convention in marrying out of personal inclination, deserve consideration—especially since they threaten our established notions of the premodern family as in institution dominated by "interest," or, in other words, by what Burgess calls "external, formal and authoritarian" controls.

We are fortunate in having one excellent source of information on this group—the legislation on marriage. Such legislation was needed because, up until the 1550s, there was no necessary institutional procedure for sanctioning the marriage bond. Engagements were made by the exchange of indications of intention (*paroles de future*), and the bargain was sealed with the *paroles de présent*, a simple statement of mutual consent. The ceremony could be performed in front of witnesses, but could as well be carried out in complete privacy. If a man and woman were living together on what appeared to be a permanent basis, they were "married," and no civil or religious authority could question the legitimacy of the union. In fact, marriage was not a civil ceremony, but a sacrament, vaguely under the jurisdiction of the church, in which consent by the partners was the decisive factor.[8]

The situation was not at all favorable to parents anxious to arrange the marriages of their children. If young people did take things into their own hands and marry without parental consent, they could embroil everyone in vexing quarrels over inheritance and dowries. Faced with this dilemma, parents turned to civil and ecclesiastical authorities for help. The first consequence of these efforts was the famous royal edict of 1556. Deploring the "very great regret, vexation and displeasure" which are the lot of parents whose children marry without their consent, the edict empowered these parents to disinherit their offspring who so disobeyed, and further suggested that judges should also punish anyone helping to arrange such a marriage.[9]

Many observers found this edict too harsh. In the first place, it was a bold attempt to legislate in an area until then reserved for the church. Further, it suggested that children should remain under the control of their parents with respect to marriage until the boys were thirty and the girls twenty-five, an unprecedented lengthening of the minority period of childhood, which, before that time, had varied between the ages of twelve and twenty (depending on the sex of the child, and on the customs of the province in which he lived).[10]

However, in other respects the law was quite cautious. Its wording indicates the strength of the old notion of marriage:

> We do not mean here to include marriages which have been consummated by carnal cohabitation before the publication of this edict, but only marriages where one claims consent by *paroles de présent* or *paroles de future*, without cohabitation or carnal union having taken place.

In addition, as Estienne Pasquier pointed out, the punishment, disinheritance, while it might save the father from disastrous lawsuits, did not really help him to strengthen his control over his children; rather, it seemed to underline the very break between parent and child which the legislation should have been designed to prevent.[11]

Pasquier wanted something more: a change in the concept of marriage itself. The problem was not that parents were unable to control their children. Getting married was so easy that no amount of parental discipline would ever hinder children determined to exchange vows. From a legal point of view, he attacked the idea that *paroles de présent* alone could legitimize a marriage and argued that the consent of parents should be considered just as essential as the fact of cohabitation in determining the legitimacy of the union. He believed that the law should invalidate all marriages made without parental consent (rather than simply leaving open the possibility that the partners in such a marriage might be disinherited) and that the offending parties should be subject to the death penalty. But after this vehement presentation, accompanied by a shower of learned citations, Pasquier wryly admitted: "I have not said . . . that the consent of the father was required, only that I hoped it would be."[12] In other words, the deeply ingrained idea that marriage was based on the freely given consent of the bride and groom was not to be eradicated by the arguments of a handful of legists.

In 1563, the Council of Trent published a clarification of church rules on marriage. The Council decreed that a priest must witness the exchange of consent in order for the marriage to be valid. Astonishingly, the church had no official part in marriages before 1563, and even afterward the priest was to play a passive role in the ceremony, as a witness rather than a participant. The Council further required the publication of the banns three times before the marriage and ordered priests to keep registers so that there would be an official record of the occasion.[18] By formalizing the public aspects of the ceremony, these rules helped parents who wanted to keep up with the marriage plans of their children.

The decrees of the Council of Trent were not published in France. They were, however, incorporated into the ordinance of Blois (1579), which required proclamations before the marriage, as well as the presence of four witnesses at the ceremony itself. The presiding priest was urged to make sure that the marriage was taking place with the consent of the parents. Most important, by a clever stratagem, the definition of "abduction" (*rapt*) was broadened to mean any marriage undertaken without the consent of the parents. Since this crime was punishable by death, and since marriages contracted as a result of an abduction were automatically null, in effect the severe recommendations of Pasquier had been made the law of the land. Finally, again testifying to the tenacity of the traditional notion of marriage, the ordinance forbade "all notaries, on pain of corporal punishment, to receive any promises of marriage by *paroles de présent.*" A generation after the edict of 1556, couples were, apparently, still exchanging vows in front of an official witness, with no sanction from church or family, and considering themselves as a consequence rightfully married.[14]

Throughout the seventeenth century, these laws were repeated and made more elaborate. The Code Michau (1626) treated the problem as one of official complicity, warning all judges and *procureurs* that if they were remiss in enforcing the laws against marriage without parental consent, they would have to stand in place of the criminals (the bride and groom). It further admonished "captains and governors who command in places under our authority" to avoid cooperating with such adventures at risk of losing their posts. Finally, it forbade the use of royal letters to facilitate such crimes. A strongly worded reiteration was published in 1639. Another law, in 1697, shifted the emphasis to the priests, who were given heavy responsibility for verifying the legitimacy of the marriage and who were themselves open to punishment if they sanctioned a union against the wishes of the parents.[15]

The wording of these documents (as well as the fact that it was necessary to republish them so regularly) indicates the magnitude of the problem. Couples determined to marry found help in many quarters, and public officials were not the only ones to be chastised for complicity. Witnesses with a "sordid interest" would agree to take part in the ceremony. Other relatives appear to have been enlisted against the parents of the bride and groom, to judge from the attacks the legislators launched against them. Even the parents themselves were often not as relentless as they should have been:

The license of this century, the depravation of manners, have always prevailed on our very holy and salutary ordinances, the vigor and the observation of which have been often relaxed, out of consideration for fathers and mothers who forgive their particular affront although they cannot forgive the insult which is made against public law.[16]

The real conflict was between public legislation on the one hand and generally accepted popular custom and usage on the other. The edicts and ordinances clearly show that legists recognized the strength of the tradition they were trying to uproot: the continuing belief that cohabitation, simple mutual consent, made a marriage. After over a century of legislation, the declaration of 1697 contains a remarkable confession:

Some archbishops and bishops have indicated to us that they find in their dioceses a considerable number of persons who live as if they were truly married. . . . [They] imagine that the acts which the notaries have had the temerity to give them of their mutual consent could confer upon them the grace of the sacrament of marriage.

All the laws in the tradition of the edict of 1556 had failed to touch this abuse:

Our *procureurs* have made little effort up to now to oblige those who commit these disorders to correct them when the parents or some other interested party have not taken the affairs of this nature to the regular tribunals of justice. As a result, these profanations remain unpunished.

In other words, long after the Catholic Reformation had transformed the church in France, and in the midst of a powerful *dévot*-oriented regime, the formal quality of marriage had still not been established; people continued to think that, in spite of the laws of church and state, individual mutual choice conferred legitimacy on the act which established particular families. As the proverb put it:

> Boire, manger, coucher ensemble,
> C'est mariage ce me semble.[17]

The relationship between law, manners, and individual choice is clarified in an anecdote recorded by Pierre L'Estoile. In 1582, Claude Tonart, a servant in the household of a Parisian notable, was rescued from the scaffold by an armed group of his friends. His crime was to have impregnated the daughter of a local magistrate. The rescuers received a good deal of public support on the basis of various extenuating circumstances, most interestingly because the girl maintained that "it was a true and legitimate marriage contracted between them, even before copulation." She added that, in any case, her father was himself guilty of sleeping with one of the chambermaids. L'Estoile was annoyed by the popular outcry: "The voice of all the people . . . is worth nothing, and it is not necessary to pause over the opinions of an ignorant and fickle population." Still, he had to admit that "this sentence of death was iniquitous and was found such by all men of address and intelligence, for in the first place the young man and woman maintained that they were married together by mutual consent." As for the question of a "bad match" (*mésalliance*), the young man being only a clerk, L'Estoile argued that the bride's family was itself not so exalted ("It is known that the mother of the girl was daughter of a very ordinary merchant and her father son of a petty official"), and, on the other hand, the boy's background was not as bad as it had at first appeared. Finally, there was the fact of the father's own philandering. All these considerations persuaded L'Estoile that Claude Tonart was innocent and the marriage legitimate.[18]

I do not mean to glorify the triumph of individual freedom in this situation. The pressures in favor of parental power and the maintenance of class lines are not to be minimized, and the earnest young swain was almost executed for transgressing these rules. On the other hand, the incident shows clearly how these commandments could at times be circumvented. Ideas about what makes a marriage, that is, mutual consent (even when verified by no public authority), were so strong that fears of filial defiance and of *mésalliances* often had to cede before them. In such cases, the very vagueness of status distinctions, which made the fear of bad marriages so pervasive, now helped to justify the situation. The touch of satiric humor in this justification—the sexual embarrassment of the father—is also characteristic, and a reading of the satires and domestic comedies of the day indicates how mockery and malicious humor helped people to ease through situations in which important norms were being violated.

I suspect that children frequently insisted on getting married against the wishes of their parents, and that cases of conflict were settled more often by a process of adjustment and compromise (some of the lines of which are suggested by L'Estoile's reasoning in the case of Claude Tonart) than they were in the courts. In other words, we should not accept without reserve the analysis of commentators like Henri de Campion. In spite of the opposition of parents and legists, "love" played a considerable part in the formation of marriage bonds in the seventeenth century.

To complete this line of argument, we should examine a few examples of marriages in families where control over the woman was maintained and where "interest" determined the issue. Even in such situations, we find the semblance of a sentimental dimension. For example, the Comte de Souvigny professed to have fallen completely in love with his bride in the ten days between their first meeting and the conclusion of the marriage agreement. Ostentatiously, he shunned the business aspect of the arrangement: "The person of my mistress was more dear to me than all the goods of the world." And yet, almost immediately afterward, he gave a brief but precise summary of his wife's dowry. Further, his editor informs the reader that this marriage gave Souvigny "the family relations which he had lacked up to that time" and marked a significant turning point in his quest for noble status.[19]

Evidently, Souvigny's pose of disinterest rings false. However, it would be wrong to see in this incident a simple case of hypocrisy. The attempt at a "courtship" was not unusual, and in practice it was quite difficult to maintain the rigid distinction between love and interest.[20] The history of the Richelieu family provides further examples. I have already referred to the strange way in which Jean de Beauvau addressed himself to Henri de Richelieu about his marriage to Henri's sister, Françoise. One might have assumed, on the basis of these letters, that she was excluded from the exchange. In fact, while wooing his "good cousin," Beauvau was also trying to cultivate the future bride, and the dossier contains several notes in which she thanks him for his "courteous letters."[21] These notes, pathetically stiff and formal as they are, nonetheless indicate that the young couple was trying to establish some sort of rapport before taking the step into marriage.

In the case of the marriage of Françoise's younger sister, Nicole, to the Marquis de Brèze, the same ritual took place. First Brèze's mother wrote to one of the brothers of the bride-to-be, assuring him that her son

had already passed several days [with Nicole] in order to demonstrate to her his love, and—surmounting his impatience—I have consented that he give yet a few more avowals of his love and that he render to her the duties and the service to which he is obligated.

The prospective groom described the matter even more baldly:

In acquitting myself of my duty to write you, I beg you very humbly to permit me to speak to you of my passion, telling you, Monsieur, that I have the honor to be with Mademoiselle, your sister, and that I employ all my industry to reveal to her my love and to hide from her my imperfections.

The most interesting letter in the series is the one which indicates Nicole's response to these diligent and rather mechanical attentions. She wrote to her brother:

I confess that you have never ceased to oblige me, and I recognize myself so unworthy of the honor that you do me and the care that you have been pleased to take with me that I remain in confusion.
. . . I have seen what you have indicated to Madame [her mother]

as well as the order you give me to consider the matter. I don't know what response she has made to you. It seems to me that the only one which a proper girl can make is to do as she is told. I will not neglect to say to you, since you find it agreeable, that this benefit [the marriage] is worth more than I am, but that (knowing nothing of the one about whom you have written me, nor of his alliances) it seems to me a good idea to take time to think about it.[22]

These letters show that "courtship" was a necessary part of the ritual of arranging a marriage. They indicate that young men were expected by their future in-laws to woo the bride-to-be with a certain ardor. Brèze's remarks demonstrate his somewhat naive attempts to "acquit" himself of this duty. The girl, on the other hand, while she was supposed to be honored and pleased by the union which her family was negotiating for her, was asked to "think about it," even to express her reservations, as if she really did have a choice in the matter.

At its inception, marriage did have a personal or sentimental dimension in the seventeenth century. Efforts to express these sentiments were compromised by the other considerations which went into contracting a match, but such efforts were made nonetheless. In theory, marriages based on love took second place to those determined by interest. In practice, couples continued to marry out of inclination, in spite of parental attempts to discipline them. Even where the parents did have control, they felt obliged to make some concessions to the feelings of their children and to arrange the semblance of a courtship. We can see that seventeenth-century marriages were not held together solely by "external, formal and authoritarian" pressures. Even where the match was most "institutionalized," an element of companionship was also present. The sentimental importance which the bride and groom attached to the act of getting married cannot, I think, be neglected in assessing family life in the seventeenth century.

III

The reasons why people get married, the way in which individual promptings (of affection or sexual attraction) are reconciled with socio-economic imperatives, is certainly important in determining the quality of the resulting relationship. At the same time, the act of marriage often does not call upon the same emotional resources that are necessary to sustain the union over an extended period of time. It is possible that the institutional pressures which the couple managed to defy or to bend to their own sentimental purposes gradually reasserted themselves as time passed and turned what was at first a close relationship into a more formal, a less intimate coexistence. Some attempt, then, ought to be made to analyze the quality of experience in the marriage itself.

The topic is not an easy one to explore. Household affairs occupy very little space in most of the memoirs of the period. Often marriage negotiations are the only aspect to be mentioned in connection with the family. Even the *livres de raison*, which have delighted conservative historians by providing a picture of industrious, pious domesticity, seem to me strikingly terse in their references to conjugal relations. There are exceptions— writers who enjoyed being with their wives, and liked to give them presents, who were deeply disturbed by the illnesses of their spouses, and struck with grief when they died.[23] However, in most individual accounts, family experience is largely neglected.

When the topic is mentioned, the tone of the discussion tends to be negative. Even its defenders outlined the objections to marriage (in order—it was hoped—to refute them) with considerably more spirit than they did the advantages of the institution. Jean Maillefer, who wrote floridly of falling in love with his wife, nonetheless warned his son against any too-hasty matrimonial decisions: "If those who get married reflected on the consequences of marriage, few would marry, and as much resolution would be required to marry as is needed for the decision to enter the most austere religious order." When a friend asked if he should take a wife, Estienne Pasquier was troubled about what advice to give. On the whole, he was in favor of the idea, but at the same time his analysis is full of a sense of foreboding:

> I speak of marriage as a blind man of colors, but since you are going to put sail to the wind in order to undertake this long voyage, you will recount it to us, not when you have arrived at your destination (which can happen only with death) but while you are on the open seas.[24]

These comments indicate a skeptical attitude toward the benefits of domesticity. They suggest that, in the seventeenth century, marriage was not closely associated with people's ideas of happiness, honor, or virtue, as it often is today. Such attitudes make sense in the light of the proposals of Ariès and Burgess. Ariès' contention that the possible advantages of marriage were once regarded with indifference certainly seems to be corroborated by these cold and sketchy discussions of family life. Burgess would make a similar point in different terms, arguing that the family was held together by institutional considerations. Husband and wife were economic associates, social allies, delegates from different kinship groups, much more than they were friends or lovers. It would be anachronistic to expect intimacy in these unions; the idea of companionship belonged in the future.

However, I think the problem deserves a closer look. People can choose to avoid discussion of a particular topic for a variety of reasons. Historians and sociologists have jumped to the conclusion that in the premodern period reticence about family life indicates a fundamental lack of interest in the matter. My own approach is to look carefully at the scattered remarks on this subject to see if there is any more complicated reason for the general disregard of domesticity.

In particular, I am impressed by the way dislike of marriage tends to coincide with negative feelings toward women. As Pasquier put it, "Marriage . . . is a way of learning how to hate women." In attempting to explain this misogyny, I think we can come to a more satisfactory understanding of the nature of seventeenth-century conjugal life. Everyone, including the most sympathetic writers, took for granted that women were physically and intellectually inferior to men. Even ostensibly feminist writings were often confined to praise for women's obedience and reliability rather than for their more positive virtues. Satirists exploited with gusto the notion of equality between the sexes, especially when this notion was suggested by women themselves. The weaker sex was vain, lazy, overly talkative, too unstable for real friendship, too feeble for genuine responsibility.[25]

Given these opinions, a radical submission on the part of women was plainly the most sensible way of adjusting household relations between the sexes. A model of humility, silence, and complete self-abnegation was held up for the wife. Like a child, she should be seen and not heard. The ideal woman carried submissiveness to its logical conclusion. As Charron put it, women should "yield and accommodate themselves to the ways and moods of their husbands, like a good mirror which faithfully reflects the face, having no desire, love or thought of its own. . . . These wives abide by their husbands in all things." The wife had only one real use. In listing the population of the household, Bodin placed her in fifth place, behind the father (the *chef*) and his subordinates (children, domestics, or apprentices, at least three in number); she was necessary, but only because the republic would perish if not repeopled.[26]

We must beware of exaggeration in these theoretical discussions. The fact that wives were described in such deprecating terms does not necessarily tell us anything about their status in actual family situations. It is true that a marked degree of deference characterized the behavior of women in some situations. For example, in certain areas of France, they were compelled to address their husbands in the third person, to serve them at table, and to stand while they ate.[27] At the same time, I think that until recently historians have been too quick to accept the extreme implications of this kind of evidence.

The legal history of the family provides a good illustration of this misjudgment. The traditional view has been that the legal position of women steadily declined throughout the later Middle Ages. They lost the right to participate in municipal affairs, to sit on certain courts or to testify before them, to substitute for husbands who were absent or who had become insane, to inherit the prerogatives of husbands who had died. Women were compelled to live with their spouses (unless they could prove that "life or salvation" was threatened by continued cohabitation) and were forced to submit to their discipline, even when it involved physical punishment. By the sixteenth century, a woman's word (on a contract, for example) had no legal force unless it was countersigned by her husband or a judge. She was an *incapable*, a lowly subject in the "domestic monarchy" of her husband's household.[28]

In its general outlines, the picture suggested by these facts is not inaccurate. From a legal point of view, women were at a tremendous disadvantage. On the other hand, they were far from defenseless. For example, the wife was assured of her share of family property. The trend in the sixteenth and seventeenth centuries was in the direction of strengthening her control over her own dowry and of more precisely defining her economic rights in the family. The wife whose husband was mismanaging her property could take the matter to court and even force a separation on these grounds. Recent research has tended to show that courts, and the law in general, were not so hostile to women's rights as once was thought.[29]

In the area of economic activity, we also find that first impressions of women's total subordination are somewhat inaccurate. Existing side by side with the image of the woman as submissive, meek, and helpless, and somewhat in contradiction to it, was the ideal of the wife as manager of the household, keeping accounts, overseeing servants, maintaining domestic life while men were busy elsewhere or not themselves capable of the job. Olivier de Serres called the able wife "a treasure, . . . one of the most important resources of the household." Fénelon's innovative concern for the education of young women was motivated by the desire to equip them to perform this set of tasks more effectively. In the sources, one often encounters cases where women were responsible for complicated affairs. In order to be free from the obligations of the household, men were often willing to leave their wives with a remarkably free hand in this sphere. The Comte de Souvigny wrote of his wife:

She had this helpful custom . . . of reading all my letters which fell into her hands, in order to let me see only what could bring me pleasure, and to take care quickly of the other things as it was necessary, without letting me know anything about them until all was settled.

In some families, the woman's status as an administrator even superseded her identity as a wife. The writer of one *livre de raison* describes an interesting request made to him by his widowed brother:

My brother . . . asked me to leave my wife with him for the government of his household . . . which I have granted to him because of the kindnesses he has shown me since my infancy. And since my office obliges me to live in the city of Besançon, . . . I have returned to my residence, going occasionally to see my brother and my wife at Dôle.[30]

Acting as household administrators did not raise wives to a position of real equality with their husbands. The tasks connected with this role required skills and initiative, but it was considered less honorable than those reserved for men. Running a house involved a multitude of vexing details, no one of which was particularly difficult. Any woman with a modicum of diligence could handle the job. Remarks about the good "housewife" were usually patronizing. In speaking of domestic tasks, Bossuet remarked, "these are simple things," but he went on to assure women that God would recognize a job well done, even at such a humble level.[31]

This notion of the wife as manager of the household represents a compromise between the desire to keep women in their place and the realization that they were necessary partners in the task of maintaining social life. The compromise was useful in that it seemed to take advantage of feminine talents while holding them in a somewhat inferior station. However, even this category proved to be inadequate in summing up the feminine role. In many biographies, a strong mother held together the family, supervising the education of her children, even securing posts for them, in the absence of the father, who was away or dead. The Richelieu family is an excellent example. When François de Richelieu (the Cardinal's father) died, his family was so poor . . . that it was necessary to pawn his medals to meet the funeral expenses. . . . He would have been the last sieur de Richelieu if Suzanne de la Porte, his wife, had not reestablished the household by good management, with which she made up for the disorder of his affairs, and by the care that she exercised in the education of their children.

Fagnier has argued that the circumstances of the Religious Wars were especially disruptive for many families and that women had to shoulder an exceptional burden of responsibility during that period. Rather than being stewards to their husbands, wives in these cases were real *chefs de la maison*. The advancing importance of feminine initiative was evident outside the household as well, and in the course of the seventeenth century there were women writers, political leaders, and even generals.[32]

Men were unable to account for these instances of feminine achievement. In some cases—when women intervened in political affairs, for example—this activity was seen as a kind of aberration, a sign of the decadence of the times.[33] In short, notions of what women were capable of, while they showed some flexibility, tended to lag behind what they were actually doing, so that the image of femininity outlined in the theoretical or general discussions of the subject underestimated and played down the role which we can vaguely glimpse women assuming in actual everyday situations.

If men had been truly indifferent to their wives, and to domesticity in general, they would not have gone to such lengths to overstate a case which a simple consultation of the facts of ordinary family life would be sufficient to refute. In fact, the inability to settle on an appropriate description of the wife's role indicates, I think, a general anxiety about the threat they, and marriage, posed for men. The contempt and condescension which superficially inform this antifeminine literature tend to shade off into an unmistakable apprehension. The real trouble with marriage was that it subjected men to their wives. Weak as women were, men somehow came away from prolonged contact with them diminished in vigor and aggressiveness. Fénelon pointed out that, because women lived in conditions of subordination, they tended to develop qualities of subtlety and finesse which endangered man's dominant position far more than would any frontal attack on masculine prerogatives. It was held that women used craft and deception to gain the upper hand over their husbands while ostensibly they continued to go through all the conventional rituals of submission. Often these fears reached grandiose proportions. After claiming that they were inferior to men, Fénelon warned that there was not an intrigue, a revolution, or a war which was not caused by "the unruliness of women"—quite a claim on behalf of such feeble creatures![34]

I have the impression that these fears often had to do with the erotic aspects of marriage. The dangers of conjugal life which I have been discussing are easily translated into explicitly sexual terms—and often were by more uninhibited seventeenth-century observers. The idea that marriage was somehow debilitating, that it made men softer, was based on the belief that sexual activity could be dangerous to the health and ought to be undertaken only at carefully spaced intervals. For this reason, Montaigne recommended late marriage and suggested that soldiers should follow a regime of celibacy.[35]

The problem was not simply physiological. Descriptions of feminine traits, of inconstancy, deception, and unruliness, hinted at a possibility which bolder satirists were to seize with a vengeance. Every husband had to face the danger of being betrayed by his wife. The sense of imprisonment in an impossible position, awaiting what was regarded as an inevitable humiliation, created that suspicious anxiety which made the husband appear so vulnerable and so absurd:

There is hardly one among us who does not fear more the shame which comes to him from the vices of his wife than from his own; who does not concern himself (astonishing charity) more with the conscience of his good wife than with his own morals; who would not prefer to be a thief and blasphemer and that his wife were murderer and heretic, than that she should be less chaste than her husband.

I would guess that many men thought what Montaigne is here able to articulate so clearly and that, in their deprecation of marriage, in refusing to let themselves get involved too intimately with their wives, husbands were prompted by this fear of sexual defeat.[36]

For whatever reasons, domesticity was not warmly regarded by writers of the seventeenth century. We can see that men did not find "mutual affection, sympathetic understanding and comradeship" in their marriages. At the same time, the preceding discussion of the quality of conjugal life helps us to appreciate some of the limitations of the historical interpretation proposed by Burgess. It seems clear that intimacy was a tremendous problem in marriages of the period. It was not easy for husbands and wives to negotiate the difficulties arising in the course of living together. However, in affirming that intimacy was an issue of some importance, I am also suggesting that people did indeed strive for closeness and trust in marriage. In voicing their contempt and fear of women, men implicitly acknowledge that these women were important to them, with the power to affect their contentment and well-being. To accuse wives so energetically of infidelity implies that one secretly harbors the desire that they be faithful and loyal. Whatever its accuracy as a description of actual family life may be, the institution-companionship theory neglects the whole matter of expectations. The seventeenth-century literature on marriage is a literature of disappointment. Against their better judgment (and in contradiction to the arguments of present-day historians and sociologists), an element of companionship continued to be associated with men's hopes for marriage.

According to the model of structural differentiation, the traditional family was loaded down with a host of responsibilities: judicial, economic, social, political. In the process of modernization, these duties have been passed out to an increasing variety of specialized institutions, eventually leaving the family with two significant tasks, the upbringing of children and the psychological satisfaction of the marriage partners. We should note that the family did not receive these assignments from some other institution. On the contrary, they are all that remains of the vast store of obligations which the family once shouldered. It has been responsible for such matters all along, but in the premodern period they were submerged under all the other facets of domesticity and as a consequence could hardly be discharged effectively. In this section, we have explored the literature on the early modern family in order to find the irregular traces of intimacy which existed (in the form of thwarted hopes and a disappointed cynicism) in spite of all the institutional pressures to the contrary. Although these aspects of companionship were relatively inconspicuous, historians should not neglect their influence on the quality of life in the seventeenth-century household.

IV

I want to round out this picture of seventeenth-century marriages with some observations on a family which was falling apart. In April, 1618, after an abortive political intrigue, Henri de Richelieu, his brother, Armand (the future Cardinal) and brother-in-law, Du Pont-Courlay, were all exiled by the king to Avignon. In October of that year, his wife, who had remained at the family estate of Richelieu, died in childbirth. The infant boy survived only a few weeks. Henri tried to get permission to leave Avignon in order to take better care of all the problems connected with this personal tragedy, but he was not allowed to travel until over two months after his wife's death.[37] In the interim, letters had to suffice, and these correspondences give an interesting picture of the nature of the bond which had just been ruptured.

It is perfectly clear that the disaster disrupted an economic arrangement. Henri was apparently in debt, and in the midst of mourning his wife, he did not neglect to take steps in order to gain control of her property. Monetary considerations had been instrumental in making the match seven years earlier, and they were no less salient when it dissolved. First, Henri wrote to a confidant of his wife, cautiously trying to discover what provision she had made for the disposal of her property:

It is with you that my poor wife has deposited by word and in writing her last intention, in order to have me know of it; I swear to you before God and his angels to follow and execute them point by point and to show you that I will love all my life those whom she has loved.

Much depended on his wife's testament: "I await the will of my wife . . . before taking a resolution on the policy I ought to follow in my affairs," he wrote to an associate. Meanwhile, he ordered steps taken to delay an inventory of his property, while comforting himself with the thought that "custom gives me the furniture by my contract of marriage." Eventually, he did receive the will. It does not seem to have contained any surprises, and Henri quickly set in motion procedures designed to safeguard the property which now belonged to him and his son.[38]

This rather cold-blooded calculation should not surprise us. The dossier provides enough evidence of Henri's distaste for marriage. In the love letters he wrote to his mistresses, he showed the usual courtier's contempt of domesticity. He attacked the "hell of marriage" and felt sorry for anyone trapped within its confines. Henri married only when he had to in order to escape a precarious financial situation. He seems to have devoted very little energy to the role of husband, and his wife's letters suggest that she saw him only infrequently. Henri's correspondences after her death indicate the fragmentary quality of the marriage "I have hardly had the chance to possess her, having spent with her only half the time since we have been married." Finally, it might be noted that, although he was the only married brother and therefore the only one capable of carrying forward the family name, Henri did not father a child until after seven years of marriage. This child was conceived in the winter of 1617–1618, at a time when, by the King's order, he was confined to his estates at Richelieu (prior to the more severe punishment of exile to Avignon). Without the royal command, he might never have become a father.[39]

Having established all of these unsentimental facts about the marriage, and confronted with a grief dressed out in a style which is highly florid, convoluted, and repetitious, one may justifiably remain unconvinced by Henri's pious lamentations on the death of his wife. And yet, stilted as they are, there is something persuasive in these letters.

When I recall the good temper of my poor wife, the charms of her nature and the contentments of which I am now deprived forever, I almost die, and pull myself together only to die each time that these thoughts come again into my mind.

His wife had possessed the face and the intelligence of an angel, and in her absence he found himself "burdened with a confusion of affairs which she used to manage with so much order and prudence."[40]

Guilt was mixed with Henri's sadness. "With such a harsh punishment, God has discharged upon me all the shafts of his ire." Since she had died in childbirth, Henri had to recognize his own indirect responsibility for the tragedy: "I have myself been the author of my misfortune, having given death to the one from whom I have received life; for in effect I have lived only since I have been with her." There are many melancholy and even suicidal passages in the letters, as well as signs of bewilderment and helplessness: "Having lost, through the loss of my wife, the source of my strength, I no longer have any resolution or courage." We know that, for a time, Henri retreated into a monastery. A friend wrote to him: "It was truly a Christian and prudent action for you to retire for several days into a holy and religious place . . . to console yourself with God." Marriage had meant more to Henri than one might have thought. As it came to an end, he wrote: "It is hard for me to recognize myself."[41]

These letters complete the point I have been trying to make. We began with a historical scheme in which the sentimental side of marriage, the belief that it is a psychological and affective union, a companionship characterized by affectionate intimacy, was seen as a uniquely modern phenomenon, to be contrasted with the formal, institutional arrangement of an earlier period. I have attempted to show, in the first place, that sentiment played a powerful role in the formation of the marriage bond in the seventeenth century, in spite of the efforts of parents and their legislative and ecclesiastical allies to protect the right of "interest" to determine the nature of the union. Further, I argued that the marriage partners continued to hope—however unrealistically—that their relationship would be marked by a degree of intimacy. Finally, I demonstrated that in at least one modest case, where marriage appears to have been hedged in by socio-economic considerations and where domesticity does not seem to have been of great importance to the husband, the response of this husband to the death of his wife plainly indicates that their relationship had involved commitments and emotional ties which had been meaningful to him.

The hopes people invest in marriage do not always square with the reality of the situation; one has only to reflect on the extent to which the ideal of companionship is realized in the marriages of our own day to see that this is the case. Marriages *were* different in the seventeenth century. They were regarded with more cold calculation, more disillusioned cynicism, than they are today. However, we should not be misled into overlooking the ways in which the basic rationale for marriage, its fundamental psychological significance for the partners, has remained relatively stable through the years.

⚜ 4 ⚜

CONCEPTION AND BIRTH

I

Demographic evidence from the seventeenth century tells us that once they had decided to live together as man and wife, couples very soon began to have children: on the average, the birth of a child followed sixteen months after the marriage had taken place.[1] In this chapter, my task is to show what kind of thinking went into the decision to become parents, what pregnancy and giving birth meant to the mother, and how the delivery itself was managed by doctors and midwives.

In discussing the mechanics of reproduction, writers were primarily interested in factors which inhibited conception. For example, Louise Bourgeois began her *Observations diverses* with an analysis of sterility, which she interpreted as a physiological problem caused by "bad humors," blocking of the cervix, or some other disability in the woman. Other authorities were more subtle, tracing the difficulty to the wife's lack of interest in sex:

The most frequent reason why the orifice [of the womb] does not open . . . to receive the seed of the man is the insensibility of some women, who do not take any pleasure in sexual activity; but when they discover a taste for it, the womb, eager and greedy for this seed, opens and makes itself ready to receive it.

These authors agree in having the possibility of conception depend on the disposition of the female. Here and in general, doctors showed an understanding of the woman's active participation in the process of reproduction. They rejected Aristotle's theory that wives were mere receptacles, and affirmed that the feminine as well as the masculine "seed" (*semence*) was necessary for conception to take place.[2]

From these tracts, one would assume that parents were interested only in increasing the birth rate. In fact, there was an audience for some of this literature: for example, childless noblewomen in search of "remedies" which would help them to conceive. However, in trying to explain the emphasis writers placed on encouraging fertility, we should also remember that, because of the church's stand on contraception, birth control was not a legitimate alternative for adults anxious to keep down the number of their offspring, or for doctors interested in giving advice on family planning. We know from other sources of evidence that fathers and mothers were not always overjoyed by conception and the birth of children. Abortions were attempted, usually by methods so primitive that they did as much harm to the woman as to her fetus. The frequent, and severely punished, incidence of infanticide, as well as the very high percentage of abandoned children, also demonstrates that some parents were not at all interested in larger families, and were prepared to take drastic steps in order to dispose of unwanted babies.[3]

It is possible that the parents' lack of enthusiasm for overly large families affected the rate of conception itself. One of the facts most firmly established by recent demographic study is that women in the seventeenth century did not conceive as often as was once imagined; the average interval between births (after the first) varied from twenty-five to thirty months. This rate, which is more measured than what we would expect if conception were subject to completely spontaneous sexual activity, suggests that parents practiced some form of birth control. However, it is not easy to specify what these methods might have been. The various magical preventives, which formed part of the folklore, could not have had a significant impact on the birth rate. A reign of continence was of course available to the couple anxious to avoid pregnancy. Although we may be skeptical of the universality of such a practice, the wife could always take "a separate bed." The rhythm method was not understood, at least not by the midwife Marguerite du Tertre, who recommended the days immediately after the end of the woman's menstrual period as the optimum time for conception, because the womb was then flushed of its impurities. Furthermore, we have no unambiguous evidence that coitus interruptus was practiced on a wide scale.[4]

Why not, then, a "child a year," the rate of birth one would expect where no effective contraceptive methods were employed? A final hypothesis has to do with the prophylactic effect of maternal lactation; women who breastfeed their new-born infants seem to cut down considerably on the chance of conceiving another child. Pierre Dionis noticed this phenomenon:

> One observes that the mothers who nourish their infants do not conceive as often as those who do not nourish them. Women usually have one infant every year, and nurses go two or three years without becoming pregnant, although they are not separated from their husbands.

The breastfeeding hypothesis seems to fit with demographic evidence in explaining the conditions under which children in the seventeenth century were, and were not, conceived, especially since the time of weaning was usually around eighteen months, or roughly nine months before the woman might normally be expected to give birth to another child.[5]

Breastfeeding may have given women a respite between pregnancies, but it should not be regarded as a method of birth control in our sense of the term. As we will see, hiring a nurse was an economic luxury which only a few families could afford. Most mothers breastfed because they did not have any choice. For these women, feeding children was just another duty, to be added to all the other burdens of daily life. It was a sign of her poverty that the lower-class mother had to take care of children while other, more affluent, women could hire a servant to perform this task. One of the secondary effects of lactation may have been contraceptive; however, women breastfed not to avoid pregnancy but because they had no other means of feeding their infants. As soon as the child was weaned, chances were good that his mother would again become pregnant.

I conclude that the woman in the old regime exerted no effective control over her own reproductive functions. She conceived, nurtured children, and conceived again according to a rhythm which in origin was biological and in practice closely related to the whim of her husband.

II

Childbirth was the most hazardous event in a woman's life, but it was also the most honorable and the most closely associated with ideas of feminine happiness. "Women have among their greatest desires the wish to see themselves with child and well honored by a successful birth." When Henri de Richelieu's pregnant wife was left alone during her husband's exile (awaiting the delivery which was to prove fatal to her), friends seemed to assume that her spirits would be bolstered by pregnancy.

It has pleased God to give you this grand reason for happiness and rejoicing at the same time that you have received some occasion for sadness [from Henri's exile]. You ought to rejoice in the one and not trouble yourself with the other.

In the days before her labor began, the expectant mother was the object of much attention. She would normally be surrounded by "a multitude" of her friends. The delivery (*accouchement*) itself was the moment in seventeenth-century social life when the importance of the woman alone was publicly and formally acknowledged with the greatest force. In pictures of the *accouchement*, festive gatherings, even including children, group themselves around the mother. One doctor did not find it beneath his dignity to advise the guest of honor about the kind of make-up and coiffure to use on this special occasion.[6]

Today, we would find such publicity bizarre, almost depraved. The way in which Marie de Medicis was forced to play the good hostess to the large crowd awaiting the birth of Louis the dauphin seems unnecessarily cruel by our standards. In fact, two world views come into play around this question. We imagine the mother in an impersonal and antiseptic hospital from which friends and relatives are excluded, her anxieties calmed by the scientific, rationalized procedures of the institution and its staff. But the woman of the seventeenth century had little in the way of science to rely on. Without it, her only comfort was to be derived from the "kinsfolkes, friends and helpers" who gathered to honor and encourage her by their respectful presence.[7]

The *accouchement* was not only a great moment for the mother, but also for women in general. In the public celebration of birth, men played a very secondary role. Their presence was often unavoidable. For example, Louis XIII was delivered under the eyes of the princes of the blood, who stepped forward and formally presented themselves to their future king even before the umbilical cord had been cut. In a society where legal and bureaucratic ties were so weak, the attendance of these princes was necessary as a proof of the legitimacy of the infant, but it was regarded nonetheless as something of an intrusion, as Henri IV's apologies to his wife make clear. Men could attend, but their proper place was in the background.[8]

The most conspicuous way in which this feminine preeminence during the *accouchement* was exercised was with respect to the role of the midwife. Surgeons present at the most important births were there as (probably disgruntled) spectators rather than as medical authorities in their own right. On such occasions, and indeed at all births, the midwife ran the show. To some extent, the relationship between midwife and surgeon can be compared to the precedence disputes so characteristic of the old regime, with each side doing its best to codify and reinforce its own claims, while attempting to cast doubt upon or appropriate the functions of the other. I think, however, that the issue was broader than this comparison would imply: we are dealing with a battle between the sexes as well as between occupational *corps*. Midwives had company in wanting surgeons in the background. Expectant mothers showed themselves reluctant to have men too closely associated with the intimate enterprise of giving birth, and their husbands were no less suspicious of masculine intruders. Throughout discussion of the subject, both sexes seem to assume that giving birth is women's work and that they should be allowed to exercise a monopoly over the ceremony of the *accouchement*.[9]

This arrangement was gradually modified in the course of the period under study. Simon de Vallambert's book on childrearing, published in 1565, inaugurated an era. Written in French, it was among the first serious attempts to provide "scholarly" instruction for midwives and nurses. "Obstetrics" was slowly taken over by men. They were much in evidence at the delivery of Louis XIII, although still in a secondary role. Two of these doctors, Jacques Guillemeau and Jean Héroard, have become historical figures in their own right, but at this time they were clearly subordinate to Louise Bourgeois, the midwife in charge of the proceedings. There were growing numbers of male midwives (*accoucheurs* or *accoucheurs-chirurgiens*) throughout the seventeenth century. Henri IV was interested in employing an *accoucheur*, but he decided against it for fear of offending his wife. However, by the 1680s, the court was setting a precedent in choosing them over their feminine rivals. Writing late in the century, Dionis saw the use of male midwives winning favor throughout society. After remarking that "princesses and women of quality" hired them, as did most women of the bourgeoisie, he added: "It is said that the wives of artisans and of the lower classes, if they had the means to pay them, would prefer *accoucheurs* to the midwives." Dionis thought the trend important enough to warrant an extended discussion, and concluded that there was nothing to choose between the two groups, an assertion which would have shocked readers one hundred years earlier.[10]

This trend does not change the general picture in the seventeenth century. For the most part, the midwife continued to be the chief helper for the mother in delivery. She represented that feminine monopoly of power which, if possible in no other sphere of activity, was maintained over the procedures of giving birth.

III

Attempts to organize the midwives and to subject them to some standard training were just developing during the sixteenth century. In the best of cases, the Parisian midwife would receive six weeks' training at the Hôtel Dieu, where pregnant women who could afford nothing better were free to come to have a child delivered. The candidate observed deliveries for three weeks and then practiced herself for three weeks, at which time she was examined by a board of surgeons and senior midwives. The more conscientious Louise Bourgeois, who was married to a surgeon associate of the celebrated doctor, Ambroise Paré, spent five years perfecting her craft in work with the "poor and the ordinary" before taking her exam. But it would probably not be reckless to assume that most women received less training—perhaps no formal instruction at all—before presenting themselves as qualified midwives.[11]

In any case, the resources of the midwife were by our standards frighteningly slim. It was hoped that she would cut her nails, wash, and remove the rings from her hands before beginning. For the delivery itself, a reclining position in bed was suggested by most doctors, although a number of variations were possible: women were known to deliver kneeling, sitting, standing, or leaning on the bed or on a chair. There was disagreement among the authorities on the advisability of inducing the delivery by applying pressure to the abdomen, with some in favor of vigorous encouragement and others more willing to let the mother and child proceed at their own pace. The midwife was supposed to apply oils or butter to the birth canal and to reach in to pull the infant along. In general, doctors did not have a great deal to say about normal births. Ambroise Paré's advice is typical: "One must leave things up to nature and the midwife."[12]

Little could be done if the delivery encountered some major snag. Midwives would offer remedies to women in special pain: concoctions involving almond oil, white wine, or more outlandish ingredients. Some authorities gave elaborate instructions in case the infant was positioned incorrectly at the moment of delivery, and these instructions make it clear that the mother in such cases was in for a trying ordeal. Occasionally, texts include illustrations of "instruments"—lethal-looking hooks and pincers. If the doctor was really at a loss, as must often have been the case, he would fall back on the universal remedies: bleeding the woman, or giving her an "enema" (*clystère*).[13]

Caesarean deliveries may have been attempted by the boldest doctors and midwives, but the serious writers were almost unanimous in rejecting this expedient unless the woman was already dead. Mauriceau saw a "too great excess of inhumanity, of cruelty, and of barbarity" in the operation, which, nonetheless, "some ignorant men still try every day in the countryside, a pernicious abuse which all the magistrates ought to combat." Louise Bourgeois' description of consultations on this subject during one birth crisis indicates the way in which Caesareans, and perhaps more broadly the whole process of delivery, were regarded: "Some spoke of the Caesarean operation, but neither the doctors nor the surgeons wanted to try, resolving that it would risk the death of the mother without providing any hope for the infant. So they left the affair in the hands of God and of nature." I think that in general, for all their learned citations, the doctors never succeeded in raising the discussion of this mysterious topic much above the point where the matter rested "in the hands of God and of nature."[14]

We can see that both mother and child were very much endangered by the act of birth. The midwife was empowered to baptise the child immediately after delivery if she felt he could not survive until a more auspicious occasion. When the infant was dying while still in the womb, she was to use a syringe to inject holy water up the birth canal and to say: "If you have life, I baptise you in the name of the Father, the Son and the Holy Ghost." It goes without saying that premature children almost always died. At six months, the prospects were hopeless. Chances were a little better for the seven- or eight-month baby, but even for children delivered after the normal term, deaths were frequent. It is true of every new-born infant that "he drawes his death after him: the which may be plainly perceived by the

cries and laments which he maketh as soone as he seeth the light."
But the observation is particularly relevant to the embattled infant born in the circumstances we have been describing.[15]

For the mother, the trial was no less dangerous. Many births
went smoothly enough: one *livre de raison* records a labor of one
half-hour, and Héroard indicates that Marie de Medicis was
delivered of one of Louis' younger brothers after only one contraction (whereas the dauphin required a labor of just under
twenty-four hours). However, to balance these accounts, there
are references to periods of labor lasting up to nine or ten days.
as well as to the great frequency with which women died in
childbirth.[16] Even the most expert observers barely understood
the process of birth and knew no effective means of intervening
if the delivery did not go smoothly. In spite of the presence of
friends and relatives, and beyond the ministrations of the midwife,
women had to pass through the ordeal of childbirth completely
alone. Ironically, in a society which put such a high premium on
bravery and endurance, and in which masculine prerogatives
were so aggressively formulated, childbearing was probably the
single experience which made the heaviest demands on the
courage and fortitude of the participant. For all their vainglorious
pretentions, men were obliged to watch helplessly from the side-
lines as women faced this ultimate trial. The paradox must be
counted among those factors complicating relations between the
sexes in the seventeenth century.

✠ 5 ✠

PARENTS AND THEIR ALLIES: KINFOLK, THE GOVERNESS, AND THE NURSE

I

Anthropologists long ago demolished whatever illusions we may have had concerning the universal importance of the nuclear family. At the same time, in thinking about psychological issues, we continue to assume that human personality is strongly influenced by the child's relationship to his biological parents.[1] In the light of these considerations, I want to introduce the personnel involved in seventeenth-century childrearing before proceeding to an analysis of the stages of infantile growth. In fact, analysis of the family in early modern France does not uncover any exotic departures from the familiar constellation of father, mother, and child. Still, within this framework, there are interesting variations which indicate some of the special features of childrearing in that period.

We have seen in a general way how important kinship was during the medieval and early modern periods. Ariès maintains that the extended kinship group commanded individual loyalty far more effectively than did the restricted nuclear family, and institutional historians have argued that this group was once active in judicial, economic, and political affairs of the highest importance. If extended kinship ties did indeed play such a prominent part in family and social life, one might expect that the child would look to more distant relatives as much as to his own parents for guidance and support. In this section, I want first to explore the question of kinship ties in the seventeenth century, to specify in what way they were significant as a principle of organizing group behavior, and then to demonstrate how they influenced arrangements made for the upbringing of children.

Family loyalty in seventeenth-century France was intense, but at the same time very unfocused. On the one hand, kinship solidarity was among the most respected principles of the period. On the other, when it came to specific situations, this principle was often ineffective in dictating individual conduct. By comparison, kinship systems in primitive societies tend to be very carefully worked out. The child is instructed in a pattern of respect and avoidance which makes clear just what duties he owes to each of his relatives, and what services he can expect in return. Whatever its sentimental importance, the French kinship system lacked the rules and regulations which would have made clear how it was to be operative in daily life.[2]

To illustrate, we can observe this system at one of its most fragile points: between groups united by marriage. Parents with marriageable children often hoped to consolidate political or social alliances with other families by arranging a match with them. There was no doubt that people related through marriage were closer than those who were not. At the same time, no one was quite sure how such closeness was to be translated into actual deeds. In these situations, where people were suddenly brought together into a state of supposedly greater intimacy, the uncertainty which pervaded the whole kinship system was especially marked.

We can get some idea of the nature of this system by looking at two alliances within the Richelieu family. Jean de Beauvau died very soon after his marriage to Françoise du Plessis. It will be remembered that the negotiations for this marriage had centered on the ties between the prospective groom and his future brother-in-law, ties which, it was hoped, would be significantly strengthened by the union. The lack of further evidence and the early death of the husband prevent us from drawing any conclusions about the success of the alliance. Six years later, however, Françoise married again, this time with less ambiguous results. The groom was Du Pont-Courlay, a noble of somewhat mediocre standing, but with a number of powerful friends. Although over twenty years older than his brother-in-law, Du Pont quickly established the closest of relationships with Henri, and from then on they were regarded as a team by the memoirists of the period. I have the impression that Henri was closer to his brother-in-law than to his real brothers. He addressed Du Pont simply as *"mon frère."*[3]

The case of the Marquis de Brèze, the other brother-in-law, provides an interesting contrast. Brèze, who married the younger daughter, Nicole, in 1617, was from an old and respected family, but the alliance does not seem to have brought as much to the Richelieus as they might have hoped. From the start, he displayed a certain touchiness about the quality of his relationship to his in-laws. Writing to Armand in September, 1618, he mentioned that his wife was ill and then added:

I hope at least that God will conserve her for me and I dare say for you more than me, Monsieur, since for all sorts of reasons she ought to be attached to you by affection and by service more than to anyone in the world.

Evidently Brèze saw Nicole's loyalties remaining with her first family.[4]

Whether he really was, or was only pretending to be, uncertain of his wife's allegiance, Brèze proved to be a disappointing and unreliable ally to the Richelieus. His independence is noted in several sources. One writer reports that "he so lacked a sense of accommodation that he told Richelieu to his face that he had married his sister, but without other consideration than her beauty." We should not take this assertion as a genuine indication of tenderness for his bride. From other evidence, it is clear that he was far from a devoted husband. Rather, the statement had a symbolic quality. To marry a woman "for her beauty," or for any consideration of sentiment, was in effect to refuse that notion of marriage in which the union brought two families into a new relationship to one another, involving fresh obligations and services. Brèze's apparently romantic statement was in fact a kind of defiance, a way of informing his in-laws that he did not regard his ties to them as binding, that he was not about to accept his bride as the carrier of a strange set of duties which he would be expected to assume.[5]

We see here some of the advantages and the misunderstandings which might result from a marriage. Depending on the personalities involved, it could bring friends closer and reinforce their resolve to work together. In the best of circumstances, the in-laws were almost assimilated to the family and were addressed simply as "brother" and "sister" in a way which seemed to seal the bargain.[6] However, the system was not categorical enough to create a sense of cooperation where before none had existed. For the most part, marriage brought together people in some sense obligated to one another, but with the exact nature of the obligation remaining uncertain, subject to careful testing and diplomacy.

All kinship ties were subject to the same problems. Blood relationships were stronger than those of marriage, but they were no more comprehensibly linked to a set schedule of mutual favors. Throughout the system, these favors had to be negotiated, with particular circumstances and personalities taken into account. This is the perspective from which we must ask about the role of kinship in childrearing. In general, the biological parents assumed responsibility for the upbringing of their offspring. At the same time, it is also possible that other relatives sometimes took part in this endeavor. Did the roster of possible services which one might demand of kinfolk include help in caring for small children?

In this connection, Henri de Richelieu's letters after the loss of his wife are again relevant. It will be remembered that the woman had died in childbirth. The most pressing problem confronting the widower was how to arrange for the care of the new-born infant. Henri was in a particularly desperate position because his brother and brother-in-law, the people he might have been able to rely on with the most confidence, were themselves sharing his exile. The third brother, Alphonse, did not enter into the crisis except for a letter of consolation.[7] His special status as a monk seems on this occasion to have put him outside the sphere of family activities. Henri had to search for other allies.

One of the first letters was to his mother-in-law. The tone was formal and correct, and the most Henri allowed himself to request was her future "good wishes" for him and his son. In answering a letter of consolation from another, unspecified, relative, he wrote:

Without this poor orphan whom she has left me, I would no longer want to live at all; I beg you in the name of God that he inherit the amity which you felt for his mother; for, just as you have written me that you would have wanted her to take care of my cousins, your daughters, I pray you to have a care for him if it pleases God to take me.

I suspect that these kinfolk were on the dead wife's side. While relations were cordial, the situation still did not allow Henri to request their immediate aid. Carefully, Henri tests the possibility: only if the infant should be completely orphaned would these relatives be compelled to intervene.[8]

With his sister, Nicole, Henri was on surer ground. In fact, she seems to have made the first move: "If I can render to you some very humble service, I will do it with more affection by a thousand times than if it were for myself." However, even here the way was not completely smooth. First, Nicole and her husband were sick. Henri wrote:

Until now, your state and the sickness of my brother have prevented me from asking you to go for awhile to Richelieu, but since necessity makes its own laws, I now beg you (providing that your health would not be affected) to take the trouble [of the trip] in order to do the things which will be necessary for your little nephew.

We are not of course dealing with a milieu in which traveling, even for healthy people, was always convenient or safe. The reference to Nicole's husband indicates another problem, although Henri tried to smooth the way with his familiar "my brother." The request to his sister found him venturing into an area where he was not sure of his rights. He tactfully added later in the letter: "If it pleases Monsieur de Brèze to go with you, that would be a great honor to me." As a wife, his sister was already the mistress of one household, and she was able to help Henri only for a brief period of time.[9]

Except for the temporary aid of Nicole, Henri could not enlist any of his kin in this emergency. Instead, he had to rely on a steward whom he did not trust, and who himself was soon called away by his own affairs.[10] The story ends with the death of Henri's son at the age of six weeks. In this particular case, we can see that the union of husband and wife defined a certain social and physical space in which the baby found some protection. When this union was disrupted, and especially when something happened to the mother, the kinship system was very hard pressed to provide alternatives. I make no argument here that the Richelieu family was "typical," although I do think that the lesson of Henri's experience is confirmed by other accounts of family life. These letters simply indicate that, whatever may be said in general of the strength of seventeenth-century family ties, the kinship network could be very unresponsive, even in situations where a life was at stake. I believe that, along with a host of other favors, the supervision of infants was negotiable among relatives, but it was one of the last services which a man could realistically expect from his kinfolk. In fact, the biological parents were primarily, and indeed almost solely, responsible for child care. Whatever else may be said of the prominent place granted to kinship ties in the historical scheme designed by Ariès, we can affirm that these ties were not strong enough to supplant the mother and father in their tutelage of very small children.

II

In some families, a governess helped in the upbringing of children. The great nobles of France, and particularly the royal family, placed their offspring in separate households with staffs of as many as one hundred people.[11] It was the job of the governess to preside over this household and to supervise on a day-to-day basis the children placed under her authority. Henri IV followed this procedure with his first-born, and Héroard's *Journal* gives an informative picture of how the arrangement worked out.

Moments after the successful delivery of the dauphin, Henri

IV commanded, "Give him to Madame de Montglat," whom he had chosen to be his son's governess.[12] This woman, the wife of the "king's first steward," was thus put in charge of the household to be organized around the young prince. It was to include the dauphin, the siblings who were born after him, as well as his half-brothers and sisters (Henri's bastards), the children's nurses, their husbands and offspring, doctors (Héroard among them), ladies-in-waiting, and a host of other retainers and servants.

In what sense was the dauphin "given" to his governess? Madame de Montglat took seriously the king's order: "I can say that Monseigneur the dauphin is mine. The king gave him to me at his birth, saying to me: 'Madame de Montglat, here is my son whom I give to you, take him.' " This "possession" entitled the governess to certain rewards, among them "all the goods which had been at the disposal of the prince," which she would receive after relinquishing control over him (around his seventh birthday). A mercenary interest was common to all the members of Louis' entourage. Each of them was entitled to a "wage" (*gage*), and to whatever "unofficial" income might be acquired by means of extortion from the dauphin: Madame de Montglat often forced her charge to coax favors from the king's ministers, and soldiers of the guard quickly stole whatever coins he was given. Numerous details make it clear that the prince's household was not so much a carefully planned nursery as it was a bundle of sinecures for various petty officials and servants.[13]

When considered in this perspective, arrangements for the care of the infant do not look promising, and from Héroard's account it is clear that many of the adults in the household were not well qualified for their task, beginning with the governess herself, whom one observer characterized as a "violent and unkind" woman. However, looking at the situation from a slightly different angle, one gets another impression of this apparently venal group. They were, after all, being paid for a particular service: to look out for the interests of the child in a world not notably attentive to infantile problems. When the dauphin was first taken to the Louvre, no preparations had been made to receive him. Héroard permitted himself one of his rare shows of temper, denouncing the incompetence of the officers who could neglect "such a precious treasure." The *Journal* is full of similar anecdotes. Because the Louvre and the royal court could not be organized around the needs of a helpless infant, it made sense to appoint a group of people with the special task of protecting the dauphin. The staff of the household may have been more or less unqualified for the job, but Louis would obviously have been much worse off without the care they gave him.[14]

The insulation this household provided between the court and the dauphin often shielded the latter even from his own parents, the king and queen. When Louis was only a few weeks old, a serious accident almost occurred: "As his Majesty, holding the dauphin in his arms, diverted himself by making the infant jump with pleasure, the baby slipped from his hands, and if the nurse had not been there to catch him just in time, he might have been killed." The *Journal* contains many other less dramatic incidents in which the entourage of the dauphin, with its more highly developed sense of the child's welfare, tried to thwart the influence of the royal couple. To give a petty but characteristic example, when the family dined together, Henri always wanted his son to eat what the adults were having and to share the wine. Héroard notes these instances without any explicit reproach, but he makes clear that, after the parents had departed, every effort was made to return Louis to his habitual dietary regime.[15]

The governess and her household are interesting manifestations of the sociology of seventeenth-century childrearing. These matters provide us with a good opportunity to test Ariès' hypothesis that family life can be related to questions of more general social and cultural history, that patterns typical of social interaction in general will be found within the home as well. The household system embodies certain paradoxes. From one point of view, the governess and her assistants were little qualified for their job; from another, we can see how indispensable they were to the infant. At times these people, who were being paid by the king to watch over his child, seem as a consequence to be mere underlings of their master. On the other hand, the financial arrangement also gave them a powerful claim to "possess" the dauphin who had been placed in their hands, a claim which emboldened them on occasion even to oppose the wishes of the father with respect to his infant son. Puzzling when taken out of context, these paradoxes make perfect sense when considered in terms of a somewhat broader frame of reference.

Think of an ecclesiastical benefice or a judicial office. In some sense, even by seventeenth-century standards, there was a contradiction between the ideological imperatives of the posts in question (spiritually and learning; impartiality and legal training) and the hard realities which actually dictated appointments. In fact, benefices and offices held a group of powerful potential enemies in some kind of tenuous loyalty to the regime. In order to "get things done," the king had to give something up. For example, he lost a measure of control over the judicial system by selling positions to the highest bidder. The magistrates might then use their powers (which they "owned") to oppose the monarchy in the short term. On the other hand, they could be counted on to keep the system going, and to support the government in a crisis, because their investments were tied up in the status quo.

On the one hand, this system looks completely corrupt since the choice of personnel is carried out according to principles which have nothing to do with the stated aims of the institution in question. On the other, business is still transacted, and not always in a way completely at variance with these stated ideals. Somehow Henri IV, who made his four-year-old nephew a bishop, also appointed many of the distinguished clerics who were later instrumental in the Catholic Reformation. At least a few of the rich men who bought their way into the magistracy turned out to be great judges. From a purely administrative point of view, it is equally hard to make a conclusive evaluation of the system. From one point of view, the king lost control (either a constructive or a dangerous consequence, depending on what you think of the monarchy). From another, he assured himself of the ultimate loyalty of the beneficiaries, who had an interest in the stability of the regime, even if they disagreed with, and resisted, its day-to-day programs.

The same patterns are evident in the administration of child care. Because he is articulate and conscientious, Héroard well illustrates some of the ambiguities of the situation. The doctor was an exemplary guardian, and for many years the usually suspicious Louis remained dedicated to him in appreciation of his loyal service. Héroard saw and reacted against the petty ways in which the dauphin was used and neglected, and in the *Journal* he often appears as a lonely champion of the interests of the child. At the same time, he tells us nothing about his own life spent at court, of his skills as a courtier (undoubtedly considerable), or of his relations with the various important people who had been responsible for his appointment in the first place. Evidently not, for these matters do not precisely square with the ethic of the selfless doctor working disinterestedly at his craft for the good of the dauphin and the king. Like the career of a pious bishop or an upright magistrate, Héroard's presence in the dauphin's household checks any reductionist impulse on the part of the historian anxious to spotlight the hypocrisies of seventeenth-century elites. On the other hand, the lacunae in the doctor's *Journal*, and the sense one has of the ambiguity of his situation, remind us of the characteristic gap between ideology and institutional practice in the old regime.[16]

Like a piece of land, a title or a revenue, the child had become the means of tying clients to their master. The dauphin, a kind of living benefice, was the glue holding together a complicated network of lord and creatures. Héroard's moving dedication to his task was one by-product of the arrangement Henri IV made for the care of his son. Another, which we should not forget, was that "all the goods which had been at the disposal of the prince" would bulk large in the inventories of the "King's first steward."[17]

Finally, to continue with the points raised by our parallel, the king had delegated to his subordinates the responsibility of raising his son, a responsibility which he was unwilling or unable to exercise directly. In so doing, he was assured that this essential task would be carried out in some minimally effective way. However, as with all such arrangements in the old regime, the king lost something in the process. The dauphin did not grow up under the eye of his parents but in a separate household where the king and queen came as visitors. The tension between the royal couple and their servants shows that (for good or ill) the former did not have entire control over the upbringing of their children.

The use of the governess and her household made sense in terms of the existing modes of social organization and in fact demonstrates the capacity of such modes to invade all areas of human experience and to determine the form taken by interpersonal relations even at a relatively intimate level. Clearly the raising of children does not take place in a vacuum but must be institutionalized in the terms made available by the society in question. Because the use of governesses was confined to a very limited segment of society, the particular mechanisms I have been examining do not have a very widespread relevance. But the principles uncovered in this examination will help us to understand the significance of a more widely employed assistant in the task of raising children: the nurse.

Before going on, we ought to ask what the presence of the governess meant to the child himself. Most conspicuously, the sense of the household universe revolving around him helped the young prince to develop early an exalted notion of his own importance, and there is no mistaking a cruel arrogance in Louis' attitude toward his servants. At the same time, another, more mournful, theme appears in the *Journal*. The dauphin's sadness, his embarrassed and usually unsuccessful attempts to escape the stratagems designed to take advantage of him, his painful sense of separation from his parents—all these attitudes give Louis the air of a hostage in an unfriendly foreign land. When someone asked why he was angry with Madame de Montglat, Louis replied: "It's because she wants to keep all my silver plate." The construction of the household in which he lived told the dauphin that noble, royal blood made him special, but also that as a child he was something inferior, a chattel to be used in the elaborate dealings which adults had with one another. After Madame de Montglat made the speech about owning him, Louis was heard to mutter: "I hope that someday I'll belong to myself."[18]

III

The most important of parental allies was the nurse. It was the almost unanimous opinion of churchmen, doctors, and moralists from Erasmus on that mothers ought to breastfeed their own infants. Some theologians even tried to suggest that a failure to do so should be regarded as a mortal sin. At the same time, these writers would reluctantly add some words of advice on how to choose a nurse, a last-minute concession indicating that the practice was far too strongly entrenched in the mores of the period to be dislodged by the exhortations of a few intellectuals. In this respect, Rousseau, who has always been regarded as the revolutionary champion of maternal breastfeeding, was no less sensitive to custom than his predecessors, and his passionate appeal to mothers was followed by some sober recommendations for selecting a nurse, and even a touch of lyricism on the joys of nursing in the fresh air of the countryside. In this section, I describe the deeply rooted practice of employing nurses, and explore some of the possible reasons for their participation in family life.[19]

The first point to note about the nurse is her poverty. "All the women who hire themselves out as nurses are peasants or women of mean estate." By contrast, the family which employed her necessarily belonged to a relatively affluent class. François Mauriceau noted that poor people did not even have the means to hire a nurse for the first week of the baby's life, during which time he believed the mother's own milk was not good for the infant. These women would have to breastfeed their children themselves right from the beginning. There was no possibility of help even for a brief period. He went on to single out among the people who engaged nurses "all the women of quality and a majority of the bourgeoisie."[20]

The relationship of the nurse to her employers varied with circumstances. The woman might be a long-term domestic of the parents, perhaps the nurse of earlier children from the same family. In many cases, however, she was a stranger. In Paris, placement bureaus arranged connections between nurses and families interested in doing business. Many writers deplored the frequent failure of mothers to investigate the character of the women they were choosing to feed their offspring. In spite of the doctors' urgings, this choice was often not made in advance of the birth. Where details are given, the parents, even those who seem especially thoughtful and attentive to the welfare of their children, contracted with the nurse after the baby had been delivered. Sometimes the father of the infant gave the money directly to the nurse's husband.[21]

These details suggest the venal quality of the relationship of the nurse to the child she was feeding and to the child's family. This quality horrified the doctors and moralists who criticized nonmaternal breastfeeding. "The nurse has for the child only a feigned and simulated love that has for aim and foundation the hope of the recompense which she expects for her trouble." Since the contract was a purely financial one, the parents ran the risk of being "cheated," and the mother was advised to pay unexpected visits to the nurse's lodgings. If the woman's sheets were dry, it was a sure sign that she had not been breastfeeding and that her milk had stopped secreting. To the nurse, the child was only a means of making some extra money, and the laws dealing with this subject formulated strict penalties against those who out of greed tried to contract with more than one family at the same time.[22]

In all the seventeenth-century literature on childrearing, nurses were the most hated scapegoats. They were vicious, slothful, and inclined to drunkenness. Children were often smothered when nurses rolled over on top of them in their sleep. Even if the nurse managed to avoid doing overt harm to her charge, the latter would still be damaged by the process of feeding itself, for it was generally believed that the child took in the nurse's ignoble character through her milk. Some observers felt a certain sympathy for nurses, but even in these cases, aversion and disgust were the dominant attitudes: "I do not know anything more deceitful than a nurse; no matter how prepossessing they may seem, necessity reduces them to it."[23]

As explanations of the practice of employing nurses, these attacks are of little help. In condemning a custom they disliked,

the doctors seem to have saved the greatest store of their indigna-
tion for the party who in real life exercised the least initiative.
They devoted much energy to violent criticisms of the depravity
and meanness of the nurses, although it is clear to any alert reader
that these women were not to blame for their own exploitation.
We must go beyond these diatribes to ask: if the nurses were
so odious, why did prosperous mothers go on hiring them?

Women had a number of reasons for wanting nurses to take
over the care of their children. Nursing was regarded as a
dangerous, debilitating undertaking for a mother fresh from
childbirth. Further, in opposition to the act of giving birth (and
in spite of the efforts of doctors and moralists), the process of
childrearing was not valued very highly and did not bring the
mother much in the way of prestige or honor. Why should the
mother "add to the pains which she had suffered in childbirth
the grievous and difficult burden of feeding" the new-born
infant? It should be remarked that this line of reasoning is based
squarely upon the assumption that childrearing is not a pleasura-
ble or rewarding experience, but simply an obnoxious task which
might well be passed on to someone else. When care for infants
meant only "the smell of the excrement of the baby . . . the
crying and the tears . . . the sleepless nights," it certainly did
make sense to call in a nurse whenever possible.[24] Given these
attitudes, the job of childrearing tended to degrade the mother
who undertook it. For a "woman of quality" to spend too much
time with infants was to run the risk of a "forfeiture of nobility"
(dérogeance).

I use the notion of dérogeance deliberately in this context.
Analysis of the role of the governess has prepared us to see
methods of arranging for the care of children in terms of the
patterns of social interaction which they represent. When he
thought about child care, the plan Henri IV worked out was
structurally very similar to the solutions he contrived for any
thorny problem of administration. In practice, the arrangements
made with the nurse were primitive compared to those with the
governess, who presided over an extensive household. Furthermore, the attitudes manifested by parents in their use of the
nurse were much more diffuse and subliminal than those of the

royal couple toward Madame de Montglat. Still, I think that the presence of the nurse is not fully comprehensible unless considered in terms of more general social attitudes.

Let us consider for a moment what happened when the nurse assumed responsibility for the child of well-to-do parents. Sometimes she would move in with the infant's family, taking her place among the other domestics of the household. Or the nurse might remove the baby to her home in the countryside.[25] In either case, she would probably find herself in a difficult position. To be capable of breastfeeding, she must necessarily have been suckling a child before the coming of the newcomer. It is possible that her own offspring had recently died, or that she had just weaned an infant, who was now able to get his nourishment elsewhere. However, I have the impression that in most instances she would be faced with the task of breastfeeding two children at the same time. While the rich mother went her own way, and the milk in her breasts gradually dried up, the nurse suddenly had to deal with an intensified problem of sustenance.

Again, arrangements within the household exactly recapitulate those found in the society at large. This way of distributing available resources was typical of French society in the seventeenth century. Just as the poor were forced to pay many times over for the wars and the extravagant life style of the rich, so the affluent mother enjoyed her freedom from the burdens of child care at the expense of the nurse, who had to supply milk to feed her own infants as well as the children of her masters.

Although the critiques of the nurse's character and performance were very outspoken, none of the writers suggested that she might give preferential treatment to her own children. On the contrary, when they did take note of this aspect of the situation, these writers condemned the nurse for precisely the opposite injustice.

> What tenderness can e'er from her be known
> Who, for another's child, neglects her own?

The contractual arrangement apparently succeeded in abrogating the natural ties between the nurse and her offspring. The interloper came first because he had paid for the milk. In speaking of this matter, Montaigne wrote:

For a very slight profit, we tear . . . their own infants from their mothers' arms, and make these mothers take charge of ours. We cause them to abandon their children to some wretched nurse, to whom we do not wish to commit our own, or to some goat, forbidding them not only to breastfeed . . . but also to care for them in any way, so that they will be able to devote themselves completely to ours. And one sees, in the majority of cases, that a bastard affection is engendered, more vehement than the natural; a greater solicitude for the conservation of the borrowed infant than for their own. As for the goats, it is common around here to see women of the village, when they cannot feed the children at their breast, call the goats to their rescue.[26]

The arrangement between the two women had an obvious social function. Seventeenth-century France was not a caste society. While there were pronounced gaps between social groups, in the daily routines of life people of different classes were constantly associating. This association was found even in the court where Louis XIII grew up: Héroard's *Journal* makes clear that the dauphin lived amid crowds of peasants and artisans, entertainers and beggars. Such instances are characteristic of that "sociability"—the mixing of ages and classes, and their "coexistence . . . in a single space"—which Ariès found to be so typical of premodern society.[27] The fact that the children of the rich were nursed by poorer women is only one among many signs of the free association of people who differed greatly in status.

However, if we look carefully at such situations, I think we find that they work to differentiate the participants one from another even as they give the appearance of bringing them closer together. Ostensibly a sign of familiar association, the nursing arrangement in fact powerfully emphasized class differences. The upper-class mother was provided with a conspicuous sign of her superiority in that she was free of a degrading occupation which other, poorer women had to perform. The nurse, on the other hand, was presented with an economic problem; or rather the difficulties of sustenance in her life were aggravated by the coming of another mouth to feed. The idea of respect for her masters and of her own lack of worth was underlined in that the nurse had to set aside her own infant and to devote her primary attentions to the intruding child in order to be acquitted of her part in the bargain. As a domesticated animal, she was alienated from her own motherhood. In spite of its air of intimacy, I think it clear that the overall effect of the transaction was a sharpened sense of the distance between the two women and between the social groups they represented.

Hiring a nurse was part of a particular style of life. It helped to define the status of the participating mothers and of the families to which they belonged. At the same time, I think that this socially oriented analysis still leaves unexplored some facets of the problem. After all, our understanding of the reasons nurses were employed comes almost entirely from the medical literature in favor of maternal breastfeeding. These critiques do not give a completely persuasive summary of the position they were trying to undermine. Why should the doctors render in convincing form a point of view they thought incorrect? Yet all the doctors grant that the use of nurses was a firmly established custom, and all of them make some attempt to explain why women chose to follow it. They do manage to convey something of the mother's position: that childrearing was difficult, unhealthy, and unrewarding. At the same time, in reviewing these arguments, I had the impression that the doctors were floundering, that they were not really sure why women would want nurses. Their arguments seemed to be filled out with implausible rationalizations, for example, that the mother might catch some disease from her child.[28] I began to wonder if perhaps the doctors were repeating with mothers the mistake they made with the nurses. They were attributing to them an initiative in the arrangement which these women actually did not possess. The reasons they put in the mouths of mothers sounded contrived perhaps because the women were not the parties most anxious to invite in the nurse.

We do know that some mothers who could have afforded

nurses still chose to breastfeed their own infants. It was also recognized that the mother who followed this course was displaying a special devotion and conscientiousness. A case in point is Cardinal Richelieu's mother, Suzanne de la Porte, who seems to have shown a marked concern for the welfare of her children. After she died, Henri sent a letter of consolation to his younger sister, Nicole, in which he said:

I will try to help you and serve you in whatever way that I can, although you will never regain anywhere what you have lost with her, since nothing can compare to the love of mothers for their children, especially for those they carried on their breast.

I suspect that attitudes toward breastfeeding among "women of quality" were more or less in flux. When Marguerite de Valois visited a friend, she was surprised when her hostess began to breastfeed an infant in the presence of the company; under normal circumstances, such behavior would be thought "uncivil." We are reminded of the arguments summarized earlier to the effect that breastfeeding was repugnant and degrading for a well-born woman. And yet the breach of manners was not really drastic: "She did it with so much grace and simplicity . . . that she received as much commendation for this gesture as the company did pleasure."[29]

These details suggest to me that women were not the prime movers in the hiring of nurses. In any case, the final authority in important family matters did not rest with them. They had reasons for wanting to call in a nurse, but their husbands were just as interested in this decision. Almost all the doctors who begged women to breastfeed their own children recognized at some point in their argument that the paterfamilias was perhaps the more important party to be persuaded. Putting a baby out to nurse had the effect of leaving the mother at the disposal of her mate. If the child remained on his mother's breast, the husband would then find himself in the position of competing for the attentions and the loyalty of his wife. He had much to lose if his spouse became absorbed in the pleasures and the duties of motherhood. The woman herself might be inclined to see the matter in this light. Simon de Vallambert remarked that nurses were often hired because of the mother's desire to retain "a slender figure, pretty breasts, firm nipples, round and smooth." I would guess, however, that the main pressure for the employ of nurses came from the husband. The practice minimized inconvenience in the conjugal life of the head of the household and was thus one of the many benefits which their wealth allowed *les gens de bien* to acquire.[30]

If we think about the second husband—of the nurse—we can see how psychological and social spheres interlock. The upper-class father buys a clear Oedipal victory, keeping the mother to himself. This victory is the more complete if the child is sent away into the nurse's house. The husband of the latter, unable to remove the first child who stood between him and his wife, is now doubly defeated by the coming of a second rival.

The logic of this model is not perfect. The father who most completely rids himself of the rivalry of his son sends him to the nurse's home. In this situation, while children may have been a nuisance, the nurse's husband still could approach his wife. On the other hand, when the father brought the nurse into his own household, he was able to supervise her private life, but he also had to put up with the distractions of a child's presence in his relations with his wife. Given these circumstances, it is not surprising that medical opinion about the kind of sex life a nurse should have was somewhat confused. Several authorities advised against intercourse for the nurse because it "troubled the blood," or caused the nurse's milk to smell, or because it introduced the possibility of another pregnancy. In practice, my impression is that these post-partem sex taboos were not observed. Several experts recognized that the advice was unrealistic and believed sexual abstinence would in any case harm the disposition of the nurse and therefore diminish her effectiveness as a guardian for the child.[31]

In the most powerful families, the father was strong enough to solve these contradictions by consigning his child to a separate household *and* separating the nurse from her mate. Dionis observed that "all the women of the first rank . . . are careful to separate the nurse from her husband." In a famous incident, Louis XIII dismissed one of the nurses of the dauphin (the future Louis XIV) because she had been seen talking with her husband.[32] The incident helps us to understand how much more than the health of the infant was involved in the practice of nursing. The decision to employ a nurse was as much as anything a sexual triumph for the father, not only within the family but also in terms of a wider network of social relationships.

We ought to look momentarily at the consequences for the children involved in this transaction. The nurse's child was beginning a difficult apprenticeship. Pushed aside by the newcomer, displaced even before the arrival of another sibling in the affections of his mother, he was already being prepared for the defeats, sexual and otherwise, which would make up his life as a man of "mean estate." For the child put out to nurse, the lesson was more complex. As was the case in the analysis of the governess, we can see certain advantages. The nurse was the child's first servant, her son whom he displaced his first underling. On the other hand, the whole procedure which we have been studying, the complicated social and psychological ritual of the nurse, finally rested on one fundamental assumption: that the infant was dispensable and could be used by his parents as an instrument for advancement and consolidation in the society around them. Within the family, he was told that his mother's breasts were forbidden and that his father did not want him around. These were the first of the hard realities which, even for the offspring of the rich, made up the curriculum of childhood in the old regime.

We are now ready to move on to an examination of actual childrearing practices. In this sphere, the seventeenth-century nuclear family retained primary responsibility. Other kin did not play a major part in the care of children. The use of governesses was confined to a handful of families. For the somewhat larger number of households who could afford to engage them, the presence of nurses oriented the system in a distinctive way, although even here the apparent departure from our model of the nuclear family really intensified conflicts among mother, father, and child rather than rendering them irrelevant. The steps taken to allocate responsibility for supervision of the very young show us something about parental attitudes in the seventeenth century and prepare us for the more complicated negotiations between adults and their offspring which arose in the course of childhood development.

PART THREE

Children

✤ 6 ✤

THE FIRST STAGE:
FEEDING AND SWADDLING

I

For every new-born infant, whether he was from a rich family or a poor one, whether he was raised by a nurse, a governess, or by his parents, the major difficulty in the first months of life was getting enough to eat. Without bottles or good baby foods, adults were very hard pressed to nourish children fully and safely.[1] Our effort to understand childhood in the seventeenth century ought to begin with a discussion of this fundamental issue.

The experience of Louis XIII, as recorded by Héroard, provides a good starting point. From the beginning, the dauphin had feeding problems. The difficulty was first attributed to the "fiber" (*filet*) under the infant's tongue. His surgeon, Jacques Guillemeau, cut this fiber in the hope of making it easier for the young prince to suck properly. In the days that followed, attention shifted to the nurse. She did not seem to have enough milk to satisfy the baby, who sucked in "such great gulps . . . that he drew more in on one try than others did in three." The woman attempted to correct this deficiency by eating more than usual, a tactic which succeeded only in giving her an upset stomach. A supplementary nurse was brought in and then almost immediately dismissed because enemies at court managed to discredit her with the queen. When Louis was eleven weeks old, and obviously undernourished, a medical conference was summoned to consider further remedies. This situation gives occasion for some sober thought. With unlimited resources at their disposal, and with the child enjoying the best possible living conditions available at that time, the doctors nonetheless found themselves confronted with a case of virtual starvation: the muscles of the dauphin's chest were "completely wasted away," and his neck was so thin that the folds in the skin had disappeared. A third nurse arrived, but she lasted only a short time; people thought she was not "clean." The fourth and permanent nurse was not in place until the baby was sixteen weeks old.[2]

This account is in no way extraordinary. For example, the operation on the dauphin's tongue was routinely performed. Almost all the medical authorities mentioned it, with Guillemeau giving the fullest explanation:

In children that are newly borne there are commonly found two strings: the one comes from the bottome of the tongue, and reacheth to the very tip and end thereof. This string is very slender and soft and it hindreth the child from taking the nipple . . . so that he cannot sucke well. This string must be cut with a sizzer within a few daies after he is borne.

Paré agreed with this advice, adding that, if not cut, the "string" would later cause the child to stutter. These comments were not dictated by the surgeon's desire for an extra commission; Vallambert's remark that the cutting was well performed with one's thumbnail indicates that the doctors thought anyone could do the job. One folklorist has maintained that the custom of cutting the infant's *filet* persisted into the twentieth century in rural France.[3]

The trouble with the nurses was also common, and in fact Louis' appetites were rather modest when compared to those of other children in the royal line. Michelet claimed that as an infant Henri IV went through eight nurses; Louis XIV may have had as many as nine. In the *livres de raison*, several families hired and discarded one nurse after another because no one among them was able to satisfy the demands of the infant she had been contracted to feed. These accounts give us another perspective on the use of the nurse. In a situation where breastfeeding was clearly the best and the safest way to nourish children, the financial ability to employ a nurse, or better yet a whole string of them, was a major advantage for a family anxious about the welfare of its offspring. If something happened to the mother nursing her own children, if she became ill or if another pregnancy interrupted the regime of breastfeeding (it was felt that carrying a child and feeding one at the same time was too taxing an undertaking for a woman to attempt), she could fall back on her family's economic reserves and bring in a nurse to help out. In a number of cases, the mother shared from the moment of birth feeding chores with a nurse, so that there were always two women available to her infant.[4]

Since their families could not afford nurses, most children must have been forced to work even harder than the dauphin to get enough to eat. Mothers seem to have felt that, because of their many other duties, they were not in a position to devote a great deal of time even to very young children. The medical literature was almost unanimously in favor of feeding children on demand, but of all the pieces of advice offered by the experts this suggestion was among the most academic. The doctors indicate that the common practice was to limit feeding to particular times and places determined by the women rather than by their offspring. Even if the poor mother managed to stay with her child at all times, it was thought that she still would not have enough milk to satisfy him. As Vallambert observed: "Because of their continual labor and poor life, [these mothers] do not have a lot of milk, so that they would not be capable of feeding the child if he did not take other nourishment in addition to the milk from the breast."[5]

This "other nourishment" was "gruel" (*bouillie*), a combination of cow's or goat's milk with wheat flour or the crumbs of white bread soaked in water. The mixture was to be baked until it thickened, then served to the infant on his mother's or nurse's finger. This staple appears to have been very widely used. Dionis commented: "There are no women who do not know how to make *bouillie*." Yet the doctors were very suspicious of it. *Bouillie* was too "viscous and thick," causing "indigestion and constipation." Women made the mixture carelessly, not sifting the flour or neglecting the baking stage.[6]

However, in a characteristic way, these experts would break

their discussion in two parts. Recognizing the strength of the custom, and apparently deciding to make the best of a bad situation, they would add all sorts of recommendations on the use of *bouillie*, for example, that egg yolk or honey added to the mixture would serve as a purgative, counteracting the "obstruction" normally caused by the food. Several of them were content with very modest prohibitions against its use, forbidding *bouillie* in the first two weeks of a child's life. Mauriceau's belief that it should not be added to the infant's diet until the second or third month seems utopian by comparison.[7]

Badly prepared *bouillie*, fed to the infant on the end of his mother's finger, must have created serious problems for untested digestive systems. However, the use of this staple was unavoidable:

> Long before the first teeth appear, even before the age of three months, . . . the women of the countryside, and the other poor women of the towns [give *bouillie* to their children] because if the latter took no other nourishment besides milk, they would not be able to go so long without sucking as they do, during the time when mothers are absent and held down by their work.

Even the dauphin was given *bouillie* only eighteen days after birth. Here, as elsewhere, the experience of the most precious child in the kingdom enables us to imagine the even more somber circumstances of his less fortunate peers. A squad of nurses barely managed to feed the dauphin, and his diet had to be filled out with *bouillie* before he was three weeks old. In spite of all the efforts of the household, Louis almost succumbed. We might well wonder how other children survived the precarious first months of life.[8]

In fact, when the infant did not get enough milk at the breast and was unable to digest the *bouillie*, he starved. The willingness to have children suckled by farm animals (a practice condoned in the medical literature) indicates the gravity of the food problem. In this respect, the story of the feeding of children represents very well the insecurity of their situation as a whole. For whatever reason, a shocking number of children died. This mortality rate has been fairly conclusively documented. In one rural area during the seventeenth century, more than one quarter of the children born at a given time did not reach the age of one, and almost a half died before the age of four. There are no equally reliable statistics for urban areas within France during this period, but from what we know of European cities in general, it seems safe to conclude that rates there would have been at least as high.⁹ The fact that infants were so vulnerable, that it was tremendously difficult to feed them properly and to protect them from disease and death, is the fundamental precondition which we of a more comfortable milieu must grasp if we are to understand what childhood was like in the seventeenth century.

II

Feeding new-born infants is first of all a biological necessity, but psychoanalysts have argued that the negotiations between parents and children at this time have important psychological ramifications as well. At his mother's breast, the infant first begins to learn what the world is like and to develop his own style of coping with reality. In their turn, adults bring something more than a set of technical resources to this situation. Attitudes toward children, and toward the obligations of parenthood, also play a part in determining how successfully the baby is nourished. I begin my discussion of these matters with a summary of Erik Erikson's theory of the initial phase of childhood. His analysis will help us to recognize the distinctive aspects of this stage of infancy in the seventeenth century.

Erikson argues that, in the first year of life, the child's most important mode of behavior is organized around the reception of outside stimuli. This mode is expressed primarily through the mouth (in the act of sucking), but it is also manifested in the functioning of the infantile organism as a whole:

It is clear that, in addition to the overwhelming need for food, [the new-born] baby is, or soon becomes, receptive in many other respects. As he is willing and able to suck on appropriate objects and to swallow whatever appropriate fluids they emit, he is soon also willing and able to "take in" with his eyes whatever enters his visual field. His tactual senses, too, seem to "take in" what feels good. In this sense, then, one could speak of an *"incorporative stage,"* one in which he is, relatively speaking, receptive to what is being offered.

As the infant grows older, incorporation or getting, the capacity "to receive and to accept what is given," gradually blends into a more active taking, evidenced most characteristically in the ability to bite with newly erupted teeth, but again in a more general way as well:

The eyes, first part of a relatively passive system of accepting impressions as they come along, have now learned to focus, to isolate, to "grasp" objects from the vaguer background, and to follow them. The organs of hearing have similarly learned to discern significant sounds, to localize them, and to guide an appropriate change in position (lifting and turning the head, lifting and turning the upper body). The arms have learned to reach out and the hands to grasp more purposefully.[10]

Erikson stresses that the infant's getting must be met by a roughly equivalent adult readiness to give. Today we tend to see this readiness primarily in psychological terms, depending on the mother's "development as a woman; on her unconscious attitude toward the child; on the way she has lived through pregnancy and delivery; on her and her community's attitude toward the act of nursing."[11] However, in the seventeenth century, before any of the psychological factors could come into play, the economic capacity of adults to give to the child, specifically to nourish him, was compromised by the primitive technology of infant feeding. Poor children were underfed by mothers who did not have sufficient milk or who were unable to suckle them regularly. The feeding of rich children might be unsettled by the inadequacy, and the frequent switching, of nurses. And all infants would have to learn from a very early age to digest an inappropriate and badly prepared gruel.

Seventeenth-century children thus started life with a dangerous handicap. Almost invariably, they were going to encounter problems of a special magnitude in their attempts to "get." Erikson has indicated some of the possible consequences of maladaptation in this stage. If the child's constant efforts to fill his stomach are to no avail, he may lapse into a state of "oral pessimism." Eventually, this pessimism can develop into a pervasive mistrust, a deeply rooted conviction that the world is a bad place and that individual initiative, because it is never adequately rewarded, is not worth the trouble.[12]

Thinking along these lines, one might argue that the food deprivation experienced by seventeenth-century children created the foundation for that fatalism which is often associated with the peasant mentality of the period. I prefer, however, to pursue another aspect of the problem. All children do not lose hope. Erikson has written: "Infantile fears . . . of 'being left empty,' . . . can give orality that particular avaricious quality which in psychoanalysis is called 'oral sadism,' that is, a cruel need to get and to take in ways harmful to others."[13] Common sense tells us that infants who were defeated by the difficulties of feeding would not grow up into unusually depressed or fatalistic individuals. More simply, such children starved, or became so weak that they were easy prey to fatal diseases. On the other hand, those who survived must have been the ones who learned how to seize with particular ruthlessness the nourishment which a not overly generous adult world made available to them. Only an aggressive development, an exaggeration of the infantile modes of getting and taking, would allow these infants to acquire enough food to live.

With these thoughts in mind, it is interesting to turn to actual descriptions of very small children in the seventeenth century. In fact, grownups had a highly developed awareness of the infant's tireless capacity for appropriation, of his tenacious parasitism. The picture Héroard sketched of a greedy Louis gulping in huge swallows of milk is not without a tinge of the sinister. It was commonly believed that birth was prompted by the hunger of the infant who, because he could no longer satisfy himself in the womb, tried "with great impetuousness to get out." Avarice was the child's principal trait: "All children are naturally very greedy and gluttonous." At the same time that they called for feeding on demand, the doctors cautioned mothers against overfeeding. While being indulgent, they could not let the unquenchable appetite of the infant hold full sway.[14]

These opinions take on their full significance when we note

that the experts thought the mother's milk was actually whitened blood. They do not seem to have understood the fact that secretion of milk in the mother's body is a self-sustaining process designed specifically to meet the special demands of the new-born infant. The nursing situation was not seen as a cooperative effort, but as a struggle in which the interests of the two parties were at least to some extent at odds. In fact, the infant prospered at the expense of his mother, from whose body he sucked the precious substance he needed for his own survival. These views explain why breastfeeding was seen as a debilitating experience for a woman, why she was counseled to hire a nurse after a difficult delivery, or if she again became pregnant. Only the healthy mother could afford to sacrifice a part of herself for the welfare of her children.[15]

In a world where people believed that resources of all kinds were fixed and in short supply, the prosperity of one person or group was always linked to the bad luck of others. From this perspective, adults were naturally disturbed by the incessant demands of small children. For example, I think that such sentiments underlie the story recorded by Louise Bourgeois about a Strasburg mother who fell asleep while nursing her child. A snake with poisonous fangs attached itself to her breast and began to suck. The woman and her husband could not remove the animal for fear that it would bite, and for ten months it continued to suck, growing to monstrous proportions on the strength of this nourishment. Bourgeois thought the incident showed "how much substance there is in woman's milk." The mother was forced to put her child out to nurse and to go everywhere with the unwelcome guest, carrying it in a basket. The child at the breast had been transformed into a serpent, symbol of evil. At the end of the story, only the magic charms of a sorceress succeeded in tempting away this covetous intruder.[16]

The fear of being bitten expressed in the story was manifested more generally by adults in a great deal of anxiety about teething. Parents reacted very specifically to this step in infantile development and regarded teething as a serious disease which might lead to all sorts of complications: diarrhea, fevers, epilepsy, spasms, and even death. Paré wrote:

Monseigneur de Nemours sent to fetch me to anatomize his dead son, aged eight months or thereabouts, whose teeth had not erupted. Having diligently searched for the cause of his death, I could not find any, if not that his gums were very hard, thick and swollen; having cut through them, I found all his teeth ready to come out, if only someone had cut his gums. So it was decided by the doctors present and by me that the sole cause of his death was that nature had not been strong enough to pierce the gums and push the teeth out.

Remedies abounded for this "disease," and parents were advised to rub the sore gums with all sorts of magical panaceas. If this did not help, Guillemeau suggested: "Rub the legs, thighs, shoulders, backe and nape of the child's necke, drawing still downwards, thereby to alter and turne the course of humours which fall downe upon the gummes and passages of the throat." As a last resort, the surgeon was supposed to cut the gums so that the teeth might more easily emerge.[17]

In these comments, doctors stress the fact that teeth are the infant's first aggressive tools, although they limit themselves to discussing the ways in which children themselves can be harmed by such sharp instruments. However, I think that the tone of the discussion, the awe with which doctors analyze the eruption of teeth, indicate an underlying fear of the child's biting impulses, the potentially dangerous use he can make of his mouth. In this respect, the interpretation of teething is consistent with the tendency to see children as gluttonous little animals and with the belief that they were sucking away the mother's blood. Collecting together these images, we have a picture of the small child as a predatory and frightening creature capable of harming the woman whose duty it was to care for him. Returning to Erikson's hypothesis, we can say that in the eyes of his elders the seventeenth-century infant was an "oral sadist."

I have no doubt that similar themes appear in the childrearing literature of all cultures. In fact, they are built into the breast-feeding relationship: the infant does suck with striking intensity, because his life depends on it; women are to some extent tied down by the demands of their very small offspring; and breast-feeding is always complicated by the child's teething. At the same time, I believe that images of the child as a greedy little animal had a special power in the seventeenth century and that they exerted a relatively pronounced negative influence on efforts to feed the very young.

I picture a mother, who herself probably did not get enough to eat, and who was forced to work long and difficult hours, turning to the task of breastfeeding with mixed feelings. The child was a parasite; he did nothing and yet his appetites seemed to be endless. He was sucking a vital fluid out of her already depleted body. This situation must have been tremendously difficult for mothers to tolerate. In turn, children sensed the anxiety of their providers, perhaps in the tense way they were held, in the tentativeness of the breast being offered to them. Aware of the unreliability of this source of life, they redoubled their efforts to "get" as much as possible. These efforts impressed mothers as especially gluttonous and devouring, and in reaction they developed an image of children as greedy little animals, who were harmful to their guardians. These fantasies worked to undermine the resolution of mothers, whose gathering ambivalence would be communicated to children, who in turn would become all the more peremptory in their demands for more milk.

Some hypothesis along these lines is necessary to account for the frequent breakdown in efforts to feed little children. The poverty of the society, while it provided the necessary, and very powerful, initial impetus for the process by which mother and child became wary of each other, is not in itself a sufficient explanation for the problem. Mothers in equally poor societies manage to keep their children close by and to feed them on demand.[18] Medically speaking, there is no reason why a woman, even if she is relatively undernourished, cannot adequately breast-feed a child. Further, we know that lactation does not weaken mothers who undertake it. This analysis is not intended as a critique of seventeenth-century mothers. Given their situation, it is entirely natural that they should have been ambivalent about children. My point is that economic or physiological arguments do not in themselves explain the great difficulty experienced in getting enough food into the child's belly. These difficulties make sense only if we picture the specifically economic factors overlaid with a set of disturbing fantasies about children at the breast. The problem was first of all in the seventeenth-century economy, but at the same time it was also in the minds and the deportment of parents.

This point is clearly illustrated in the royal court, and in the houses of the rich, where nurses, who almost certainly got enough to eat, were often unable to produce enough milk for the children they were supposed to breastfeed. Poor living conditions cannot explain these failures which the literature documents with such regularity and which adults of the time seem to have accepted as a matter of course. The situation of the nurse must have created conflicts of its own. Given their low status, and the constant critical scrutiny of people like Héroard, who were alert to any sign of their inadequacy as providers, these women may well have had trouble relaxing and devoting themselves wholeheartedly to the task of feeding the children of their superiors. On the other hand, I suspect that some part of the problem was independent of the woman's identity as a nurse, but instead grew out of her image of children, her sense of them as demanding and dangerous little animals, a sense she shared with all other mothers, of the time.

In describing this way of looking at children, I am anxious to avoid exaggeration. Adults were not entirely alienated from their offspring. Fears of predatory infants operated on the periphery, rather than in the center of, parental awareness. The case of teething offers a good illustration of the point I am trying to get at. The mother's qualms about her infant's sharp teeth have been inferred from writings where the overt point is to express sympathy for the discomfort of the child. In fact, adults empathized with infants in the midst of teething. Guillemeau thought there was no pain so intense, and when the dauphin's teeth started to push through the gums, Héroard made a point of sitting up with him during the night holding his hand. Dionis saw lists of remedies for this "disease" as means of satisfying the "impatience of mothers and fathers." According to him, parents waited with great anticipation for the emergence of the child's first tooth, and when it did appear, there would be a celebration and presents for the nurse.[19] Whatever its latent meaning, the manifest intent of parental concern on this occasion was to comfort the child.

I see parents in this phase of childrearing operating somewhere between a confident mastery and an incapacitating state of anxiety. They were burdened with certain misgivings, which could impair their performance in significant ways, but these fears were not allowed to get out of hand, to trigger a complete rejection of the obligation of feeding infants. Parents were threatened, but they managed to retain their composure. The meaning of this intermediate state of mind will, I think, be more clear when we have had a chance to consider a later phase of infantile growth, where parental fearfulness was allowed a wider, and more destructive, freedom of expression.

In any case, a moment's thought will help us see how much value there was in the collective repression of the image of children as devouring and rapacious animals. How could it be otherwise in a milieu where the infant's capacity for grasping and getting was so vital to his survival? Parents might be put off, but they could not overreact to the child's aggressive sucking, to his parasitism or biting. If parents could not deal with their own fears of infantile avarice, they would be all the less well equipped to help their offspring surmount the many obstacles of the first months of life. In fantasy, a mother might escape through the aid of a sorceress the unwanted attentions of the serpent, but in real life she would try to retain the infant at her breast.

III

In his analysis of the first phase of childhood growth, Erik Erikson maintains that the incorporative mode of behavior is expressed most obviously through the mouth, but that it is also manifested in the activity of the infantile organism as a whole. The child must be seen as a personality, facing a total existential situation, and not simply as an oral creature who must be fed. By contrast, in the seventeenth century infantile experience was grasped by adults primarily in terms of feeding. The discussion of the doctors concentrated heavily on the problem of how best to nourish the child. In the same spirit, parents contracted with nurses to serve simply as suppliers of milk, rather than as maternal figures in a broader sense, because they believed that the infant's alimentary needs were the only ones worthy of serious attention. The fact that small children needed conversation, companionship, and play, as well as nourishment of a more tangible sort, was not well understood by adults of the period.

Of course parents were amused and diverted by infants and did take notice of them in situations other than those connected with feeding. On the other hand, I think it is significant that in the seventeenth century the notion of "playing" with children had an ambiguous ring. Some critics thought that in this play adults betrayed a careless, self-indulgent attitude. In casting about for the words to describe their impressions, these observers hit upon a comparison which we have already encountered in the discussion of feeding: parents treated children like pets, or little animals. Montaigne argued: "We have loved [infants] for our own amusement, like monkeys, not like human beings." And Fleury commented: "It is as if the poor children had been made only to amuse the adults, like little dogs or little monkeys."[20]

This comparison of the child to an animal is something more than a useful device, a way of characterizing the infant at the breast. The image appears throughout seventeenth-century literature on children. In a total sense, the small child was an intermediate being, not really an animal (although he might often be compared to one), but on the other hand not really human either. This quasi-evolutionary model of the ages of life was so ingrained that adults often hardly noticed its presence in their own speech. Thus in describing the battle of Paris, Jean Burel wrote that the Parisians "were besieged by the King of Navarre so closely that they were forced to eat animals: dogs, horses, everything right up to, and almost including, little children."[21] In the chain of being, a separate link—infancy—connected the animal and the human worlds without belonging completely to either one.

I have already argued that, with respect to the specifically oral forms of this image of the child as little animal, in an area where infant survival was very much at stake, parents struggled with their negative feelings and managed to stay in touch with their offspring. Once the child had been safely fed, however, it is possible that adults gave vent to their aversion and disgust and treated the infant with the callousness which his subhuman station deserved. We must try to ascertain whether the feeding of infants was somehow special, or if, on the other hand, parental attitudes in that area carried over into the whole of relations with the child during the first year of life.

I think the best way to approach this problem is through an examination of the practice of swaddling. The eighteenth-century philosophes have already experimented with a similar tactic. In turning their attention to childrearing, they found evidence of negligence on every side, but nowhere more obnoxiously manifested than in the practice of swaddling. In detailing the evils of the custom, these critics conjured up a whole gallery of cruel images: the infant was wrapped up tight and tossed "in a corner"; or the nurse hung a crying baby in swaddling clothes from a nail on the wall, so that the bands tightened, suffocating the child and choking off his cries; or the nurse placed the swaddled baby in his cradle and rocked him until he fell into a groggy sleep.[22] In all these instances, swaddling represented a general point of view toward children, a deficiency in that sympathy or generosity which the philosophes thought a child had a right to expect from his elders. While reserving judgment on the exact meaning of the practice, I follow the eighteenth-century critics by discussing swaddling in this symbolic sense, as a key to understanding what adults thought of the first stage of life.

The swaddling of infants, which to us is one of the most exotic features of childrearing in the seventeenth century, was utterly taken for granted by the adults of that period. Doctors, who showed such a lively interest in the various controversial issues of childrearing, barely took notice of swaddling and offered only a few scraps of advice on the subject; as Mauriceau put it, "There are no women who do not know all about something which is so common." In describing Louis' birth, Héroard mentions that the infant was swaddled soon after being washed and fed, but he never refers to the clothes again. In an account otherwise rich in detail, there is nothing on the regime of swaddling: how the wrapping was done, when during the day the clothes

126

were removed, not even a hint as to when in the life of the dauphin the practice was terminated. Although swaddling has almost completely disappeared in modern France, the custom was once so deeply rooted in everyday life that it was put into practice almost automatically. This combination of factors makes it a particularly useful, as well as difficult, subject for the historian interested in the distinctive qualities of childrearing in the old regime.[23]

The swaddling band (called the *maillot*) was a roll of cloth about two inches across. The infant was wrapped up with this length of cloth, arms straight at his sides and legs extended, with a few extra turns around the head to hold it steady, so that only a small circle of his face would be left exposed. Doctors advised that the pressure of the band should be equal on all parts of the body, to avoid crippling the infant, and that especial care should be taken in wrapping the chest and stomach so that breathing would not be impeded. The swaddling was left in place at all times during the first weeks of an infant's life except when it was necessary to clean and change him. Vallambert suggested that if an infant cried excessively, one could "unswaddle him, and massage and move his limbs, for that often causes the crying and the screaming to stop." At some time early in his life (according to doctors, between the first and fourth month), the infant's arms would be freed and the wrappings applied only to his legs and torso. Finally, when he was eight or nine months old, or at the latest around his first birthday, the infant would be left unswaddled for good.[24]

Intuitively—and wrongly—we imagine that such a regime would leave infants deformed or retarded. Actual details on the physical development of babies in the seventeenth century are very scarce, but Héroard's *Journal* does suggest something of the dauphin's progress in this respect and helps to show that swaddling did not stunt the growth of children. At first, the doctor describes Louis performing acts compatible with a regime of swaddling: listening, staring, speaking, laughing. At four months, Louis was "playing" with the king and queen, and in one session Henri studied the feet of his son, which, he had been told, resembled his own. At five and a half months, "he dances gaily to the sound of a violin." Obviously this was not real dancing, but perhaps some rhythmic movement of the arms. A week later, he stretched out his hand for an object (a book) for the first time. Louis was throwing things at the age of six months and was also being put to bed with his arms free (it will be remembered that while he was teething Héroard sat up holding his hand). At eight months, the dauphin was fitted for his first pair of shoes, and six weeks later the "leading strings" (*lisières*), which would be used by adults to help him learn to walk, were attached to his clothes.[25]

This circumstantial evidence seems to fit well enough the schedule suggested by the doctors. No later than five and a half months after his birth, Louis' arms were left unswaddled so that he was free to "dance," to grasp a book, to be held by the hand. In fact, he may have been completely unswaddled by this time since Henri IV was able to study his feet; but it is also possible that the dauphin was specially unwrapped for his parents' visit. In any case, the *maillot* was definitively discarded by eight or nine months when Louis was fitted for shoes and *lisières*.

Swaddling had little effect on subsequent motor development. Apparently children did not spend much time crawling. There are almost no pictorial representations of a stage between swaddling and walking, and, on the other hand, every effort seems to have been made to help children learn how to walk. Around his first birthday, the dauphin was indeed walking with "firmness, held under the arms." When Louis was nineteen months old, Héroard describes him running, and in going from place to place he was now led (*mené*) as often as carried (*porté*). The descriptions offered of his play corroborate the impression of the dauphin's rapidly growing dexterity, "fencing" with Héroard (ten months), playing the violin and the drum (about a year and a half), and striking a blow of fifty-five paces with his "bat" (*palemail*) when he was just over two.[26]

Swaddling obviously did not cripple children. In fact the practice performed a number of positive functions. From the recent literature on the subject, we know that (like a high-walled cradle or a play-pen) swaddling limits potentially dangerous motor activity; that (like a carriage) it makes children easier to carry;

and that it provides a measure of security and reassurance by relieving the infant of responsibility for the control of his limbs in a period when he does not yet have sufficient physical mastery to handle the job completely on his own.[27]

All of these reasons may have been considered in the seventeenth century, but they were not mentioned by experts in their terse discussions of the practice. Among the reasons which were given for swaddling, the first and most important seems to have been that it kept the baby warm:

> Nor then forget that wrappers be at hand,
> Soft flannels, linen, and the swaddling band,
> T'enwrap the babe, by many a circling fold,
> In equal lines, and thus defend from cold.

This function was very important; we are dealing with a world in which even the royal palaces were so poorly insulated that children had to be admonished to stay close to the fireplace on the coldest days. One doctor cautioned against freeing the child's arms during the winter. Even if he was past the age of three or four months, the baby was to remain fully swaddled "until he is older and it is not so cold."[28]

Doctors also argued that swaddling was necessary to help the infant's limbs grow straight. Apparently this belief in the effectiveness of the wrapping is not unfounded, especially when one considers the prevalence of rickets among young children at that time. There was also some notion that swaddling prevented the child from hurting himself by striking a hard object or by falling.[29] More generally, swaddling immobilized the child under reasonably beneficial circumstances and thus served as a substitute for the constant attention which the unhindered baby would have required from its elders. This substitution may often have been dictated by a lack of interest in children and could therefore be interpreted (in the tradition of the philosophes) as a sign of parental neglect. However, in this respect as in others, we must be careful to distinguish matters of choice from those of necessity. For many poor women, the *maillot*, no less than *bouillie*, was an essential device which enabled them to spend long periods of time at work and away from their infants. For any society which could not afford to be too child-centered, swaddling, or some other practice which relieved adults of the need for constant supervision of children, was inevitable and can hardly be construed as a sign of some special parental malice and neglect.

In fact, swaddling can be interpreted as an antidote to the more extreme forms of parental ambivalence. We have seen how much contempt adults were likely to feel for children and how they seemed to regard their offspring as little animals. Swaddling allowed parents to defend against the consequences of their own distaste. This distinctive custom helped to place infants. It defined with a more reassuring precision the limbo of childhood, leaving it distinct from the sphere of adult life, but also firmly marking it off from the animal kingdom. As Mauriceau observed, children were swaddled for fear they would otherwise never learn to stand erect, but would always crawl on all fours like little animals.[30] Swaddling embodied the promise of a future humanity and saved infants from a descent to that animal world into which their own strangeness and frailty threatened to propel them.

In the same spirit, adults wanted children either in swaddling clothes or walking on two feet. Crawling was discouraged precisely because it made more ambiguous that distinction between infants and animals which adults knew in their hearts they had to maintain. We have already seen how a kind of collective repression protected parents from their fear of the predatory appetites of growing infants. With its numerous benefits, and as a means of defining the first stage of life, swaddling operated on an even more general plane as a way of caring for infants and at the same time of binding up the anxiety which adults experienced in dealing with the animality of small children.

IV

In the light of these arguments defending swaddling, we might ask not why parents adopted such an irrational technique, but rather why swaddling was so abruptly abandoned. Writing in

1718, Dionis seems to have assumed that everyone knew all about the custom and that parents needed no advice in its uses. However, at the end of the century, Scévole de Sainte-Marthe's English translator wrote: "This antient method of swathing children with tight bandages is now justly laid aside." While the custom was to persist in rural areas, the philosophes had succeeded in completely discrediting it among authorities on childrearing.[31]

How had this transformation been achieved? Buffon's critique is a good example:

Scarcely is the infant out of the womb of his mother, scarcely is he at liberty to move and to stretch his limbs, when he is given new bonds. He is swaddled, put to bed with his head fixed and his legs extended, his arms at his sides; he is wrapped in linen and bandages, to the extent that he cannot change position. He is lucky if he is not squeezed so hard that he is unable to breathe, and if he has been placed on his side, so that the water which he has to pass through his mouth can run out of its own accord, for he is not able to turn his head.[32]

There are no new facts here. Doctors of an earlier period were aware of the dangers Buffon mentioned and were content to caution parents against them. For the rest, a different construction is being put on the same details. The immobility which appalls Buffon was simply taken for granted by everyone before 1700. In the interim, the issue of the child's freedom had become all important.

It seems clear to me that the philosophes overstated their case against swaddling. Seventeenth-century medical advisors were sensitive to the possibility of discomfort for the child and ready to advocate measures, like the temporary removal of the wrappings, to soothe crying infants. Furthermore, we have seen that there was more than a little substance to the justifications of swaddling, which did keep children warm and which could insure that their limbs would grow straight. By contrast, many of the claims of the critics—for example, that swaddling would cripple children—are clearly inaccurate. In the light of these considerations, I feel justified in having treated the practice from a functional point of view.

At the same time, I think that the philosophes have directed our attention to a significant (if secondary) implication in the use of swaddling. One of the most pervasive themes in the literature on childhood for this period is that the parents or the teacher had the responsibility of "molding" or "fashioning" the child, of making him "take the fold" in an acceptable way. Swaddling, of course, literally does shape the infant, helping his limbs grow straight. In addition, midwives were in the habit of handling the soft skulls of new-born children to give them the proper shape. And after being swaddled, the infant was deposited in a narrow crib, which reinforced the effects of the wrappings. Finally, after the swaddling was removed, young girls were dressed in tight corsets, so constricting that they were often physically harmful to the wearers.[33]

I am persuaded that in their desire to make the child "take the fold," parents tended to multiply the methods for achieving this end. These efforts indicate a certain apprehension about what would happen if the baby were left free to develop according to his own inner impulses and capacities. While they overlooked the advantages of swaddling and simplified many aspects of the controversy, the philosophes were on to a genuine issue when they insisted that the wrappings were an attempt to interfere with the freedom of the infant. In this respect, swaddling is related to the fear of the child's undisciplined orality, of his primitive sucking and biting. Adults were afraid of the infant's natural impulses and were tempted to deflect his growth from its regular, and possibly dangerous, channels. In this chapter, I have in general placed the emphasis on the ways in which the temptation was overcome or given rein only in an attenuated form. However, the practice of swaddling does hint at a parental concern which would be exercised much more vigorously when the child was a little older and had survived the dangers of the first stage of life. We will have more to say of this concern in the following chapter.

~~७~ 7 ~~२२~

THE SECOND STAGE:
BREAKING IN THE CHILD

I

One of the most controversial aspects of psychoanalytic theory concerns the sequence of infantile development. Analysts like Erikson maintain that the child moves through a predictable timetable of psycho-social and psycho-sexual phases which are closely related to physical maturation. Critics have argued that even the biological aspects of childhood growth are open to question. It is not at all clear that the infantile libido is concentrated in turn on different bodily zones (the mouth, the anus, the genitals) and even less certain that a distinct psychological crisis can be associated with each of these steps.

Thinking along these lines, I was interested to discover in Héroard's *Journal* that the dauphin was weaned in his twenty-fifth month, four weeks after he had been whipped for the first time. Up to this point, discipline had not been a matter of great concern for the adults around Louis. When the child cried or misbehaved, he was soothed by his attendants or, more simply, fed until he quieted down. The formal ritual of whipping had a completely different tone and meaning. These beatings were administered with a switch on the buttocks of the child as he bent over. Usually one blow sufficed, although in more serious cases several might be required. After the gravest offenses, the dauphin was compelled to expose his rear end so that the blows would fall on bare flesh. During Louis' third year, the whippings dominate Héroard's account in a way which suggests that the child had entered a qualitatively different phase in his relations with the adult world.[1] This striking change in the tenor of child-rearing provides us with tentative confirmation of the Eriksonian hypothesis that around his second birthday the infant passes from the first into the second phase of childhood. In the present chapter, I explore some of the ramifications of this development.

We should note first of all that the changes described by Héroard were not special to Louis' case. With respect to feeding methods, medical authorities suggested that the infant should be weaned between his eighteenth and twenty-fourth month, and in the *livres de raison* when the event is mentioned, it falls within this period. Caution is necessary here. We have seen that economic factors forced poor mothers to introduce *bouillie* into the diets of their offspring at a time which some doctors considered premature. By the same token, lower-class families without the means to hire a nurse and in which the mother was not free to attend the infant were forced to wean children before the suggested time. Nonetheless, it seems clear that under ideal circumstances, where parents had free choice, the child's feeding schedule would resemble that of the dauphin.[2]

The whippings described by Héroard were also not unusual. Sources agree that this was the favored means of disciplining children. Pierre Charron spoke of the "almost universal" custom of "beating, whipping, abusing and scolding children and holding them in great fear and subjection." We are of course dealing with a society in which physical violence was not so automatically deplored as it is in our own day. Since even the most reputable adults so readily struck one another, there is no reason to suppose that they were any more gentle with their offspring. The punitive discipline of the schools was notorious. And in those cases where we can follow the regime of childrearing within individual households, adults seem to have accepted complacently the notion that fearfulness was an essential component in the mentality of the good child and that no efforts should be spared in trying to inculcate this "virtue."[3]

All in all I cannot believe that the whipping of the dauphin was unusual. It might be argued that his parents more than others would have been touchy about issues of authority and therefore more inclined to punish misbehavior with rigor. But on the other hand, we should also note that the dauphin as a future king was, more than any other child, entitled to a certain amount of respect. In any case, the reasoning of Henri IV on this matter did not show any special stamp of royalty. At one point, he wrote to Madame de Montglat:

I have a complaint to make: you do not send word that you have whipped my son. I wish and command you to whip him every time that he is obstinate or misbehaves, knowing well for myself that there is nothing in the world which will be better for him than that. I know it from experience, having myself profited, for when I was his age I was often whipped. That is why I want you to whip him and to make him understand why.[4]

Surely other fathers were capable of such logic. If the dauphin was regularly beaten, I would assume that most children were no less severely treated.

Various transgressions could lead to a whipping: too much crying or carrying on, refusal to eat, unwillingness to show affection toward adults like the queen or, more frequently, the king himself. The most ubiquitous complaint was that the child had been *opiniâtre:* stubborn, obstinate, headstrong. Héroard wrote: "Awake at 8:00, he is obstinate, is whipped for the first time"— but not the last. Obstinacy comes up often in discussions of childhood. Occasionally lying gets a vote as the most reprehensible of infantile felonies, but even then obstinacy is a close second. The word (and its opposite, to be *sage*) acquired an almost cosmic significance for children. Louis was told that men were placed in prison for obstinacy and that Christ went to the cross because mankind in general was *opiniâtre.*[5]

I think these developments fit very well into the scheme Erikson has outlined for the second stage of infancy. According to him, at about the age of two, the child is rapidly developing physical and intellectual skills which enable him to move about, to talk, and to express his own individuality more forcefully. The organ modes for this stage are elimination and retention, the modalities, holding on and letting go: "The development of the muscle system gives the child a much greater power over the environment in the ability to reach out and hold on, to throw and to push away, to appropriate things and to keep them at a distance."[6] Having already perceived the general distinction between himself and the external world, that momentous realization which Freud characterized as the end of primary narcissism, the child now experiences with the development of his own means of inner and outer control a highly intensified need to define these two spheres with increasing sharpness, to single out a certain area as his own and to assert his rights of autonomy and self-government within this area.

In terms of ego strengths or "virtues," Erikson would say that here the infant is attempting to exercise his will. Because of the strangeness of this newly emerging capacity, the child is not adept in its use. Since his tools both physical and intellectual are only partially formed, it will be hard for him to delineate that area in which he is indeed able to govern himself. As a result the stage is characterized by a constant vacillation between periods in which the child tries to do too much, an effort which he may pursue with exasperating "obstinacy," or too little, preferring to regress into a passive, oral dependency.

The adult world must be able to adjust to these vacillations, to encourage appropriate independence while at the same time offering support when the child's failures make him so anxious that he needs the will of another to help him maintain control. As Erikson has put it:

The infant must come to feel that the basic faith in existence, which is the lasting treasure saved from the rages of the oral stage, will not be jeopardized by this about-face of his, this sudden violent wish to have a choice, to appropriate demandingly, and to eliminate stubbornly. Firmness must protect him against the potential anarchy of his as yet untrained sense of discrimination, his inability to hold on and to let go with discretion.[7]

If this interaction is well regulated, the child will move on with a sense of autonomy, a feeling that he is master of his own house and that in the world he is allowed a degree of freedom appropriate to his own competence. Such a person will be capable of a judicious self-control and will not feel that he is overcontrolled by external forces.

However, if the infant feels defeated in his attempt to be autonomous, he will be left with a permanent legacy of shame for "having exposed himself prematurely and foolishly."[8] In this defeat, the child is made aware of his smallness and weakness most painfully just as he tries for the first time to assert his rights over against other, stronger individuals. For adults, the problem here is that the infant's stubborn obstinacy can so quickly give way to despairing self-doubt, to a sense of having failed irrevocably.

In the *Journal*, Héroard describes occasions when Louis' parents seem to have understood what was going on in the mind of the infant. For example, the dauphin was walking with his father who wished to take his hand. The child obstinately refused, and Henri lost his temper. Then the dauphin grew frightened, demanded pardon of the king, and embraced him. They continued their walk more amicably, but Louis still declined to take Henri's hand. In this instance, the father managed with an effort to adjust to the willfulness of his son. Louis did not want to fight, but he did not want to hold hands either—and he was permitted the gesture.[9]

Usually the results of such conflicts were not so fortunate. A cycle of stubborn defiance and harsh punishment was much more characteristic. To some extent, Louis' aggressiveness made strife inevitable, as would be the case with any healthy child. He often fought with other children, especially with his hated half-brothers and sisters. There were also blows aimed at adults: his governess, the queen, then the king himself. At the same time, it is impossible to overlook the role played by the impatience and impulsive anger of the adults in these incidents. Henri IV often abused his son without apparent reason, and in general his responses to the delinquencies and provocations of the dauphin were excessively harsh. Several times he baited Louis, ending by throwing water in his face. When the dauphin refused to kiss him, the king was so angry that he whipped the infant himself, a rare occurrence. A few days later, when Louis refused to take the king's hand, the latter furiously seized his son's hat and threw it to the ground.[10]

Adults were no more judicious, no less defiant and impulsive, than their children. When he lost his temper with the dauphin, Henri recognized only one rule: the governess was to administer the whippings. Even this rule was ignored if the king's anger went completely out of control. Earlier, I argued that one function of the governess and of the separate households rich families organized around their children was to protect these children from parental mismanagement. Whatever deeper reasons there may have been for the governess's disciplinary role, its most conspicuous surface effect was that it saved the infant from really damaging physical punishment. One may wonder what happened to children whose fathers were not able to pay others to help them deal with their own rage. It should also be noted that contemporaries regarded Henri IV as an especially easy-going father, a notion which, I think, should prompt some sober thoughts on the quality of discipline in other households.[11]

This evidence suggests that adults were not at all sympathetic to the child's emerging autonomy and little prepared to deal with it in a spirit of mutual regulation. On the contrary, infantile willfulness was conceived as a threat, a sign of wickedness, to be combatted—with obstinacy. Jacques Guillemeau wrote of the first months of life:

He is not fit . . . to be employed in any businesse while he sucketh; because he wholly depends upon the helpe of another. Afterward, when he comes to more yeares, he growes stubborne, and unruly, and wants a Master to give him instruction.

The first duty of the parent was to stand firm in the face of this natural insubordination. Adults seem to have felt genuinely threatened by their offspring: "The sole concern of children is to find the weak spot in their masters. . . . As soon as they have been able to get the better of them, children are on top of their elders, and they stay on top."[12] Given this climate of opinion, grownups were bound to react harshly to any signs of infantile self-assertion.

The battle between old and young was joined over a variety of issues. We have seen how the feeding of new-born infants was regarded by adults with a good deal of ambivalence, but also that in practice the problem was always how to get enough nourishment into the child. However, once the baby was a little older, food took on a different significance. For example, after being weaned, Louis was alternately forced to eat foods he did not want and forbidden to have things which he had requested. At the table, he was expected to fight with his half-brothers for the scraps which the king dispensed from his plate. For other adults as well, food deprivation became a favored means of punishment, ranking just behind whipping. The gentle Fénelon and the very punitive Madame Acarie agreed that children should be discouraged from singling out certain foods as preferred or distasteful. Madame Acarie carried this policy to its logical conclusion, forcing her children to eat disliked foods day after day and systematically denying them those which they seemed to enjoy.[13]

Such dietary rules were not dictated by that fear of the infant's avarice which we encountered earlier. Parental anxiety was not connected so much with food as with the infant's growing ability to exercise his will, to choose, for example, what he liked and did not like to eat. What the child wanted was by definition bad, and Madame Acarie denied her offspring favorite clothes and toys as well as chosen foods. When the daughter of Sainte Chantal showed "a sign of vanity and of joy" in trying on a dress, her mother took offense because such signs were "proof of our lost innocence." Thus, in their most pious moments, parents went so far as to equate the child's natural search for autonomy with the principal of original sin.[14]

I am convinced that this fear of the child's will, the consternation and anger which his first gestures of independence called forth, were general cultural themes. Feeding the very tiny infant involved adults in an area where, given the universality of problems of sustenance, they were unusually vulnerable. Yet parental uneasiness had to be mastered if the infant was to be kept alive. As a result, adults seem to have acted with at least a relative composure in dealing with the first stage of infancy. However, in studying the next phase, one is struck by the air of conflict and of breakdown, by panicky inflexibility on the part of adults and demoralization among the children. In the following sections, I attempt to explain why this phase of infancy should have been such a source of difficulty for parents of the seventeenth century.

II

Before getting into this broader question, however, I would like to explore a related theoretical problem. For Erikson no less than for Freud, the primary issue in the second phase of infancy is management of the bowels. The organ modes of retention and elimination are centered in the anal zone, just as incorporation was expressed most characteristically through the mouth. In our society, the first issue of infantile self-control (and thus the first occasion on which the child's autonomy is tested) tends to arise in connection with toilet training. If guided properly, the infant can assert his own will and gain a certain mastery by learning how to regulate the holding on and letting go of his bodily wastes in a way which makes him feel good and satisfies the society around him. At the same time, psychoanalytic literature has demonstrated how easily things can go wrong here. If the parents are overly anxious in their desire to push the child into a self-control in excess of his muscular and psychological capacities, they deprive him of autonomy in the first moment when it might have been successfully asserted and leave him with a sense of having been defeated in his own body even before the issue with the world around him is joined.

"Anality" is implicit in the infantile loss of autonomy. Erikson suggests that doubt as well as shame haunts the individual who was damaged in this period of childhood, a doubt which retains its dynamic connection to the anal zone:

Where shame is dependent on the consciousness of standing upright and exposed, doubt . . . has much to do with a consciousness of having a front and a back—and especially a "behind." For this reverse side of the body, with its aggressive and libidinal focus in the sphincters and in the buttocks, cannot be seen by the child, and yet it can be . . . magically dominated and effectively invaded by those who would attack one's power of autonomy and who would designate as evil those products of the bowels which were felt to be all right when they were being passed. This basic sense of doubt . . . finds its adult expression in paranoiac fears concerning hidden persecutors and secret persecutions threatening from behind (and from within the behind).[15]

In other words, if parents find it hard to deal with problems of infantile autonomy, the struggle will often center around the child's control of his own body, and especially of the anal zone.

On first glance, this hypothesis does not seem to have much to do with seventeenth-century childrearing. Since there were no smoothly functioning disposal systems to carry away unpleasant sights and smells, that society was in a completely different relationship to its own excrement. Houses did not have toilets; people used chamber pots and *chaises-percées*, and the contents ended up in the streets. There were no public rest rooms and no really effective sewage networks. Legislative efforts to alleviate the problem—by requiring people to use what sewers there were, by developing a system of garbage collection, or by having the streets paved—were unsuccessful. As a result, daily life was carried on amidst the inescapable smell, the feel underfoot, the sight in every corner, of human and other excreta. An observer described the royal palace in this way:

In the neighborhood of the Louvre, in several parts of the court, on the great stairway, and in the passageways, behind the doors, and just about everywhere, one sees a thousand ordures, one smells a thousand intolerable stenches, caused by the natural necessities which everyone performs there every day.

As one critic remarked, "We are squeezed, pressed, encircled from all sides, and can breathe only the stinking air from behind our walls, from our mud and from our sewers."[16]

Under the circumstances, it was inconceivable that children should be held to rigorous hygienic standards. Such standards would hardly have made sense to the adults themselves. Because it was impossible to shroud the act of elimination in a shamefaced privacy, this act could not be invested with the moralistic importance of a taboo. In fact, doctors tended to think that infants should be changed two or three times a day, but they had to admit that most mothers and nurses were much less interested in cleanliness and would be content with an occasional shaking out of the swaddling clothes. Among other functions, these clothes left the infant wrapped up with its own excrement so that adults need not have been bothered by it. After the child had been unswaddled, bed-wetting could become a problem, and children may have been severely punished for such infractions; Guillemeau claimed that out of fear boys sometimes tied a string around their penises to prevent nocturnal eneuresis. I suspect, however, that punishment for bed-wetting was administered because parents were directly inconvenienced by these incidents (as we shall see, parents and children would probably be sharing the same bed). So long as this lapse was avoided, parents were content with very minimal standards. In any case, the doctors who do discuss the problem indicate that it should be taken seriously only if the infant had not achieved control by the age of four or five. Further, these discussions concern only bed-wetting, and no reference is made to other forms of incontinence.[17]

Apparently, the child had to submit only to a very mild regime of toilet training. In the *Journal*, the matter is hardly mentioned. When the one-year-old Louis defecated on the carpet, Héroard made a joke of it. When the dauphin was five, "It was forbidden to all persons, of whatever quality, condition, or nation, to relieve themselves in the enclosure of the chateau [St-Germain-en-Laye, where Louis spent most of his childhood] except in the places destined for that use." On the same day, Louis was caught urinating against the wall of the lower chamber: "He finds himself surprised, blushes, does not know what to say, acknowledging that he has contravened." Louis seems to be mildly ashamed (perhaps even a bit surprised by his shame), but the issue is not taken seriously. Ariès has called attention to the pictures in which boys urinate publicly without causing any kind of scandal. We know that, like most infants of the time, Louis grew up amid a crowd of his peers. In such situations, children tend to learn what rules the society has set down from one another.[18]

These facts present us with a dilemma. Earlier, I attempted to develop an argument about the problem of autonomy in seventeenth-century styles of childrearing. Yet in connection with toilet training, which in psychoanalytic theory is closely associated with this problem, there seems to be no particular tension or conflict. Just when we might expect parents to be especially rigid, they turn out to be uncommonly relaxed. On the other hand, something must be wrong with my formulation of this theoretical anomaly if rigorous toilet training in our sense of the term would have been impossible both to conceptualize and to put into practice in the seventeenth century. With the best, or the worst, will in the world, no parent of that time could have made an issue of cleanliness training. In spite of its prominence in psychoanalytic theory, this issue has no meaning in a seventeenth-century context. We must consider the possibility that parents of that era chose to deal with infantile anality in other ways which were more congruent with the conditions of their lives.

In this respect, we should note that after the cutting of the umbilical cord, the first thing which happened to the new-born infant was that his bowels were flushed out. Before being washed or swaddled, he was given a cathartic of honey, white wine, or almond oil in order to make him pass the *meconium*. From the moment of birth, failure to expel what was inside threatened the health and even the life of the infant:

Oftentimes, if there were not helpe to make a free passage, in the fundament, yard, or other naturall places, that are sometimes closed up, there could neither sustenance bee received nor excrements expelled, which would cause the child to be stifled, and choked up.

From the beginning, adults were interested in what the child was harboring in his intestines and anxious to encourage him to rid himself as soon as possible of all "superfluities."[19]

After the child's birth, the doctors continued to take alarm if the process of evacuation should even momentarily slow down. Purgations were recommended to cure a variety of diseases and even to soothe the cranky baby who seemed to be crying too much. These remedies often were employed for purely preventive reasons; one doctor advised that children should be purged daily during the first month of life, then somewhat less frequently later on. If oral formulas did not have the desired effect, *clystères* or suppositories were suggested. Even roots or beet stalks might be inserted up the anus of the infant who seemed reluctant to eliminate. In the same spirit: "If the bladder of the childe be too full of urine, his belly will be hard, and strout out; and then let the nurse sucke the end of his yard, and press downe his belly."[20]

The doctors were also very anxious about the formation of stones (with some justice, in view of the child's diet) and wanted to make sure that waste matter was voided before it could solidify. They described techniques of conducting rectal examinations and of inserting probes up the urinary canal in order to extract stones, or even to check on their suspected presence. One may wonder what prompted these invasions. In a spirited analysis of how to verify a woman's virginity, Laurent Joubert discussed the tightness of an unpenetrated vagina, comparing it to "when one puts a finger in the anus of a little child to test it, on account of stones."[21]

In fact, adults were extraordinarily interested in that matter which the infant was storing up inside. On the one hand, they felt a sharp repugnance for this waste material. It was thought that children should be purged especially before eating "for fear that the milk will be mixed with some ordure, and be corrupted, and that some bad vapors will be elevated to the brain which could very much harm the infant." At the same time, when these "ordures" had been extracted, adults were likely to subject them to careful examination. Urine analysis was based on a complicated symbolism. The sample should be taken in the morning and stored in moderate temperatures out of the light. After several hours, it was to be evaluated for smell, color, amount of foam, transparency, and so on. Each variation said something about the inner state of the donor.[22]

Feces were cross-examined no less thoroughly. At its most fanciful, this study became a kind of psychological analysis, a seventeenth-century projective test. The bowels of children were thought to harbor matter which spoke to the adult world insolently, threateningly, with malice and insubordination. The fact that the child's excrement looked and smelled unpleasant meant that the child himself was somewhere deep down inside badly disposed. No matter how placid and cooperative he might appear, the excrement which was regularly washed out of him was regarded as the insulting message of an inner demon, indicating the "bad humors" which lurked within. The fact that this evil could be flushed from its hiding place constituted a victory for adults, ostensibly over the "humors," but perhaps more fundamentally over the infants themselves.[23]

We can see that parental indifference to toilet training did not signify a lack of interest in the child's anal zone. While they were not rigorously toilet trained, children were nonetheless deprived early in life of complete control over their own bowels. Potential self-regulation was disrupted by purges and rectal examinations. Doctors were not alone in sponsoring these measures. Remedies "for curing an infant who does not want to go to the toilet" were part of the folklore, finding their place among potions designed to relieve toothaches and to counteract mad dog bites. Cleanliness was not an issue, but infantile self-control, especially with respect to the modes of retention and elimination centered in the anus, obviously did attract a tremendous amount of concerned attention from the adult world. If purges and *clystères* failed to make the point, the fact that punishment was concentrated on the anus would remind the child of how interested his elders were in that part of his body. No wonder the French were known as the greatest "spankers" (*fesseurs*) in the world.[24]

Throughout seventeenth-century sources, we find the traces of this preoccupation expressed with great freedom in a variety of symbolic, and not so symbolic, ways, in jokes, proverbs, and insults. The comic possibilities were exploited with a special thoroughness, by Molière, in his portraits of hypochondriacs and their beloved *clystères*, by the court jester who told Henri IV, "You have to go to Rome . . . [where] you will take a nice *clystère* of holy water in order to . . . wash away all the rest of your sins," and even by the three-year-old dauphin. Héroard noticed him looking through a picture book and finding one drawing of "a halberdier who lowered the breeches of another and put a finger in his anus." Louis immediately got the point, translating the picture into a joke at the expense of one of the soldiers of the guard. Already he knew that to let another person put anything up your anus was to suffer a humiliating mortification.[25]

When Bodin refers to the young man who "defecated in the soup of his mother," the modern reader may be amused. However, this incident proves that the jokes covered a painful reality. Bodin was trying to show the breakdown of authority in French society, and with satisfaction he was able to report that the son was burned at the stake by order of the *parlement* of Toulouse.[26] With an unerring logic, the criminal had reduced the issue of authority to its primal terms. His choice of a gesture was designed to indicate that he had indeed retained control of that area of his body against which adults had inaugurated their campaign of repression. This idea may seem farfetched to us, but the worthy *parlementaires* took it seriously enough. Both the victim and his executioners knew that "anal" issues were not isolated from the child's struggle for self-determination. Their acts, and the rest of the evidence considered in this section, confirm the psychoanalytic prediction that the anal zone is dynamically linked to problems of infantile autonomy.

III

Our next task is to determine how this conflict was brought to a head and in what way parents and children reached an agreement on the issue of autonomy. In the dauphin's household, the regime of whipping came to a decisive turning point shortly after Louis' third birthday.[27] We know enough today not to take too seriously the idea that children's lives are determined primarily by a few traumatic events, and I single out one particular incident because of the more general trends it so aptly represents. Even so, I am impressed by the way in which this story leaps off the pages of the *Journal*, how it seems to be followed by a series of significant changes in the attitude and behavior of the dauphin, and how it was often recalled by Héroard as Louis grew older. In his entry for October 23, 1604, the doctor wrote:

Awake at 7:30, up at 8:30, he becomes sullen, does not want to take his frock. His nurse calls him: "Monsieur Tabouret, Monsieur Tabouret [her pet name for the dauphin], take your frock." He breaks out laughing and gets dressed. At 9:15, he breakfasts. He asks if it's raining. He feared the rain. Led to the king and queen, in the chapel, taken back to the room at 11:00. Dined at noon, led to the king, who was going to the hunt, very well behaved. He wants to put on boots like the king, and wants to go down to the privy and nowhere else, sees his little drum, . . . wants it (it was one of his greatest pleasures).

The passage concerns a willful little boy: he does not want to get dressed, he wants to put on boots like his father's, wants to go to the privy (and nowhere else—here will has a specifically anal referent), wants to play with his drum. Then the king returned from the hunt and for the third time that day called his son to attend him:

So he went to find the king against his will, by force. The king says to him: "Remove your hat." He is reluctant to remove it, the king takes it off, he is irritated. Then the king takes his drum and drumsticks, and things got even worse: "My hat, my drum, my drumsticks." To spite him, the king puts the hat on his own head: "I want my hat." The king hits him with it on the head. Now he is angry and the king against him. The king takes him by the wrists and lifts him in the air, stretching his little arms out to the sides: "Hey! you're hurting me! Hey! my drum! my hat!" The queen returns his hat, then his drumsticks to him. It was a little tragedy.

The taking of the drum ("it was one of his greatest pleasures") recalls the automatic way adults were likely to react against the preferences in food, clothes, or toys of their young children. It touched the dauphin on a sore spot: his right to his own possessions, to a small domain where he was in charge, with claims of ownership and execution just like an adult ("he wants to put on boots like the king"). As we have seen, all children at this stage take these issues seriously. Holding on to what "belongs" to them is a vital aspect of self-identification and self-preservation. Even as he was being roughly handled, Louis continued to try to "hold on" by insisting that the hat, drum, and sticks were his.

The dauphin was carried away from the scene. The rest of

the day was filled with tantrums and whippings. During a lull, his nurse tried to extract a moral: "Monsieur, you have been obstinate, you shouldn't, you must obey papa." Louis was incensed: "Kill mamanga [his name for the governess], she is bad. I will kill everyone! I will kill God!" He was finally put to bed at 10:30, slept unevenly, complained of pains in his shoulder, and was unable to lift his arm or to hold what was put in his hand.

This incident seems to sum up all of the themes which we expect to encounter in the life of a child at this age. Louis was caught up in an erratic and willful struggle with the world around him in which he was trying, not always judiciously, to experiment with modalities of holding on and letting go. In attempting to settle on an appropriate definition of his freedom, he collided disastrously with adults who were unwilling to adjust with him. I want to stress the dangerous violence of the king's response, the primitive impulsiveness of his anger. The event occurred just about a year after the regime of whipping had been inaugurated, and even to a three-year-old, it must have been obvious that some accommodation would be necessary with an adult world so little master of itself.

Héroard remarked several times during the next months that the dauphin was afraid, still remembering the incident of October 23. This fear was not far below the surface as Louis began to develop the self-discipline which would enable him to avoid future catastrophes. When the king used his glass, "he was very angry, but he controlled himself and calmly let it pass." The next day, "he wanted to cry but restrained himself out of respect for the king." Another time, "bursting with rage," he shouted at a nobleman: " 'I'm going to kill you, just wait, with my scissors!' then, repenting of the word 'kill' for which he had been chastised, 'I'm going to poke out your eyes.' " Louis was watching carefully, trying to learn how to deal with his own dangerous impulses and sensitive to the hints of the adults around him. In church, he saw the king striking his chest and asked his valet why. " 'Monsieur, . . . because he was angry and hit someone; he has offended God and now he demands pardon.' [Louis] . . . struck his own chest, saying 'I have offended God, pardon me.' "[28]

A society cannot be content to control and to punish children. It must also indicate the avenues along which further growth and initiative will be permitted. In the *Journal*, approved initiative is summed up by the notion of service. Before the incident of October 23, there had been many evocations of the child's role as servant. Louis made a habit of singing or playing his drum for the king, and, beginning at the age of about sixteen months, when the dauphin dined with Henri, he presented him with his napkin before the start of the meal.[29]

After the beating, a much more concentrated effort was made by adults to force the child to embrace the role of servant. Louis was asked: "Monsieur, who is the master of papa?" "God is." "And who is yours?" "I don't want to say." Héroard adds: "It was never possible to make him acknowledge a master. The day before, the king had made him angry when he said: 'I am the master, and you are my valet'; that very much irritated him." Irritation or no, Louis was learning quickly. For the most part, when he was questioned, "Who are you?" he responded, "The little valet of papa." His letters to the king now always included the assurance that he was "good, no longer obstinate," that he wanted only to obey him, and that he was his devoted servant.[30]

During the first years of his life, Louis' relations with the king had been very amicable, full of play and signs of mutual affection. But after the beating and for about two years, this closeness gave way on the one side to haughty reserve and arrogance and on the other to fear and subservience. It was precisely at this time that Louis was symbolically liberated in having his leading strings removed: " 'I can now run all alone . . . I have no leading strings, I'll get around all by myself'; he was completely delighted." Having been directed on the road toward a childhood of compliant submission, Louis could now be safely unleashed.[31]

The dauphin's personal solution to the problem of autonomy could hardly have been unique. With a unanimous voice, theorists argued that childhood obedience was essential to the survival of society. In this spirit, Bodin defined a republic as a collection of "several households" in each of which the authority of the father was unquestioned. Of all possible command situations, the father's mandate over his children was special: he was the only chief in all society who received power directly from nature. This authority was primary:

Just as the well conducted family is the true image of the republic, and the domestic power similar to the sovereign power, so the governmental right of the household is the true model of the government of the republic. Just as with each individual member doing his duty the whole *corps* will prosper, so with families being well governed, the republic will thrive.[32]

No wonder so many voices urged the child to obey his parents!

The theme of parental authority continued to appear throughout the political theory of the seventeenth century. In justifications of monarchy, the fifth commandment did yeoman service, and when Filmer claimed that the Stuarts derived their power from the fact that they were the descendants of Adam, the first father, he was only carrying to a logical extreme an argument which on both sides of the Channel had always been a staple of the absolutist case. The 1639 royal declaration on marriage neatly linked the themes articulated by Bodin and Filmer:

Marriages are the schools of states, the source and the origin of civil society, and the foundation of the families which make up republics, which serve as sources forming their administration and in which the natural reverence of children for their parents is the bond of legitimate obedience of subjects for their sovereigns.[33]

Law and ritual helped to reinforce paternal authority. We have already reviewed the ways in which parents could legally control their children's marriage plans. Minors had to live under the same roof with parents, were without property rights, and had no legal recourse against physical abuse. Bodin even claimed that parents had the power of life and death over their offspring, making them less than serfs. Seconding the exhortations of legists, churchmen, and politicians were all the routines of the household, and in at least one case the most venerable rituals. Here is a "coming of age" in the south of France:

The father, being on the chair, and his son kneeling before him bareheaded, put the hands of his son between his, and then, acceding to the petition and requisition of the other, by his clear wish, frank and free will, emancipated him and put him in liberty and outside paternal power, save naturally the honor, respect and unity which his son owed to him . . . as a sign of which the father, spreading his hands, released those of his son, putting him in full liberty.[34]

We should not imagine that the family system compelled anything like a universal obedience. As soon as children grew up, they were likely to challenge the power of their parents. We have seen how strict laws prohibiting marriage without parental consent only partially hindered young people determined to marry on the basis of their own inclination. The same pattern of legal prohibition and individual contravening of the law no doubt applies to the relations of parents and children in general. Pasquier's dictum is often cited: "The true images of God on earth are fathers and mothers with respect to their children, and just as obedience is the principal sacrifice which God desires of us, so it is between parents and their children." But this statement hardly describes the actual state of parent-child relations. Pasquier's letters refer often to cases in which his own and his friends' children defied their parents while the latter looked on fatalistically and told one another that patience and conciliation were the only sensible tactics.[35]

However, if older children were relatively free, their younger brothers and sisters could only submit, waiting for the day when growing up would enable them to claim the same liberties. A certain leeway might be allowed young adults, who were to some extent able to control themselves, but the anarchic little child could not be trusted so far. In any case, he was too small to force concessions from the adults around him. Historians have often cited the fact that children and servants were mixed together in the households of the old regime, both under the authority of the father. As Ariès puts it:

The idea of childhood was bound up with the idea of dependence: the words "sons," "varlets," and "boys" (*fils, valets, garçons*) were also words in the vocabulary of feudal subordination. One could leave childhood only by leaving the state of dependence, or at least the lower degrees of dependence.[36]

In other words, the painful steps by which Louis gradually learned to placate his father were taken by other infants as well. He was not alone in having to submit. For young children in general, being the father's servant was the only role which society allowed them to assume.

IV

It seems to me that the foregoing discussion leads up to one major question: why did adults find it necessary to insist so emphatically on the obedience of children? Eriksonian theory suggests the beginnings of an answer. In his most thorough attempt to relate the second phase of childhood to the quality of social life, Erikson writes:

We have related basic trust to the institution of religion. The basic need of the individual for a delineation of his *autonomy* in the adult order of things seems, in turn, to be taken care of by the *principle of "law and order,"* which in daily life as well as in the high courts of law apportions to each his privileges and his limitations, his obligations and his rights. The sense of autonomy which arises, or should arise, in the second stage of childhood, is fostered by a handling of the small individual which expresses a sense of rightful dignity and lawful independence on the part of the parents and which gives him the confident expectation that the kind of autonomy fostered in childhood will not be frustrated later. This, in turn, necessitates a relationship of partner to parent, of parent to employer, and of parent to government which reaffirms the parent's essential dignity within the hierarchy of social positions. It is important to dwell on this point because much of the shame and doubt, much of the indignity and uncertainty which is aroused in children is a consequence of the parents' frustrations in marriage, in work, and in citizenship. Thus the sense of autonomy in the child . . . must be backed up by the preservation in economic and political life of a high sense of autonomy and of self-reliance.[37]

In short, parents need certain specific cultural and political supports if they are to accept with equanimity the first manifestations of infantile will. If we look for a moment at the kinds of reinforcements available to parents of the old regime, I think we can understand why they reacted as they did to the second stage of childhood.

In the seventeenth century, childrearing took place in a hierarchical society characterized by a very uneven distribution of wealth and dominated by forces of political and religious authoritarianism. It was not a social order in which most individuals found it possible to maintain "a sense of rightful dignity and lawful independence." For the vast majority of French subjects in this period, the concept of "law and order" could hardly have had much relation to their own very precarious existence. Such a social order naturally influences styles of childrearing. The adult who in his own life had little experience of genuine self-determination and only limited opportunity to observe it in the conduct of others, was not able to tolerate his child's efforts to be self-determining. The difficulty parents experienced in dealing with infantile will grew out of the inequitable character of their experience "in marriage, in work, and in citizenship."

Admittedly, these are sweeping statements. One might well object that I am arguing almost tautologically: if the society is authoritarian, methods of childrearing (and probably every social relationship) will also be authoritarian. All known societies contain some element of hierarchy. For generations, historians have been debating about the nature of the social system whose character I seem to be taking for granted. Many have argued that individuals of the old regime were used to the graded ranks into which they were born and did not feel differences in status and power as hindrances to close personal ties or to living a satisfying and happy life. These historians claim that modern criticisms of the old regime are anachronistic. With our legalistic and bureaucratic notion of the way a society works, we lack the means to understand a world held together by mutual loyalties, a shared tradition, the "existential bond" between master and servant.

Paternalism is implicit in these defenses of the old regime. To its champions, this system worked like a large family. Rulers were similar to benevolent parents, often autocratic, but at the same time attentive to the welfare of their "children." A study of childrearing, and particularly of the stage of autonomy, can give us an especially informative slant on the problem. If the concept of paternalism has been called into question, then presumably the best setting in which it might be evaluated would be within the family itself. Here the human consequences of old regime hierarchy should be most characteristically demonstrated.

I would maintain that in the seventeenth century people felt strongly the contrast between the loyalties and duties incumbent upon them as a consequence of their station in society on the one hand, and their natural inclinations on the other. Institutional arrangements always implied a gradation of rank and were thus held to be incompatible with friendship, in which equality between the partners was so important. Far from accepting the fact that personal relations were almost always arranged according to hierarchical principles, individuals were made acutely uncomfortable by this situation. In personal letters, writers often distinguished sincere and spontaneous affection from the more perfunctory good will which went with the formal relationship to their correspondent. Thus Madame de Sévigné, in sending good wishes to her daughter, stipulated that, "In this case, maternal love plays less of a part than inclination."[38]

As the quote indicates, the family was caught up in this system. To be a brother, son, or wife was a status, with its special obligations, its place in a grid of rule and submission. Members of the family were supposed to love one another; paternal, maternal, fraternal love were all often cited as models of human fellow feeling. At the same time, even within the family, it was terribly hard to imagine a relationship of mutual affection which was not simultaneously one of ruler and ruled. Like the bond between master and servant, between seigneur and peasant, between king and subject, family ties, while steeped in a folklore of pious harmony, implied as well the power to dominate others, to claim rewards, or, on the contrary, the awareness of a helpless dependence.[39]

This line of argument will help to explain further the distinction which, as we have seen, observers made with such clarity between marriages of love and those of interest. Marriages of love implied spontaneous affection between the two lovers, who were concerned primarily with their own happiness. Marriage of interest involved social and financial considerations to be arranged for the benefit of families. These observers understood very well that in a social system which attempted to subordinate the wishes of marriageable children to the ambitions of their parents, and in which the wife was regarded simply as the means of cementing alliances between families, marriage could not at the same time be expected to provide for the happiness and the emotional satisfaction of the partners.

Fraternal relations were compromised by similar pressures. As the dauphin was being forced to acknowledge himself as his father's valet, it was also being pointed out to him that his brothers, who were younger and hence subordinate, would serve him just as he served the king. Books of etiquette often struggled with the problem of fraternal affection and the rights of primogeniture. How do you reconcile "natural" ties with the principle which arranges brothers one above the other in a hierarchy of prerogatives? Corneille built the play *Rodogune* around this dilemma. The twins Seleucus and Antiochus are the model of fraternity. Since they do not know who is older (the oddity of the situation demonstrates how hard it was in the seventeenth century to conceive of real equality), they can be familiar and trusting in relations with one another. Their mother, however, decides to disclose the order of birth, and the two brothers are thrown into a panic. They know that if this information is revealed, one will become the arrogant master, the other, his resentful servant (full of "shame and envy"), and their accord will be ruined.[40]

We can see that gradations of rank within the household were interpreted simply as a matter of power and of usage, and that people believed this situation discouraged close and mutually satisfying relationships among family members. Ideally, those of lower rank should have accepted the eminence of their superiors and been warmed by the benefits they received from an admittedly unequal partnership. In fact, inequality within the domestic unit filled people not with love and warmth, but with resentment and a feeling of "shame and envy."

Among the members of the family, the infant is the most prone to these feelings. His physical and intellectual inferiority is a basic fact of nature as is his subjection to the will of older, stronger adults. Precisely because it is so completely unearned by any merit, but instead is derived from an amoral biological fact, parental authority might legitimately be expected to embody whatever sense of justice adults profess to respect. The child has to obey; in what ways do grownups persuade him that he ought to obey?

It seems to me that no one could deny the paramount importance of force and intimidation in the upbringing of the dauphin. The beating Louis received at the hands of his father demonstrated the lengths to which adults were willing to carry the matter: an obstinate child was in physical danger. Grownups relied heavily on their ability to frighten the young prince. They rightly assumed that he remembered what had happened the last time he had been too defiant. Childish fears were exploited in a variety of petty ways. For example, when it was discovered that Louis was afraid of someone (a hunchbacked member of the guard, or a mason in the king's service), that person would be summoned whenever it was necessary to make Louis toe the line.[41]

The whippings continued, gradually settling into a fixed ritual. Louis was beaten first thing in the morning the day after his infractions: "Scarcely were his eyes open when he was whipped." Often he would get up early and hide or block the door in order to avoid these sessions. When it became impossible for Madame de Montglat to handle the dauphin, his father instructed soldiers of the guard to hold him while the whippings were administered. Louis was beaten even after becoming king of France, and at the age of ten, he still had nightmares about being whipped. As late as January, 1614, adults continued to threaten Louis with the switch, but by this time his physical development was at last putting a stop to such means of punishment.[42]

As I suggested earlier, formalized coercion was probably better for the infant than the erratic and unrestrained cruelty which no doubt characterized discipline in families where parents had to deal directly with their offspring. But even in the royal household, it is obvious that fear was one of the principal forces steering the child into that social role which adults required him to assume. Such fear was not incompatible with love. Louis always demonstrated an intense feeling for his father, and it would be foolish to pretend that their relationship was entirely negative. Yet this love (corresponding to the sentiment which many historians have thought tied together master and servant in the old regime) does not change the fact that terrorizing children was inhumane and wrong. At the core of its domestic life, I think we find a telling indictment of the old regime.

We now have a better idea of how life cycles "interlocked" in the seventeenth century. It is no accident that fathers whipped their sons for their own good, because they themselves were whipped as children. These fathers had been thwarted in their own infantile efforts to be autonomous. Punished for attempting to establish selfhood, and deprived of control over their bodies, they were left with a pervasive sense of shame and doubt. Such sentiments fit the adult life they could lead in a hierarchical society indifferent to the dignity of the individual and held together principally by coercive means. In turn, people formed along these lines were necessarily going to respond to their children's search for independence with rigid counterassertions and panicky violence. The inability of the king himself, the only man in the society who was without a master, to break out of this vicious circle attests to the power of the cycle of unfreedom.

Herbert Marcuse has written: "In every revolution, there seems to have been a historical moment when the struggle against domination might have been victorious—but the moment passed. An element of *self-defeat* seems to be involved in this dynamic."[43] When healthy and stable adults are oppressed, there is a possibility of resistance and revolt. But the fact is that authoritarian systems work through parents to get at the child before the man. Marcuse traced the propensity for self-defeat back to the Oedipal stage and to the beginnings of human guilt. In view of what has been said here about the second stage of infancy, I think this propensity can be linked to an even earlier phase of childhood. When infantile autonomy is crushed, the result is not and cannot be planned resistance. On the contrary, this crackdown leads the small child to question himself, to be ashamed, to doubt his own worth and the possibility of future success. Standing on these sandy foundations, the individual will never be able to demand what is his due. In this way, a repressive status quo is anchored in the conflicts of the anal stage.

8

THE THIRD STAGE:
INFANTILE SEXUALITY

I

In Héroard's *Journal*, the proximity of weaning to the beginning of corporal punishment signals Louis' passage from the first to the second phase of infancy. No similarly dramatic coincidence helps us to pinpoint the next qualitative change in the life of the dauphin. However, during the child's fourth and fifth years, some kind of development was unmistakably taking place. At this time, the young prince was physically able to participate in a wider range of court functions (his own christening, for example). In addition, his play became more purposeful. Pretending to be a courtier or a general, Louis was experimenting with the adult roles he would later be expected to assume. The dauphin was also making intellectual progress, thinking, and asking questions, about a variety of topics—and especially about sex.

These developments can be squared with Erikson's analysis of the third stage of childhood.[1] At best, the infant now has a sense of autonomy, a degree of confidence in his ability to control his body and a chosen segment of the milieu, and is ready for more purposeful activity. An intrusive organ mode asserts itself: the child aggressively explores the physical world; his approaches to other people take on a challenging quality; he enters a phase of intellectual ferment, manifested in an often disconcerting curiosity. The child is fascinated by the styles of adulthood, wants to emulate and even to surpass grownups. Because of the very considerable role experimentation which it encourages, this stage is related to problems of identity. Here infants and adults must begin to agree more specifically about who the child is and what kind of person he will be in later life.

Sexual issues are crucial to this whole process. As usual, Erikson gives his discussion a biological base. Just as incorporation is linked to the mouth and retention-elimination to the anus, the intrusive mode is centered in the child's genitals. This unprecedented erotic drive lends a special urgency to the project of recognizing and mimicking adult roles. Wanting to be grown up in sexual as well as in other ways, the infant dreams of replacing his father and possessing his mother. In the best of circumstances, children accept the fact that these hopes cannot be realized and begin to map out alternate routes to the power and competence they desire but cannot yet obtain. By identifying and internalizing the characteristics of adults around them, they trade dreams of immediate gratification for the promise of a maturity to come. This crisis thus imposes upon parents and children a difficult mutual task: infantile initiative must be preserved even though the one project the child most wants to put into effect is blocked by reality. The way in which he absorbs the constraints which parents, and his own limitation as a child, force upon him at this time is important in determining what kind of personality the infant carries on into adulthood.

No aspect of psychoanalytic theory stirs as much controversy as the attempt to derive important segments of human personality from the starting point of infantile sexuality, especially from the Oedipus complex. Before proceeding with our study of seventeenth-century childhood in the Oedipal phase, we must consider criticisms of Freudian theory on this point and decide how they relate to the present work. As I see it, such criticisms can be grouped in three categories. What might be called the philistine school simply denies that sex is a significant determinant in the functioning of the normal personality, and refuses to believe that such a topic can be rationally discussed, especially with reference to children. On the other hand, critics within the clinical field are often sympathetic to psychoanalytic emphasis on the general importance of sex in shaping human behavior, but are also anxious to subject specific analytic concepts to a careful,

osity about sex. He was allowed to explore what we would call pornographic picture books, and no one prevented him from playing sexually with his younger sister. When he was a little older (about five), his forays became more ambitious: "Put to bed, he asks to play, plays with Mademoiselle Mercier [one of his ladies-in-waiting], calls me, saying that Mercier has a cunt as big as that, showing his two fists, and that there's a lot of water inside." As a result of these explorations, as well as of the marked outspokenness of the adults around him, Louis knew a great deal for a five-year-old. He was acquainted with prostitution, adultery, and sexual intercourse, which he had obviously been allowed to observe.[4]

It should be apparent that the mores of seventeenth-century France, at least within the court, differ from those we take for granted today. Can psychoanalysts have anything to say about this ostensibly unrepressive milieu? In commenting on the *Journal*, Philippe Ariès has written:

This lack of reserve with regard to children surprises us; we raise our eyebrows at the outspoken talk but even more at the bold gestures, the physical contacts, about which it is easy to imagine what a psycho-analyst would say. The psycho-analyst would be wrong. The attitude to sex, and doubtless sex itself, varies according to environment, and consequently according to period and mentality.[5]

This observation seems at first glance to be based on the sophisticated relativism which, as we have seen, even many sympathetic critics of psychoanalysis have adopted. At the same time, Ariès craftily evades the issue by refusing to tell us what possible interpretation we are being asked to reject. The reader is left to "imagine" what a psychoanalyst might say about the *Journal*.

From other passages, I gather that Ariès believes a Freudian analyst would indiscriminately label seventeenth-century practices as "perverse" or "corrupt," whereas, in fact, "all that was involved was a game whose scabrous nature we should beware of exaggerating: there was nothing more scabrous about it than there is about the racy stories men tell each other today." Such remarks suggest that we are dealing with the philistine rejection of psychoanalysis rather than with a well-informed assessment of its historical limitations. Analysts have of course been among the first to push beyond the moralistic prejudices implicit in terms like "perverse" and "corrupt." Further, Ariès hardly convinces us of the innocuous nature of the "game" Héroard describes by comparing it to "the racy stories men tell each other today." In the next breath, the reader expects to be assured of the meaninglessness of dreams and slips of the tongue.[6]

As usual, however, it would be rash to reject Ariès' interpretation too hastily. His point about historical relativism is a good one. If adults are not themselves repressed, if they treat sexual issues spontaneously and naturally (like a "game"), then they certainly are to be distinguished from the patients who have found their way into therapy and whose conflicts provided Freud with the clues upon which he based a theory of personality. We assume that neurotics, and indeed all adults, are more or less repressed. We would be inhibited in those instances where our seventeenth-century predecessors seem to have been so outgoing, ashamed where they were simply amused. According to Ariès, the sexual transactions recounted by Héroard were not complicated and agonizing negotiations involving basic psychic issues. On the contrary, they were trivial games, hardly noticed by either parent or child. We should follow their example, ignore the solemn interpretations of the analysts, and pass over these bawdy anecdotes without giving them too much serious consideration.

Naturally I do not plan to follow this advice. The argument is persuasive, but at the same time we have to look a little more carefully before denying the importance of infantile sexuality in the seventeenth century.

II

All the source materials employed in this book share one vexing characteristic: they tell us about a limited segment of old regime society. The problem in this chapter is especially acute since we are forced to rely even more heavily than usual on Héroard's

Journal, which describes only a very special milieu: the royal court. Ariès swiftly deals with this problem: "There is no reason to believe that the moral climate was any different in other families, whether nobles or commoners; the practice of associating children with the sexual ribaldries of adults formed part of contemporary manners." And yet, where questions of morality were concerned, there was a marked gap between court and country in the England of James I, just as in France the debaucheries of Henri III were hardly typical. In short, I do not believe that we can assume that the *Journal* describes a representative sample of seventeenth-century sexual morality.[7]

It is true of course that throughout society the lack of privacy in domestic life affected sexual practices (just as it influenced issues of toilet training). We can affirm that most children of that time slept in the same room or even in the same bed with adults and were therefore conversant from an early age with the details of erotic activity among their elders. Some upper-class families were exceptional in providing children with their own bedrooms. However, separate beds or even separate rooms would not shield the infant from sexual realities if his parents did not attempt to hide these realities. Louis the dauphin may have had his own bedroom, but, at the same time, he was in no way screened off from adult intimacies. As a result of the physical construction of the household (the lack of privacy) and of the freer attitudes toward the subject, sex in the seventeenth century, outside as well as within the court, was treated with a greater openness than it is today.[8]

On the other hand, powerful ideological forces were set in opposition to this permissiveness. Nowhere in the literature on childrearing do we find any justification of the kind of licentiousness described in Héroard's *Journal.* To be sure, moralists were put on the defensive by the strength of the customs they were attempting to combat. Thus François de Sales thought that ideally all children should have separate beds, but he was content with the more modest recommendation that they should sleep alone "as much as possible, or with persons in whom you can have as much confidence as in yourself." Writers like de Sales, Jacqueline Pascal, or Jean-Baptiste de la Salle may have recognized the difficulties in enforcing rules of modesty, but that did not prevent them from attempting to maintain high standards of purity for children. La Salle, for example, argued that infants should be advised to sleep demurely and well covered, so that anyone approaching would not be able to discern "the outline of the body." He also advised against "nudity," meaning the tendency to expose something other than the face and hands. A rigid purity in word and gesture was the norm. It was hard to believe that mothers like Marie Chantal and Madame Acarie were any less demanding.[9]

My remarks are not intended to introduce an exhaustive discussion of sexual customs throughout society—a research project in itself—but rather to provide some perspective on the material found in Héroard's *Journal*. In fact, not all adults were so careless as those around the young Louis when it came to children and sex. Granted that manners were in general relatively lewd during the seventeenth century, I still assume that for this period the court milieu represents an extreme limit of sexual liberality. Ariès would presumably agree that in no other area would one find a greater permissiveness. Keeping this fact in mind, I think that Ariès can be refuted simply by sticking to examples drawn from Héroard's picture of court life. If the evidence shows that, even in this free and licentious atmosphere, sex was a source of anxiety and conflict for both adults and children, it would necessarily follow that the same conclusion also applies to the rest of society, where mores were almost certainly more sober and conservative.

We have seen how openly adults treated their own sexual needs and those of the dauphin, how little they interfered with his autoerotic activity, and what free rein they gave to his curiosity. At the same time, the *Journal* amply demonstrates that this "freedom" had its limitations, and that Louis' sexual initiatives encountered various obstacles. Some were implicit in the fact that he was a child. Louis seems to have spontaneously decided to impose other restraints upon himself. Finally, in a third category, we find those hindrances which were the product of adult efforts to socialize the young prince. In examining these obstacles, we should be able to decide if sex was indeed a harmless "game" for children in the seventeenth century, or if, on the other hand, it had a more serious impact on them and the adults responsible for their care.

In the first place, it is clear that in spite of his explorations Louis understood little of sex. The nature of erotic love, the process of conception and of birth—these are dilemmas beyond the reach of the child's intelligence. The dauphin knew roughly what happens when people copulate, but tended, as do children in many cultures, to interpret what he saw as a violent assault. Birth was even more perplexing. Louis was not sure how the baby entered his pregnant nurse: "By the ear," he guessed. Later he told her, "I will enter through your mouth, then I'll go into your belly, you will say that you're pregnant and then you will have me." He also was not sure what role the penis played in all of this, imagining that it might be a source of milk with which he could feed those who attended his *levée* or that sex had something to do with urination. Louis' investigations impressed him with the size of women's orifices: "He tells me to write again that the cunt of Saint-Georges is big as this box [it was the one where his silver toys were kept], and that the cunt of Dubois is big as his belly." In his mind, he connected this inner space with the other great childhood mystery—death. "Madame de Montglat warned him that if he was not *sage*, God would blow him far away, with one breath. 'Oh!' he said, 'I will return to mama's belly.' "[10]

It is also apparent that the sexual anarchy of the court did not prevent Louis from developing certain reservations about erotic activity. At some point during his second year a new element of modesty entered into the usual incidents: "He throws down little Marguerite, kisses her, throws himself on her, then, being picked up, is ashamed and goes to hide." Louis began to recognize and to try to avoid certain people:

He runs into Madame the Marquise de Verneuil, who asks him for his hand to kiss, then his nipple. He haughtily refuses both requests. He was told to obey several times by Madame de Montglat. Finally he gives in for form's sake.

The dauphin also learned to fend off the queen's fool. At first, like the others, she had no trouble in engaging him in sexual games: "She plays with him, he laughs. She pulls up her skirts, he sees the tops of her stockings. He begins to laugh and joke." But later he found her less amusing, saying that he did not like crazy people, and refusing the role of foil. When she asked, " 'Will you be as bawdy as your father?' he responds coldly, after a moment's thought: 'No.' "[11]

We cannot know what was going on in the dauphin's head as he drew back from these erotic encounters. From a psycho-analytic perspective, one might surmise that the infant was frightened by his libidinal impulses and spontaneously felt the need to develop his own monitoring devices in order to regulate these anarchic inner drives. Analysts believe that all children are afraid of what will happen if they let loose all the energy inside them. Looking at the matter from this perspective, we might surmise that the threat of disintegration was especially acute to a child in Louis' circumstances since adults were constantly in-vading his privacy and provoking erotic impulses which he was not at all practiced at integrating and controlling.

However, in this particular case, we have no way of testing such conjectures. As an alternative, I prefer to concentrate on the way adults reacted to Louis' sexual activity rather than on the inner dynamics of the child himself. In fact, the anecdotes cited above, while they may indeed show the dauphin developing self-regulating capacities, also hint that grownups were encouraging his efforts to be more circumspect. After throwing down "little Marguerite," he is ashamed: the word implies a social situation. Louis blushed not so much because of the promptings of some inner voice but rather because he sensed that onlookers were displeased with what he had done. We are thus presented with something of a mystery: among the gallants, mistresses, and jesters of the court, who is the frowning observer causing Louis to feel so uncomfortable?

The nurse is one possible candidate:

The Dauphin does not want to kiss Madame the Marquise de Verneuil, does not want to approach Madame the Marquise, hits her with his *palemail*. . . . He never wants to let the Marquise touch his nipples, his nurse had said to him: "Monsieur, do not let anyone touch your nipples or your cock; they'll cut them off." He remembered this.[12]

However, in looking at the *Journal* as a whole, we can see that the nurse was not a consistent disciplinarian on this issue or on any other. The same might be said of his governess, Madame de Montglat, who could be very stern, but who hardly took notice of the dauphin's sexual adventures. She and most of the other members of the household seem to belong to the category established by Ariès: they treat sex lightly (like a game) and show little interest in helping Louis define some workable system of self-control.

We can cite one exception to this statement: Héroard himself. Ariès is wrong in maintaining that no one tried to teach the dauphin "decency in language and behavior" until he had "attained the fateful age of seven," and he is unfair in implying that the "worthy doctor" was a naive chronicler who wrote down everything he saw without making any judgments of his own. Héroard was not a complacent observer of the mores of the court, but a firm, even a severe, critic whose views are readily apparent just beneath the surface of his understated prose. From about the age of three, Louis was aware of Héroard's potential disapproval. Madame de Montglat asked: " 'Monsieur, what will the newlyweds do?' 'If Monsieur Héroard wasn't there, I'd tell you.' 'Monsieur,' I say to him, 'there's no danger' "; and Louis gave a little pantomime of sexual intercourse.[13]

When Louis was a little older, Héroard became more outspoken: "In conversation with Mesdames de Vitry and de Saint-Georges, the Dauphin says some new words, and shameful phrases, unworthy of his upbringing, saying that papa's is much longer than his, that it is this long, indicating half the length of his arm." When Monsieur de Montglat kissed the dauphin on the mouth, Héroard wrote in the margin: *"temeritas et impudentia."* When the dauphin was put in the bed of Madame de Montglat, "between her and her husband," the note was *"insignis impudentia."* The doctor was embarrassed for Henri himself:

The king returns from the hunt. Louis goes to see him; *pro pudore erubescit; manu obducit faciem* [Rex] *ostentans manu p . . . et dicens: Ecce qui te talem qualis es fecit* [he blushes with shame, covers his face with his hands; the king stretching out his penis with his hand, and saying: Behold what made you what you are].

I do not have any doubt that Héroard disapproves of the king's acts, which he fastidiously translates into Latin. These quotes clearly establish the doctor's conservatism in sexual matters. Louis was aware of this conservatism, and any careful modern reader will also recognize its traces in the *Journal*.[14]

Héroard's presence is of great value because it shows that even in the most liberal sexual atmosphere of the day there was available a not unfamiliar range of attitudes toward erotic expression. The freedom of word and gesture of a Verneuil or of the king was balanced by the doctor's rectitude. With Ariès, I am struck by the "outspoken talk" and the "bold gestures." But more striking still, I think, is the coexistence of this eroticism with more cautious attitudes toward sex: not the excessiveness of sexual behavior so much as the contrasts between different points of view. The example of Héroard is especially telling because he expresses little interest in religion and gives no sign of being a zealot.[15] We read of the feats of discipline engineered by mothers who were (literally) saints with a certain sense of irony, and I suspect that observers in the seventeenth century also found such behavior "special" (if in an exemplary way). Because Héroard's actions are so matter-of-fact, they seem all the more convincing. His marginal comments are not the rantings of a fanatic moralist but are, I believe, the signs of a conventional and relatively widespread set of attitudes toward sex.

The following incident illustrates how the court world was sharply divided on moral issues, and how this split left Louis, and, I assume, other children as well, in a very awkward position: "Monsieur de Verneuil . . . advises [the dauphin] to kiss the girls, the little Vitry and the little Frontenac." But Héroard's wife said to the dauphin:

"Monsieur, do you remember what Monsieur Héroard said to you about this kind of thing the other day?" Without saying a word, the dauphin covers his ears. Monsieur de Verneuil says to him: "My master, don't listen to them!"

Someone else kidded Monsieur de Verneuil: " 'It will be necessary to go to Rome to ask pardon of the Pope.' 'Ho! yes,' answers Monsieur de Verneuil. 'Ho! my master will marry the little Frontenac and I the little Vitry.' " Louis was taken back to his room. A little later, Monsieur de Frontenac (the father of his "bride-to-be" playmate of a few moments ago) approached him. Louis "is afraid it was about his daughter, is ashamed, and begins to cry."[16] We can see that adults were by no means unanimous in prompting the infant to abandon himself to his impulses. On the contrary, Louis heard an almost paralyzing chorus of conflicting advice: amid a general celebration of sexual license, certain adults continued to defend the principle of continence. No wonder Louis tried to cover his ears.

This analysis can be carried a step further. I think careful examination will show that even the king, for all his boisterous sensuality, was interested in imposing certain moral prohibitions on the dauphin. In Héroard's account, the relationship between Henri and his son is continually emphasized. In the simple catechisms with which Madame de Montglat instructed Louis, filial piety held a prominent place. Héroard thought that the destinies of father and son were joined together. The dauphin woke up "full of melancholy and out of sorts. . . . He seems to have a sense of the mortal danger . . . which threatened the king," who had just narrowly escaped an assassination attempt on the Pont Neuf. When Louis had a bloody nose, the doctor wondered if it had something to do with the severe case of diarrhea which the king was suffering the same day. Héroard wrote: "We have noticed several times that whenever something happens to the king, an accident without manifest cause befalls the dauphin."[17]

By contrast, the relationship between Louis and his mother was startlingly cold. After giving birth to the dauphin, the queen often visited her new son, but he was six months old before she embraced him for the first time. Moments of intimacy were not unknown: "The queen arrives at 1:30, finds Monseigneur the Dauphin at the foot of the stairway. She suddenly blushes red and kisses him on the side of the forehead." A more typical incident occurred when Louis was about four, and the queen abruptly ended one of his visits to the Louvre:

He goes to the queen who asks him if he wouldn't prefer to return to Saint-Germain than to remain near her. He answers "yes," coldly, says goodbye to her, and at 1:00 is put on the litter and leaves.

On another occasion, finding himself in the chambers of the queen, and "hoping to dine with her, he waits until 1:00, not wanting to leave at all." Héroard does not tell us if Louis succeeded; probably not, if the general impression conveyed by the *Journal* is correct.[18]

I have the impression that Henri was the effective agent in maintaining the distance between mother and son. When the dauphin saw the queen, she was almost always in the company of her husband. With one or two exceptions, Louis never wrote to the queen, but instead asked the king, in his many letters to him, to greet Marie on his behalf. At one point, Louis asked if she would ever write to him. "The response was that she wrote only to the king." Louis said that if she wrote him with inkstains on the letter, he would still keep it. No such luck: the queen belonged to his father.[19]

People around Louis lent their support to the separation. No one waited for blood to gush from the dauphin's nose when Marie was stricken with diarrhea, and there were no catechisms about loving one's mother. When Louis was about five, his parents almost drowned as their carriage capsized in crossing the Seine. The next day, Madame de Montglat told Héroard that she had noticed Louis did not cry upon hearing of the danger to his father.[20] Nothing was said of the tears he might have shed for his mother. When it came to the queen, people did not want Louis to be too sentimental. The moral was clearly drawn for him. The dauphin was physically separated from his mother, discouraged from developing any kind of deep affective ties with her, reminded constantly that she belonged to papa: thus did absolutism attempt to sabotage the Oedipus complex.

Perhaps this is a special case; it would be foolish, for example, to call Marie de Medicis an "ordinary" mother. Still, I believe that this configuration of family life has a general relevance. In a number of individual cases, writers of the seventeenth century were very much attached to their mothers. Invariably, they came from families in which the father had died when the children were relatively young, thus leaving the wife to take over the household as well as the affections of her children. On the other hand, writers who speak with particular warmth of their fathers often at the same time ignore mothers who were just as long-lived. Wherever the father was alive and well, children's efforts to be close to their mothers seem to have been systematically blocked.[21]

The nurse also played a part in this configuration. We have seen that the hiring of a nurse had a lot to do with the husband's sexual prerogatives. Erotic freedom in the court was for the child a matter which revolved around domestics like the nurse, or semi-respectable people like the king's mistresses and jesters. It was seldom expressed within the nuclear family itself. A separate household for the child provided an arena in which Oedipal tensions could be dissipated without threatening the father's rights to the mother. The nurse was in constant and intimate attendance to the child, caring for him, sharing meals, play, conversation, and often her bed with him. In some sense, she replaced the mother in his affections. Thus we find Louis bragging that "he was not a simpleton: he slept with Doundoun [the nurse] when [her husband] was away."[22] Such dreams of glory were permissible with respect to household servants, but only in this area was the sexual anarchy of court life left unqualified. Because he imagined that his own domestic prerogatives were threatened, the king firmly thwarted Louis' efforts to explore the possibilities of a greater intimacy with his mother.

Debate with Ariès might be carried a step further. The game of sexual license portrayed in Héroard's *Journal* can be dismissed by historians unfriendly to psychoanalysis. However, these scholars are then under some obligation to explain why the dauphin was later such an unhappy, and ineffective, husband. Louis was humiliated by his wife, suffered long periods of impotence, and eventually, after many years of marriage, fathered a child almost by accident. He was a lonely, isolated person, whose life was brightened only by an occasional infatuation with virtuous would-be nuns, or court favorites like Cinq Mars. I am sure that careful analysis would enable us to follow the process whereby the child who was treated like a little pet by adults of the court grew up into the king known to contemporaries as Louis the Chaste.

Even without such an analysis, we have enough evidence to counter Ariès. I have attempted to demonstrate that the erotic freedom of the court did not in itself solve any of the dauphin's problems. This kind of freedom, no matter how unqualified, cannot make the child into a man. The dilemma for infants is in part that their wishes and ambitions always leap out ahead of physical and intellectual growth. Take the matter of infantile curiosity. No matter how much exploring Louis was allowed to do, he could not solve the mysteries of physical love, of conception, and of birth. The dauphin was baffled by these events and tended to make up for his lack of understanding with a wealth of confusing fantasy.

Posing the question on a social level, I have also argued that adults of the court were by no means united in advocating complete licentiousness. The example of Héroard indicates that attitudes toward sex were more complex than historical myths about an old regime state of nature would tend to suggest. Finally, I think it has been established that parents themselves very specifically distinguished between good and bad kinds of infantile sexuality. One of the luxuries of upper-class life may have been that the infant was permitted certain liberties with household domestics, but in no source, and especially not in the *Journal*, do we see children relating warmly or provocatively to their mothers so long as an able-bodied father was there to control the quality of relationships within the family.

Evidently "sex varies according to period and mentality," and in the old regime, because the vocabulary of our conventional domestic repressions, based on privacy and sexual reticence, was relatively lacking, the whole debate over issues of morality took place in a climate significantly more outspoken than anything we know today. But even in the most erotic sector of this culture, in the royal court, sex had its limits. Flexible about certain matters (autoerotic activity, sex play among children or between children and some adults), parents were as rigid as any Victorian about issues they regarded as important, such as the quality of the relationship between mother and child. Much of the licentiousness in the handling of the dauphin was in fact part of the exploitation of the infant, who, like an endearing little pet, was made to amuse its owners. As if to condemn this "game," Louis began, as soon as he was able, to draw back, to dissociate himself from sexual activity, and to settle into a suspicious aloofness. On the other hand, where the child showed a real desire for closeness—in relations with his parents, and especially with his mother—he was coldly and summarily rebuffed. Far from documenting the infant's freedom, Héroard's discussion of the sexual aspects of seventeenth-century childrearing adds another dimension to our understanding of the subjugation of the very young.

III

In conclusion, I wish to bring together the themes we have been considering, to show how parental management of Oedipal issues tells us something generally about this stage of infantile growth, and how the stage as a whole illustrates certain characteristics of seventeenth-century childhood.

In all of childrearing, there is a special paradox: parents must nurture and train the infants who will some day grow up and replace them, rendering them obsolete. The truth underlying psychoanalytic discussion of the Oedipus complex is that two generations cannot occupy the same space at the same time. As one advances, the other must get out of the way, give up its prerogatives, prepare for senescence and eventually for death.

This grim reality is brought home to grownups with especial force during the third stage of infantile development. For the first time, the child has an inkling of what it means to be an adult, an understanding he demonstrates in increasingly accurate imitations of his elders. This playing with the styles and roles of maturity is a foreshadowing, almost in the form of a rehearsal.

The infant begins to anticipate what adulthood is like, and to be impatient for the day when he will be grown up himself, capable of taking over a world now monopolized by his parents. The phase is naturally going to arouse the anxieties of mothers and fathers. In the child's play, his experiments and questions, they catch a glimpse of a time when their helpless offspring will be self-sufficient and strong and they, with the task of childrearing successfully completed, will no longer have a position of power in the family.

This paradox was made all the more difficult to manage by the particular circumstances of family life in the old regime. As we have seen, seventeenth-century culture knew no way of rewarding the "good family man." This status did not hold out any particular promise of honor or praise. On the contrary, the literature on domesticity dwelt on the dangers and possible humiliations of the household. Men in families felt threatened, their self-respect compromised by the fact of being husbands and fathers.

The problem of intimacy made family life even more unenviable. Husbands of the period did not know how to trust or be comfortable with their wives. The brittle authoritarianism of the household and the general denigration of domestic pleasures only partially succeeded in concealing the uneasiness of the paterfamilias. Rituals of feminine submission were thought to mask the forces of incipient revolt, and even well-behaved wives were suspected of insubordination or, what was worse, of sexual delinquency. Surrounded by the props of a male chauvinist culture, men still wondered if their wives were tricking or defying or humiliating them in some secret way.

I think that this fear of intimacy was responsible for the particularly overwrought quality of sexuality in the period we have been discussing. Whether in the indulgences of court libertines or in the self-denial of zealous moralists, erotic issues were resolved not in a spirit of confident mastery, but with a certain desperation. Earlier, we saw that economic pressures kept down the number of marriages. In addition, I believe that the apprehension aroused by the prospect of domestic intimacy also prompted men to steer clear of marriage and to seek out the honorable alternative of a celibate life. In any case, within the household, the fragility of conjugal relations was intensified by the confusion and anxiety found at the intimate center of the marriage bond, in the sexual transactions of the husband and wife.

The coming of children cruelly taxed the resources of this none-too-solid conjugal arrangement. The father found that his already precarious position was being rudely challenged. A heavy burden of domesticity was made all the more disagreeable by increases in the size of the family he was to oversee. The dubious loyalty of his wife was now further undermined insofar as she had simultaneously to serve him and his children. This consideration helps to explain men's reluctance to face the responsibilities of child care, the decision to send new-born infants away with a nurse, the tendency to fight against the child's developing selfhood.

The most difficult moment for fathers came when children entered the third stage of development. The often grandiose and phallic initiatives of the young caught men in the area of their greatest sensitivity. If all infants taxed the limits of family solidarity, those in the Oedipal stage were especially difficult to cope with because their demands focused on the sexual relations which were found at the core of this troubled domesticity, where adults felt the most insecure. In separating his son and wife, Henri IV was exercising a power which, I would speculate, all husbands and fathers of the period must have envied. The king was protecting a precarious relationship with his spouse, guarding conjugal rights which he thought would not survive the ingenuous and yet insistent challenge of his first-born.

On the other hand, all parents realize that they cannot afford to ignore children completely. Mixed in with their fear of the young is an awareness of the need to provide infants with a minimal level of care. Even when pervasively undermined by cultural conditions, the generative impulse will not be totally eradicated. For example, with respect to the third stage, the infant's initiatives contain an urgent request. In wanting to compete with and perhaps to surpass his parents, the child also very much needs their guidance in order to make the kind of identifications which are the key to growing up. Here parents have an opportunity to tell the child who they are, to define themselves, to interpret for him the world of adulthood. To ignore this infantile request would be to confess that one had no values, no achievements, no belief in the world to which children aspire. Antagonized by the child's rivalry, parents also sense that they have in this aspirant a pupil of rare attentiveness. For adults with any kind of pedagogical impulse, with any pride in the world they have made for themselves, this opportunity will be hard to pass over, even if it does bring them face to face with the possibility of their own deposition.

Seventeenth-century parents were no exceptions to this rule. They wanted to teach their children, and to serve as exemplars for them. At the same time, these adults were very strict about the conditions under which relations with children in the third stage of growth would be undertaken. We have already seen how the difficulties of conjugal life were subsumed under the façade of a rigid authoritarianism. The same process occurred between parents and children, as the infant's initiative was channeled ruthlessly into obedience and service. If children wanted to be around their parents, to have a chance to learn from their example, they had first to show themselves properly humble and submissive.

For example, in the case of the dauphin, the beating of October, 1604, should be considered the turning point between the second and third Eriksonian stages. Sensing that the child's advancing physical and cognitive skills would soon enable him to confront them more purposefully, adults wanted to make clear from the start what the ground rules for this new stage would be. The beating forcefully illustrated the penalties for disobedience and insubordination and thus served as a kind of initiation into the Oedipal stage. Louis was forewarned. If he wanted to be around his parents, and especially his father, he had to play the docile valet, to stifle the urge to imitate too impertinently, to question too searchingly, to express his own impatience and resentments.

For about two years after the beating, Henri had almost nothing to do with his son. Their infrequent relations were completely dominated by the stereotyped rituals of master and servant. After the child had been properly quarantined, Louis was permitted a somewhat more extensive relationship with his father. When he was about five or six, the king apparently decided that the point had been made and began to instruct his son, to serve somewhat more self-consciously as exemplar for the young prince. I describe the details of this apprenticeship in the next chapter. For the time being, my point is that during a period of about two years the strains of this stage of infantile growth seem to have brought interaction between parents and child almost to a standstill. Luckily for the dauphin, his elders could afford to pay others to assume a duty they were themselves unable to perform. We may wonder at the dilemma of children more closely involved with parents in the midst of this fateful crisis in their lives. Parental duties which the king was able to discharge only imperfectly were, I would imagine, performed with even less distinction in other households.

The lessons of the third stage of infantile growth might well serve for the process of childrearing as a whole. Like a magnifying glass, parenthood picks up all the confusions and irrationalities of the adult world and brings them destructively into focus on the minds and bodies of young children.

<small>๛</small> 9 <small>๛</small>

OUT OF THE HANDS OF WOMEN

I

Sources in the early modern period often single out the age of seven as a special turning point in the child's life.[1] No one official ceremony confirmed this step, but the observer senses nonetheless that some kind of "graduation" was taking place. In the child's sixth, seventh, and eighth years, his status was qualitatively changing. He found himself with a new set of responsibilities and in a different relationship to the adult world. Our discussion of the stages of childhood ought to conclude with an analysis of this graduation: What were some of the dimensions of this transformation, which brought to a close the first age of life?

Héroard's *Journal* suggests some of the ways in which children were growing up at this time. Take the question of clothes. After his swaddling band was discarded, the dauphin dressed in the frock boys wore during infancy. Just before Louis' fifth birthday, Héroard took off his "children's bonnet" and told him: "Monsieur, now that your bonnet has been removed, you are no longer a child; you begin to become a man. You mustn't be childish any more." The doctor was a bit premature, and after a few days Marie de Medicis ordered the bonnet back on. Six months later, however, the dauphin had his first long socks and, around his sixth birthday, his first high-collared robe. Soon after reaching the age of seven, Louis "is dressed in a doublet and breeches, leaves childhood clothes, takes the cloak and sword."[2]

Historians have often underlined the importance of clothes as indications of a person's status in the old regime.[3] With a change of clothes came a change in quality as well. We should not overestimate the significance of the dauphin's grownup outfits: the "cloak and sword" did not stay on permanently, and Louis was still many years short of full manhood. Still, the new wardrobe suggests that adult expectations and the child's picture of himself were going through a substantial evolution at this time.

Louis indirectly demonstrated his understanding of this approaching change in status through a series of experiments he performed with girls' clothes: "He has himself dressed as a picardian chambermaid, puts on a mask, calls himself Louise, follows Mademoiselle de Vendôme, who says that he is her chambermaid. He avoids talking in order not to be recognized." For dances, he frequently dressed as a shepherdess or a peasant girl. Before this time, adults had not been indifferent to "effeminate" behavior. When Louis was about four, Héroard wrote: "He was born for the functions of war, completely virile, and I have never detected in him, however small he was, any feeble or feminine action." Adults also tried to discourage him from taking part in girls' games and dances. However, no one seems to have objected to the six-year-old dauphin's fascination with feminine clothes.[4]

I suspect that adults were forbearing here because they realized that the child was coping in his own way with fears of growing up. Bruno Bettelheim has argued that boys who are about to assume adult masculine roles and duties experience an accentuated need to deal with their own femininity, their envy of women, and that such sentiments may lead to ritualistic imitations of the opposite sex:

It is possible to see in these customs a ritualized last effort to enjoy a social and possibly also a sexual role other than the one prescribed by society and imposed by biology. Now, on the threshold of adulthood, boys and girls are given a last chance to play both sexual roles. . . . Afterward, each person must settle down permanently to the single behavior assigned to his sex.[5]

If this hypothesis applies to the present case, the various costume changes indicate that Louis grasped the significance of the step lying just head of him, one which would bring him into the world of men.

Growing up also meant that the dauphin's education was increasingly emphasized. Two concepts are involved here: *éduca-tion* (moral training), and *instruction* (reading and writing—what we mean by "education"). Almost as soon as Louis could talk, Madame de Montglat began to teach him moral lessons in the form of maxims and proverbs, which the dauphin memorized and repeated. The technique was often employed in the old regime. It led easily into church catechisms and eventually into the more complicated Catholic observances. Louis went to confession for the first time at the age of five.[6]

As for education proper, Héroard and others often helped Louis to compose letters by guiding his hand, but apparently more for their own amusement than for the purpose of teaching him how to write. From about the age of five, Louis was oc-casionally given formal reading lessons, but these irregularly scheduled sessions do not seem to have had any tangible results. Shortly after his seventh birthday, a tutor appeared to teach the dauphin Latin. However, it is interesting to note that even here education was not taken too seriously. The tutor applied himself sporadically, and when Louis complained about the lessons, he was assured that they would last only three or four years.[7]

This relative indifference to schooling fits the child's life plan. The dauphin was not to be a scholar but a king, and his real teacher was therefore Henri IV himself. Henri's attitude toward his son had always been closely related to the infant's stage of development. To recapitulate, at first the king was delighted with Louis, playing with him, soothing him when he became angry, evidently enjoying his company. Then, as the dauphin grew up, began to move around freely and to assert his will, relations be-tween the two became more tense. There was much fighting, defiance, and bad feeling, coming to a head in the incident of October, 1604. Afterward, father and son drew apart and for about two years had very little to do with each other.

When the dauphin was about five, Henri began to get interested again in his chastened and increasingly dutiful son. The king undertook to instruct Louis in the virtues of audacity and cour-age: he forced the dauphin to flick out a candle with his fingers, saying "the one who wants to be papa's favorite has to snuff out the flame"; to fight with his older half-brothers; to jump a moat which was too wide for him. Henri told his son that he must not be afraid of anything and watched to make sure that Louis did not show any apprehension when, for example, there was a sudden clap of thunder. The dauphin also went to the hunt for the first time (in a carriage) and started to take riding lessons. Finally, he began to attend sessions of the King's Council. In all these incidents, we see adults attempting to cultivate in Louis the skills and attitudes he would need in adult life.[8]

All of the signs of growing up were epitomized by the graduation "out of the hands of women" and into "the hands of men." The possibility of such a change was first mentioned when the dauphin was six. It was often discussed in the months ahead, but did not actually take place until January, 1609, when Louis was seven years old. Madame de Montglat relinquished control over the household, which was now to be under the tutelage of Monsieur de Souvré, the court noble chosen as the child's "governor." In many ways, the dauphin's life went on unchanged under the new regime. Souvré instructed him as Madame de Montglat had done on points of etiquette (e.g., not belching) and the whippings continued. Still, a significant step had been taken. Given the low estimation of women, to affirm that the child had passed "into the hands of men" was another way of saying that he was now worthy of the serious attention of the adults who really counted in society.[9]

I think the significance of this "graduation" can be pinned down more precisely. In the first place, we should make clear what had not happened. In spite of the emphasis put on the precocity of seventeenth-century children by historians like Ariès, we can affirm that the seven-year-old was far short of being considered an adult. Physical maturation still lay several years in the future.[10] The dauphin had a governor and was under an exacting system of discipline, even after having left the hands of women. When he became king, at the age of nine, and indeed throughout his teens, Louis continued to be regarded as something less than a fully self-reliant adult.

However, the child had made some gains. First, he seemed intellectually more competent. Assessments of the infant's cognitive capacities tended to be markedly disparaging. One author noted that in the first age of life (that is, until the age of seven) the infant "cannot talk well or form its words perfectly, for its teeth are not yet well arranged or firmly implanted." But as this first age came to an end, adults then (as they do now) noted a qualitative difference in the child's mental functioning: he was developing a capacity for abstract and logical thought, and was therefore teachable. Those children who were going to school would begin around this time, as children do today.[11]

Second, the child was physically more mature. Erikson speaks of an age of industry:

[The child] has mastered the ambulatory field and the organ modes. He has experienced a sense of finality regarding the fact that there is no workable future within the womb of his family, and thus becomes ready to apply himself to given skills and tasks, which go beyond the mere playful expression of his organ modes or the pleasure in the function of his limbs. He develops a sense of industry.[12]

In the seventeenth century, this age must have been awaited with an especially keen sense of anticipation. Because problems of sustenance were so universal, the burden of providing for the care of dependent children was particularly taxing. When the child was old enough to help earn his keep, one can be assured that he was quickly pressed into service as an apprentice, through employment in another household, or beside his own parents. Passing into "the hands of men" for these children simply meant going to work. Here is another qualitative change: the child ceased to be exclusively a consumer and began to help produce the goods which kept the society alive. The dauphin was not under this kind of pressure because his family was rich, but at this time even Louis was introduced to some of the professional skills which he would need as an adult.

Finally, parents saw their children evolve in a way even more fundamental than the intellectual and physical changes we have been discussing. When Henri de Campion's daughter died at the age of four, he was stricken with grief:

Despite her age, she was so diverting that those who saw her took great pleasure from her. . . . I would not speak of these things, which many will find unworthy of being written, if her loss did not make me seek out this consolation.

We may wonder why Campion anticipates objections to this display of emotion. Survivors were always expected to show "constancy" after the loss of someone close, but apparently people found excessive outpourings of feeling over the death of small children particularly undignified: "If it is said that such keen attachments can be excused for fully realized human beings (*des personnes faites*), but not for children, I respond that my daughter undoubtedly had more good qualities than any other child of her age." Campion did not defend infancy; he simply maintained that his daughter was exceptional. Usually, such deaths did not have quite the impact of adult mortality. In the *livres de raison*, the demise of children was often mentioned with sorrow, but in the books I have consulted, the departed infant was always described in impersonal terms. Campion was almost alone in seeing the child as a distinctive personality with special traits and potentials, a *"personne faite,"* in other words, as a fully individualized human being.[13]

Campion's precocious four-year-old daughter was a person in his eyes, but most infants seemed to be something less than that. Montaigne wrote bluntly that they had "neither movement in the soul, nor recognizable form in the body, by which they could render themselves lovable." Charron went so far as to claim that "the faculties of the soul are opened" only after the child had reached the age of four or five. Bérulle summed up the opinions of a century when he characterized childhood as "the meanest and most abject state of the human condition."[14]

I hope that earlier discussion has made clear how hard pressed adults were by the various challenges of bringing up small children. Feeding and caring for them, as well as dealing with their aggressive and sexual impulses, severely taxed parental patience, understanding, and physical ability. Cause and effect are of course difficult to separate, but I think that much of the repudiation of children, the refusal to see them as completely human, was prompted by the nagging awareness that they, the parents, were not able to fathom the secrets of this stage of life and were conspicuously unsuccessful in keeping children alive and well. The various ways in which adults categorized children as little animals amounted to an unconscious confession of failure. Finally, out of frustration, adults located the fault in infancy itself, dismissing it as a kind of disease: "Only time can cure a person of childhood and youth, which are truly ages of imperfection in every respect."[15] It must have been with relief that they saw some of their offspring grow up. The "graduation" we have been discussing might be interpreted in this sense. Adults began to feel at home with the six- or seven-year-old child who was physically more robust and self-sufficient, and intellectually more approachable. In other words, he was "cured" of the malady of infancy which had made him so incomprehensible and frightening to his elders.

PART FOUR

Conclusion

ᨄ 10 ᨄ

SOME REFLECTIONS ON
CHILDHOOD AND HISTORY

I

This study has been organized around the interplay between certain psychological and historical theories. In the present chapters, I assess some of the results of the endeavor. In the first place, we are now in a position to measure the strengths and weaknesses of Philippe Ariès' work on the history of childhood. It will be remembered that Ariès believes children in the premodern period were treated with an indifference which gave way, somewhere between the ages of four and seven, to a relatively complete integration into adult life. In some respects, this notion seems to be confirmed. If "indifference" signifies a reluctance or an inability to analyze infantile needs and a comparatively insensitive treatment of the very young, then seventeenth-century parents were indifferent. Furthermore, the process of growing up did allow these parents to accept more comfortably the presence of their offspring, who were to be regarded from then on as functioning members of the community rather than as exasperating parasites.

However, the child had made some gains. First, he seemed At times he seems to be favorably disposed to the old style of parenthood (qualified as "gay indifference") and unimpressed with the concern for children which has gradually replaced it. In the light of this reasoning, we are to imagine that because adults did not make an issue of infantile vulnerability, children were free to grow up as they pleased. Taking our cue from the psychoanalytic interpretation of the first years of life, as it has been spelled out by Erik Erikson, we have followed the actual course of childrearing in seventeenth-century France. Far from viewing the unfolding of infantile potentials with benign indifference, grownups in that period were deeply disturbed by some aspects of the orality, the obstinacy, and the sexuality of their offspring and made determined efforts to mold or to thwart altogether such inclinations. In spite of the fact that babies were strange, that infancy itself tended to be regarded as a kind of infirmity, adults could not and did not want to abandon children to their own deserts. Rather than leaving them in peace (the implication of "indifference"), they became very involved, as do all parents, in the task of childrearing. It is not true that they had no "awareness of the particular nature of childhood." This awareness may not have been especially enlightened, but adults of the seventeenth century clearly did bring to parenthood a ground plan, a set of beliefs about what infants were like and how they should be encouraged to develop in appropriate directions.

On the other hand, Ariès' most significant achievement was to locate childrearing practices within a social context. While disagreeing with many of the particulars of his interpretation, I have attempted to maintain the same kind of connection between family matters and old regime society. Thus, the institution of marriage has to be understood in terms of the social and economic relations among families; the governess and the nurse were employed according to administrative and status habits which were manifested in a variety of situations outside the household; the feeding of infants was linked to problems of sustenance, discipline to patterns of authority, and the regulation of infantile sexuality to the moral codes of the adult world. These arguments help to substantiate the hypothesis that methods of childrearing are part and parcel of the culture in which they are formulated and cannot be treated in isolation. Given its socio-economic and ideological setting, treatment of children in the seventeenth century could not have been reformed without a change in the society as a whole. Aspects of childrearing in that period are distinctive. We recognize them as the characteristic products of particular social and political conditions. In this respect, the basic assumption of Ariès' work—that childhood has a historical meaning—has been amply confirmed.

In the course of my work, I have taken as a point of reference Erik Erikson's theory of psycho-social development. The method points the way to a better understanding of matters which historians have tended to ignore, and which even Ariès treats in a superficial way. At the same time, historical research enables us to appreciate more clearly the advantages and limitations of Eriksonian theory itself.

First, it will be remembered that I took as a working hypothesis Erikson's suggestion that adults will respond to each stage of infancy in a distinctive way, that parental conduct varies according to the nature of the demands made by the child as he grows up. This approach, which stresses the unique qualities, the individuality, of each phase of childhood development, has led to results I did not anticipate at the outset of the project. In general, scholars arguing over the cultural importance of child-rearing seem to share one common assumption: that childhood should be treated as a unit. Those who believe that customs for raising infants are related to social and historical trends take for granted that the method can be applied with equal success to all stages of infantile growth, while opponents are skeptical in an equally total way. My own loyalties obviously lie with the first group rather than with the second. At the same time, in the course of my work, I have been forced to consider the possibility that cultural realities bear directly upon the child at certain specific points in his development, but affect him only tangentially during the remaining phases of growth. Childhood and society are always related, but the connections are much more obvious in some psycho-social stages than in others.

In particular, I have the impression that the second Eriksonian stage has been the most pertinent to the study of childhood in the old regime. We learn from an analysis of all phases of maturation, but at the same time Erikson's argument seems most convincing when he is attempting to demonstrate the interrelationship of the anal zone, the infantile mode of retention-elimination, the human potential for autonomy and selfhood, the social configuration of "law and order," and finally the parents' experience "in marriage, in work, and in citizenship." As I see it, the analysis of these factors brings us as close as we ever get to the essence of childrearing in seventeenth-century France.

There are several possible explanations for the particular salience of this aspect of Erikson's theory. For example, one might argue that because of its distinctive characteristics, seventeenth-century society chose to define with a special clarity issues associated with the second stage of childhood. It is also possible that *all* societies tend to stress these issues and that the emphasis found in the present study is related to a universal fact of childrearing. However, without ruling out these hypotheses, I wish to call attention to a third interpretation: that the prominence of socio-historical factors in the second stage is inadvertently built into Eriksonian theory itself.

Erikson believes that enlightened treatment of children in this phase of growth depends on "a relationship of parent to parent, of parent to employer, and of parent to government, which reaffirms the parent's essential dignity within a hierarchy of social positions." This formulation covers a lot of ground. In effect, it links the second stage of childhood to the quality of domestic life, and to the economic and political experience of the parents. The passage thus contains a whole sociology in miniature and suggests that this aspect of infantile development effectively monopolizes all important sociological and historical categories. Furthermore, of all the childhood potentials, autonomy is the one which most transparently relates to the realities of social existence as they are usually understood. Political theorists have long puzzled over the problems of individual freedom versus collective solidarity. I do not find it implausible that this debate, and the conflict it attempts to resolve, should be associated with the child's situation as he tries to balance his own need for freedom, for an area in which he is sovereign and self-governing, against the necessity of complying with the often constraining demands of his parents. For these reasons, the second Eriksonian stage seems to be especially relevant to the study of society.

Prospects are less clear for the other phases. Whereas parental conduct in the second stage depends on political and social experience, adults dealing with younger, new-born infants do so largely in terms of religious considerations. As I understand it, Erikson is thinking here of religion as a world view which individuals, and societies, accept as their own, a kind of collective *Weltanschauung*. There is no precise institutional concomitant to this element of social order, unless the historian is willing to entertain the notion that organized churches are to be considered primarily as philosophical clearing houses, designed to deal with the metaphysical questions of their parishioners, rather than as functioning organizations with their own power resources, similar to states and economic corporations. Erikson's notion of religion is thus "sociological" only in a Hegelian sense; that is, as an almost metaphysical idea embodied by certain historical actors and institutions, a vague "spirit of the times." Similarly, "trust" is not an easy virtue to conceptualize in terms of social life. How can one measure the degree of trust or hope which a society seems to allow its individual members? Unlike autonomy, this human strength is not related in any obvious way to the familiar categories of collective experience. For these reasons, the historian is not going to find this aspect of the sociology of childrearing very easy to employ.

The third phase of infancy is also hard to relate to social questions. In his general discussion of infantile sexuality, Erikson promises to link each stage to "related elements of social order." He delivers the goods for each of the first two cases (religion, and "law and order"), but, as far as I can tell, discussion of the third never seems to crystallize around a corresponding aspect of group life. This leads to an ironic situation. The Oedipus complex is the pivot of psychoanalytic theory, Freud's greatest discovery, and the insight which has been most enthusiastically borrowed by nonclinicians. But on reflection, I am persuaded that the real logic of psychoanalytic, or at least of Eriksonian, thought should lead sociologists and historians to look primarily to earlier stages of psycho-social growth for the information relevant to their own investigations. Parents communicate with their newborn infants as carriers of a world view, almost as philosophers, who in handling the child instill in him some sense of the setting in which he is going to live, whether it is a good place or a bad one, whether he should hope for the best, or on the contrary

193

adopt a stance of suspicion and mistrust. In the second phase, the parents speak as political animals, acting out of their sense that the community is (or is not) a just and well-ordered arena in which the individual is allowed to guard his integrity and self-respect. In the third phase, the relevant frame of reference is not the world (that is, the general milieu in which life unfolds), and not the community (a particular political, economic, and social order), but is instead the household itself. Parents speak not as philosophers or political theorists, but simply as husbands and wives, fathers and mothers. The message conveyed to the child at this point concerns not so much the cosmos or the body politic as it does the domesticity which his parents have experienced and which must serve as the model for his own future family life.

Erikson's reasoning thus almost compels the historian to make his most extensive sociological interpretations in connection with the second stage of childhood. I believe that infantile autonomy was the major childrearing problem in seventeenth-century society. At the same time, I am not sure that any other conclusion would have been possible, given the dynamics of Eriksonian theory. It may be that Erikson has captured the essence of the problem, that there was something about the nature of child-rearing in old regime France, or perhaps something in all cultures, which accounts for the fact that grownups were then most concerned about the social implications of the second stage of infantile development. On the other hand, it is also possible that Erikson has overlooked or not adequately conceptualized the sociological determinants of other periods of childhood and that his system should be regarded as a provisional step in the progress toward a fuller understanding of the relationship between psychology and society.

This critique of Erikson suggests to me that historians should approach psychological topics with an experimental predisposition. The major questions are still open, and in fact historically oriented research can help to answer them. The problem of "generativity" is a good example. I have argued that we cannot count too much on the innate desire of parents to care for their children, that the upbringing of the very young is not always characterized by that intuitive wisdom which Erikson has taught us to expect. In seventeenth-century France, adults did indeed take up the responsibilities of parenthood. On the other hand, accounts of family life show how poorly prepared they were for the job, how the conditions of daily existence seriously hindered their efforts, and how children suffered from the resulting breakdown in parental care. If these grim details have not invalidated the Eriksonian model, they at least test the limits of a system which puts so much emphasis on the inherently reciprocal and self-sustaining qualities of the childrearing relationship.

Psychoanalysis fails here not solely because of its deficiencies as a tool of historical analysis. When I turned my attention to the seventeenth century, I was shocked by many aspects of childrearing, but mixed with the shock was a sense of recognition. There is nothing historically unique about the mistreatment of infants. Today the case histories of disturbed and retarded children are filled with illustrations of a childrearing frighteningly divorced from the platitudes of our official view of parenthood. Infants are still starved, beaten, and sexually abused in our own day. More important, where the grosser forms of physical mistreatment have been eliminated, an equally frightening psychological cruelty can be found. Such case histories, and no doubt the unwritten histories of many children who never come to the attention of clinicians, indicate that styles of parenthood in our society have been remarkably unaffected by that cultural revolution which, we tell ourselves, has brought about a fundamental transformation in methods of childrearing. We do not need to go back into history to test the plausibility of Eriksonian theory. An equally persuasive critique could, I am sure, be drawn from the details of contemporary family life.

I think that the problem here can be explained by the fact that most psychoanalysts after Freud have shown little interest in relating the particular cases which come before them to a comprehensive theory of society. Clinical literature has given us an unparalleled sense of the private suffering which takes place in our culture. No age before the present has so tirelessly explored the terrain of individual alienation and unhappiness. However, we have only the most rudimentary sense of the social roots of this malaise. Isolated cases, even a great many of them, cannot be entirely understood, and certainly not ameliorated, unless they are considered together as parts of a system. When we deal with the distant and relatively alien society of seventeenth-century France, it is not hard to accept the notion that the plight of children was related to the character of the social and political order in which they lived. We lack the corresponding understanding of parenthood and society today. As I have attempted to demonstrate in the critique of his concept of generativity, even Erikson falls short in this respect. We often do not begin to grasp the magnitude of a problem until someone attempts to solve it. With due respect to his pioneering work, I prefer to stress the incompleteness of the project he has inaugurated. If these reflections seem to raise questions rather than to resolve them, if they sound more like an introduction than a conclusion, it is because I believe the next assignment is to build the politics of psychological thinking in the present.

NOTES

INTRODUCTION

1. Philippe Ariès, *Centuries of Childhood: A Social History of Family Life*, Robert Baldick, trans. (New York, 1965), © 1965 by Alfred A. Knopf, Inc.; see also the original *L'enfant et la vie familiale sous l'ancien régime* (Paris, 1960). Erik Erikson, *Young Man Luther: A Study in Psychoanalysis and History* (New York, 1962). Erikson's latest contribution in the same vein is *Gandhi's Truth: on the Origins of Militant Nonviolence* (New York, 1969).

2. Information on the Richelieu family is found in the papers of Michel Le Masle, one of the Cardinal's secretaries. Included are letters from an early period of Richelieu's life and also the correspondences of other members of the family. These papers are in the Bibliotheque Nationale (fonds français 23199–23201).

3. Jean Héroard, *Journal de Jean Héroard sur l'enfance et la jeunesse de Louis XIII (1601–1628)*, Eud. Soulié and Ed. de Barthélemy, eds., 2 vols. (Paris, 1868). Unless I indicate otherwise, all quotes from the *Journal* are drawn from the first volume. Bibliographical details on Héroard are found in the preface of the above edition.

4. Roger Mercier, *L'enfant dans la société du XVIIIe siècle (avant L'EMILE)* (Dakar, 1961).

CHAPTER I

THE PSYCHOLOGICAL BACKGROUND:
ERIK ERIKSON'S THEORY
OF PSYCHO-SOCIAL DEVELOPMENT

1. In the following discussion, I draw heavily on the very clear and concise summary of ego psychology, and of Erikson's position within it, by David Rapaport, "A Historical Survey of Psychoanalytic Ego Psychology," which serves as an introduction to Erikson's *Identity and the Life Cycle: Selected Papers*, Psychological Issues, No. 1 (New York, 1959), 5–17.

2. Rapaport, "Ego Psychology," 8.

3. Sigmund Freud, *Civilization and Its Discontents*, James Strachey, trans. (New York, 1962), 24.

4. Erikson, *Identity*, 150–151.

5. Heinz Hartmann, *Ego Psychology and the Problem of Adaptation*, David Rapaport, trans. (New York, 1964), especially Chapters 2–4.

6. Erik Erikson, *Insight and Responsibility: Lectures on the Ethical Implications of Psychoanalytic Insight* (New York, 1964), 111–157 (Chapter IV: "Human Strength and the Cycle of Generations").

7. For a discussion of this shift in emphasis, see Erikson, *Identity*, 114–116. The stages of life are delineated in *Childhood and Society* (New York, 1963), 247–274 (Chapter VII: "Eight Ages of Man") © 1963 by W. W. Norton; see especially the helpful footnote, 273–274. Also, *Identity*, 50–100 (Chapter II: "The Healthy Personality"), a helpfully reworded version of the chapter in *Childhood and Society*.

8. Erikson, *Childhood*, 67.

9. *Ibid.*, 48–108 (Chapter II: "The Theory of Infantile Sexuality"); again, the material is recapitulated with slight changes in Chapter II of *Identity*.

10. Erikson, *Childhood*, 114–165 (Chapter III: "Hunters Across the Prairie"); quotes taken from page 137.

11. *Ibid.*, 72; Erikson, *Identity*, 58.

12. Erikson, *Childhood*, 250.

13. To keep all these schedules straight, consult the "worksheet" in Erikson, *Identity*, 166; also the chart in Erikson, *Insight*, 186. Jean Piaget's timetable of cognitive development might be integrated into the Eriksonian scheme. See *Insight*, 115.

14. For a superb review of the anthropological literature on childrearing, see Milton Singer, "A Survey of Culture and Personality Theory and Research," in *Studying Personality Cross-Culturally*, Bert Kaplan, ed. (Evanston, 1961), 9–90. For examples of such work, *Childhood in Contemporary Cultures*, Margaret Mead and Martha Wolfenstein, eds. (Chicago, 1966); *Personalities and Cultures: Readings in Psychological Anthropology*, Robert Hunt, ed., American Museum Sourcebooks in Anthropology (New York, 1967).

15. For analysis along these lines, Alfred Lindesmith and Anselm Strauss, "A Critique of Culture-Personality Writings," *American Sociological Review*, XV (1950), 587–600; Harold Orlansky, "Infant Care and Personality," *Psychological Bulletin*, XLVI (1949), 1–48.

16. Exception should be made for psychoanalytically oriented family therapy, where schizophrenic disorders are seen as the consequence of mutually reinforcing patterns of interaction involving all members of the family. For an example, see Theodore Lidz et al., "Schizophrenic Patients and Their Siblings," in *Perspectives in Psychopathology: Readings in Abnormal Psychology*, James Palmer and Michael Goldstein, eds. (New York, 1966), 21–41.

17. For discussion of the nature of parental responses during the first three stages of life, see Erikson, *Insight*, 114–122.

18. Erikson, *Childhood*, 94–97.

19. Erikson, *Insight*, 116.

20. Erikson's strongest statement of this position is in *Insight*, 130–132.

21. Erikson, *Childhood*, 73.

22. The controversy between Freud and his successors is analyzed by Herbert Marcuse, in *Eros and Civilization: A Philosophical Inquiry into Freud* (New York, 1955), 217–251 (Epilogue: "Critique of Neo-Freudian Revisionism"). Also published, under the title "The Social Implications of Freudian 'Revisionism,'" in *Dissent*, II (1955), 221–240. See debate between Marcuse and Erich Fromm in the same volume of *Dissent*, 342–349, and in the following number, III (1956), 79–83.

CHAPTER 2

THE HISTORICAL BACKGROUND:

PHILIPPE ARIÈS AND THE EVOLUTION

OF THE FAMILY

1. Pierre Gaxotte, *Le siècle de Louis XV* (Paris, 1933), 445.

2. Franz Funck-Brentano, *L'ancien régime* (Paris, 1926), 113. See also Charles de Ribbe, *Les familles et la société en France avant la révolution*, 2 vols. (Tours, 1879).

3. Joachim du Plessis de Grenadan, *Histoire de l'autorité paternelle et de la société familiale en France avant 1789* (Paris, 1900), 376, 380. See also Léon Moreel, "La notion de famille dans le droit de l'ancien régime," *Renouveau des idées sur la famille*, Robert Prigent, ed., Institut national d'études démographiques. Travaux et documents, No. 18 (Paris, 1954), 24–25.

4. Hippolyte Taine, "L'ancien régime," in *Les origines de la France contemporaine* (Paris, 1896), I, 163–179.

5. Gaxotte, *Louis XV*, 446; for a rehabilitation of the eighteenth-century family, Edmond Pilon, *La vie de famille au dix-huitième siècle* (Paris, 1923).

6. For these points see Marc Bloch, *Feudal Society*, L. A. Manyon, trans. (Chicago, 1965), I, 125–130, 133; Funck-Brentano, *L'ancien régime*, 67ff; Roland Mousnier, *Etat et société sous François Ier et pendant le gouvernement personnel de Louis XIV*, vol. II, *Les Cours de Sorbonne. Histoire moderne et contemporaine* (Paris, 1966), 166–168; Peter Laslett, *The World We Have Lost* (New York, 1965), 2–3; Lawrence Stone, *The Crisis of the Aristocracy, 1558–1641* (Oxford, 1965), 591.

7. William Goode, *The Family*, Foundations of Modern Sociology Series, Alex Inkeles, ed. (Englewood Cliffs, 1964), 107.

8. Marcuse, *Eros*, 81–89. For an analysis conducted in the same spirit, Barrington Moore, "Thoughts on the Future of the Family," *Political Power and Social Theory: Seven Studies* (New York, 1965), 160–178, and especially 165–166.

9. Such obvious statements are perhaps unnecessary. And yet there is a tendency among American social scientists to throw all "extremists" into the same basket. Thus Leon Bramson quotes the same passages I have cited from *Eros and Civilization* and then claims that Marcuse's analysis of the

displacement of the father "is clearly a plea for an authoritarian family." *The Political Context of Sociology* (Princeton, 1961), 136.

10. Ariès, *Centuries*, 396, 414–415.

11. *Ibid.*, 72–73, 341, 398, 405–406.

12. *Ibid.*, 86, 315–328.

13. *Ibid.*, 43, 86, 385.

14. *Ibid.*, 368.

15. *Ibid.*, 9, 128; see also page 368. For a helpful amplification on the questions Ariès has raised in connection with children, see Georges Snyders, *La pédagogie en France aux XVIIe et XVIIIe siècles* (Paris, 1965).

16. Ariès, *Centuries*, 34ff, 128–219.

17. *Ibid.*, 42, 47, 50, 92.

18. *Ibid.*, 114–119, 129–131.

19. *Ibid.*, 154, 251–252.

20. *Ibid.*, 171, 254–261, 318. Contemporary American schools have been criticized in the same spirit. See Edgar Friedenberg, *Coming of Age in America: Growth and Acquiescence* (New York, 1965), 41.

21. Ariès, *Centuries*, 355–356. For a more detailed treatment of this issue, see Georges Duby, *La société aux XIe et XIIe siècles dans la région maconnaise* (Paris, 1953), 136–137, 263ff.

22. Ariès, *Centuries*, 353, 364.

23. On elites, *ibid.*, 81, 88, 132, 328–331. On absolutism, *ibid.*, 171, 252. Other historians have joined Ariès in relating absolutism and the family; Mousnier, *Etat et société*, 182; Pierre Petot, "La famille en France sous l'ancien régime," *Sociologie comparée de la famille contemporaine*, Colloques internationaux du centre national de la recherche scientifique (Paris, 1955), 14.

24. Ariès, *Centuries*, 93, 406, 415.

25. *Ibid.*, 10.

26. *Ibid.*, 9.

27. Talcott Parsons, "The American Family: Its Relation to Personality and to the Social Structure," in Parsons, Robert Bales et al., *Family, Socialization and Interaction Process* (New York, 1955), 9–10, 16; for a critique, see Moore, "Thoughts on the Future of the Family."

28. Neil Smelser, *Social Change in the Industrial Revolution: An Application of Theory to the British Cotton Industry* (Chicago, 1959), 2.

29. Ariès, *Centuries*, 128–132.

30. For Ariès' attempted solution to this problem, see *Centuries*, 369–370.

31. *Ibid.*, 99, 261–262, 314.

32. *Ibid.*, 406.

33. Philippe Ariès, *Histoire des populations françaises et de leurs attitudes devant la vie depuis le XVIIIe siècle* (Paris, 1948), 550, 553–554.

34. *Ibid.*, 477, 509, 511; see also Ariès' article, "Attitudes devant la vie et devant la mort du 17e au 19e siècle," *Population*, IV (1949), 463–470. Ironically, the weakest link in Ariès' presentation is the demographic evidence. Recent studies have demolished the myth that families of the old regime had "a child a year." See Chapter 4, note 4.

35. Ariès, *Populations françaises*, 516.

36. I am inclined to this view not only on the basis of the citations already given but also because of a talk I had with M. Ariès during the winter

of 1966–1967. At that time, he enthusiastically recommended to me J. H. Van Den Berg's *Metabletica*, which turned out to be a vastly inferior facsimile of *Centuries of Childhood*, dedicated to the task of upholding traditional methods of childrearing at the expense of their modern counterparts. See the English version, *The Changing Nature of Man: Introduction to a Historical Psychology (Metabletica)*, H. F. Groes, trans. (New York, 1961).

37. Ariès, *Centuries*, 327–328.
38. *Ibid.*, 406.
39. *Ibid.*, 365.
40. *Ibid.*, 71, 238, 329, 411.
41. *Ibid.*, 15–32.
42. I prefer Erikson's early work to the later and more explicitly "historical" biographies on Luther and Gandhi because I believe that the biographical format is a clumsy and limiting methodological device. In my own case, I found that a general study of the seventeenth century offered many more possibilities than the biography of Richelieu which was my original project. However, most historians who are interested in Erikson have followed his biographical approach. See Richard Bushman, "On the Uses of Psychology: Conflict and Conciliation in Benjamin Franklin" and Cushing Strout, "Ego Psychology and the Historian," both in *History and Theory: Studies in the Philosophy of History*, V (1966), 225–240, and VII (1968), 281–297; Bruce Mazlish, "James Mill and the Utilitarians," *Daedalus*, XCVII (1968), 1036–1061.

CHAPTER 3
CHARACTER OF
THE SEVENTEENTH-CENTURY FAMILY

1. On intimacy, see Erikson, *Childhood*, 263–266; *Identity*, 95–97; *Insight*, 127–130.
2. Ernest Burgess and Harvey Locke, *The Family: From Institution to Companionship* (New York, 1953), vii. Moore discusses Burgess and Parsons as representatives of the same point of view in "Thoughts on the Family," 160–161.
3. J. Hajnal, "European Marriage Patterns in Perspective," *Population in History: Essays in Historical Demography*, D. V. Glass, D. E. C. Eversley, eds. (London, 1965), 101–143; Gérard Duplessis, *Les mariages en France*, Cahiers de la fondation des sciences politiques, No. 53 (Paris, 1953), 13. On the way religion encouraged celibacy, see François de Grenaille, *L'Honneste mariage* (Paris, 1640), 20, 33; Pierre Charron, *De la Sagesse*, Collections de moralistes français . . . , vols. 7–9, Amaury Duval, ed. (Paris, 1820), I, 349; also, Ariès, *Centuries*, 356–362.
4. BN, fonds fr., 23201, folios 144, 146. See Introduction, note 2.
5. For example, Gustave Fagnier, *La femme et la société française dans la*

première moitié du XVIIe siècle (Paris, 1929), 68. On marriage contracts in general, *ibid.*, 53–56; Mousnier, *Etat et société*, 160.

6. Robert Arnauld d'Andilly, *Mémoires* (Hamburg, 1734), I, 98–102.

7. Henri de Campion, *Mémoires*, M. C. Moreau, ed. (Paris, 1857), 231.

8. Mousnier, *Etat et société*, 160–164.

9. On the edict of 1556, Mousnier, *Etat et société*, 162–165. For a copy of the edict, Isambert et al., *Recueil général des anciennes lois françaises depuis l'an 420 jusqu'à la révolution de 1789* (Paris, 1821), XIII, 469–471.

10. For an interesting discussion of the edict, and reactions to it, see Estienne Pasquier, *Les Oeuvres d'Estienne Pasquier, contenant . . . ses lettres; ses oeuvres meslées et les lettres de Nicolas Pasquier, fils d'Estienne*, II (Amsterdam, 1723), 49ff. On the minority question, Mousnier, *Etat et société*, 164; Régine Pernoud, "La vie de famille du moyen âge à l'ancien régime," *Renouveau des idées sur la famille*, Robert Prigent, ed. (Paris, 1954), 30.

11. Isambert, *Recueil général*, XIII, 470–471; Pasquier, *Oeuvres*, 51.

12. Pasquier, *Oeuvres*, 54.

13. Fagnier, *La femme*, 84; Mousnier, *Etat et société*, 177, 180.

14. Isambert, *Recueil général*, XIV, 391–392; Mousnier, *Etat et société*, 179.

15. Isambert, *Recueil général*, XVI, 273–274, 520–524; XX, 287–295.

16. *Ibid.*, XVI, 274, 521, 523; XX, 288.

17. *Ibid.*, XX, 297; Pernoud, "La vie de famille," 29.

18. Pierre L'Estoile, *Journal de L'Estoile pour le règne de Henri III (1574–1589)*, Louis-Raymond Lefèvre, ed. (Paris, 1943), 307–308.

19. Jean-Gangnières, Comte de Souvigny, *Mémoires du Comte de Souvigny, lieutenant-général des armées du roi*, le Baron Ludovic de Contenson, ed. (Paris, 1906–1909), II, 72; III, xiii.

20. Fagnier, *La femme*, 71; Snyders, *La pédagogie*, 234.

21. BN, fonds fr. 23200, folios 142, 143, 147.

22. *Ibid.*, 115, 120.

23. Souvigny, *Mémoires*, II, 333; "Journal domestique d'Elie de Roffignac (1588–1589)," and "Journal domestique de Martial de Gay de Nexon, lieutenant-général à Limoges (29 janvier 1591–4 mars 1603)," both edited by Louis Guibert in *Bulletin de la société scientifique, historique et archéologique de la Corrèze*, XV (1893), 349, 607; "Livre-Journal de Pierre de Bessot, 1609–1652," Tamizey de Larroque et al., eds., *Bulletin de la société historique et archéologique du Périgord*, XX (1893), 149–150; Jean Maillefer, *Mémoires de Jean Maillefer, marchand bourgeois de Reims (1611–1684)*, Henri Jadart, ed. (Paris, 1890), 47.

24. "Il y a de bons mariages, mais il n'y en a point de délicieux." La Rochefoucauld, quoted in Fagnier, *La femme*, 136; Grenaille, *L'Honneste mariage*, especially book II (97–192); Maillefer, *Mémoires*, 32 ff., 109; Pasquier, *Oeuvres*, 14.

25. Pasquier, *Oeuvres*, 14; Fénelon, *De l'Education des filles* (Paris, 1821), 3; *Les Caquets de l'accouchée* (Paris, 19th century), 191ff; for a minority view, Montaigne, *Essais*, Pierre Michel, ed. (Paris, 1965), III, v, 127. Also Léon Abensour, *La femme et le féminisme avant la révolution* (Paris, 1923), xi.

26. Pasquier, *Oeuvres*, 14; Charron, *De la Sagesse*, II, 62; Jean Bodin, *Les Six Livres de la République* (Paris, 1576), 8.

27. Fagnier, *La femme*, 162.

28. *Ibid.*, 154; Petot, "La famille," 12–13; Moreel, "La notion de famille," 23; Abensour, *Le féminisme*, iii–iv.

29. On the basis of his research with marriage contracts and other sources relating to family life in Bordeaux during the seventeenth century, Robert Wheaton has called this trend to my attention; see also Moreel, "La notion de famille," 24; Petot, "La famille," 13.

30. De Serres cited in Albert Cherel, *La famille française. Pages de nos bons écrivains de 825 à 1924: Le moyén âge et le XVIe siècle* (Paris, 1924), 178; also, Montaigne, *Essais*, III, ix, 209; Fénelon, *De l'Education*, 7ff., 168–169; Souvigny, *Mémoires*, II, 322, 332; "Livre de raison de la famille Froissard-Broissia de 1532 à 1701," *Mémoires de la société d'émulation du Jura*, 4ème série, II (1886), 85; for other examples, Etienne Bernard, "Un père de famille sous Henri IV. Lettres domestiques d'Etienne Bernard, 1598–1609," Henri Drouot, ed., *Annales de Bourgogne*, XXIV (1952), 166; see also Fagnier's interesting chapter, "La vie professionelle," *La femme*, 93–134.

31. Bossuet cited in E. Bougaud, *Histoire de sainte Chantal et des origines de la Visitation*, I (Paris, 1867), 111; see also Charron, *De la Sagesse*, III, 65–66. "Whatever the strictly male tasks are, they are defined as *more honorific*" in *all* societies. Goode, *The Family*, 70.

32. Michel de Castelnau, *Mémoires*, Le Laboureur, ed. (Paris, 1660), II, 297; for other examples of mothers running the family, Maillefer, *Mémoires*, vi; Jeanne du Laurens, "Généalogie de messieurs du Laurens . . . ," Charles de Ribbe, ed., *Une famille au XVIe siècle* (Tours, 1879), 72–82; André du Val, *La Vie admirable de la bienheureuse soeur Marie de l'Incarnation* (Paris, 1893), 13; Campion, *Mémoires*, 4ff. Treating the problem more generally, Fagnier, *La femme*, 29, 152; Abensour, *Le féminisme*, ix; Lucien Febvre, "Aspects méconnus d'un renouveau religieux en France entre 1590 et 1620," *Les annales: ESC*, XIII (1958), 639–650.

33. Cardinal Richelieu, *The Political Testament of Cardinal Richelieu. The Significant Chapters and Supporting Selections*, Henry Hill, ed. and trans. (Madison, 1961), 116–117.

34. Charron, *De la Sagesse*, I, 347ff.; Grenaille, *L'Honneste mariage*, 14; Pasquier, *Oeuvres*, 1235, 1265; *Les Caquets*, 113–116; Fénelon, *De l'Education*, 7, 148–149.

35. C. A. Er. Wickersheimer, *La médecine et les médecins en France à l'époque de la renaissance* (Paris, 1906), 304–305; Montaigne, *Essais*, II, viii, 16.

36. *Les Caquets*, 119; Montaigne, *Essais*, III, v, 86.

37. The letters are found in BN, fonds fr. 23200, folios 86–105; the king's order to Henri (7 avril 1618) and the latter's response (26 avril) in *ibid.*, 308–309; see also Adrien Marcel, "L'exil de Richelieu à Avignon," *Mémoires de l'académie de Vaucluse*, 2ème série, XXVII (1927), 102.

38. BN, fonds fr. 23200, folios, 87, 100, 102; for details on the marriage of Henri, Bonneau-Avenant, *La Duchesse d'Aiguillon, niece du Cardinal de Richelieu, sa vie et ses oeuvres charitables* (Paris, 1882), 30.

39. The love letters found in BN, fonds fr. 23199, folio 11; 23201, folio 70; his wife's letter found in BN, fonds fr. 23201, folio 162; Henri, on being home only half the time, BN, fonds fr. 23200, folio 91; on the chronology of his various exiles, *ibid.*, 308–309.

40. BN, fonds fr. 23200, folios 89, 91, 96.
41. *Ibid.*, 87, 90, 92; the friend's letter in BN, fonds fr. 23201, folio 173.

CHAPTER 4
CONCEPTION AND BIRTH

1. Pierre Goubert, *Beauvais et le beauvaisis de 1600 à 1730* (Paris, 1960), I, 33. In thinking about the issues raised in this chapter, I have drawn heavily on Bruno Bettelheim, *Symbolic Wounds: Puberty Rites and the Envious Male* (New York, 1962).

2. Louise Bourgeois, *Observations diverses sur la stérilité, perte de fruict, foecondité, accouchements et maladies des femmes et enfants nouveaux naiz* (Rouen, 1626), I, 2ff: François Mauriceau, *Traité des maladies des femmes grosses* . . . (Paris, 1675), 43, 57; Ambroise Paré, *Oeuvres complètes* (Paris, 1840), II, 633–635, 734.

3. See the case of the childless wife in Souvigny, *Mémoires*, II, 330ff. On abortion, Mauriceau, *Traité des maladies*, 186; Hélène Bergues, "Sources et documentation," *La prévention des naissances dans la famille, ses origines dans les temps modernes*, Institut national d'études démographiques, Travaux et documents, No. 35 (Paris, 1960), 149–161. On infanticide, Pierre L'Estoile, *Journal de L'Estoile pour le règne de Henri IV (1589–1610)*, Louis-Raymond Lefèvre, ed. (Paris, 1948), I, 424, 477, 491, 528, etc. On abandoned children, Bergues, "Sources et documentation," 167–170. Reliable figures on the number of *enfants trouvés* appear only in the eighteenth century. Conclusions for an earlier period therefore involve a certain amount of conjecture.

4. On birth rates, Pierre Goubert, "Recent Theories and Research in French Population between 1500 and 1700," Margaret Hilton, trans., *Population in History: Essays in Historical Demography*, D. V. Glass and D. E. C. Eversley, eds. (London, 1965), 468–469. On methods of birth control, *Les Caquets*, 120; Marguerite du Tertre, *Instruction familière et tres-facile . . . touchant toutes les choses principales qu'une sage-femme doit scavoir pour l'exercise de son art . . .* (Paris, 1677), 35; Ariès, *Populations françaises*, 496–497; *La prévention*.

5. Our understanding of the prophylactic effects of lactation is still very tentative. See summary of the problem in Robert Potter et al., "Lactation and Its Effects upon Birth Intervals in Eleven Punjab Villages, India," *Journal of Chronic Diseases*, XVIII (1965), 1125–1140; see also Pierre Dionis, *Traité général des accouchemens, qui instruit ce tout ce qu'il faut faire pour être habile accoucheur* (Liège, 1721), 455.

6. Laurent Joubert, *Première et seconde partie des erreurs populaires et pensées vulgaires touchant la médecine et le régime de santé* (Lyon, 1608), 411; Paré, *Oeuvres*, II, 733; letter to Henri's wife is from Sébastien Bouthillier, BN, Fonds fr. 23201, folio 214; see also folio 197; on the *accouchement*, *Les Caquets*, 9; J. Lévy-Valensi, *La médecine et les médecins français au*

XVIIe siècle (Paris, 1933), 211 (for an engraving of an *accouchement*); Dionis, *Traité général*, 211.

7. Héroard, *Journal*, 1–6; Jacques Guillemeau, *Childbirth or, the Happy Delivery of Women* . . . (London, 1635), 88.

8. Héroard, *Journal*, 3; Louise Bourgeois, "Récit véritable de la naissance de messeigneurs et dames les enfants de France . . . ," in Gustave-Jules Witkowski, *Les accouchements à la cour* (Paris, 1922), 149.

9. Mauriceau, *Traité des maladies*, 239; Bourgeois, *Observations diverses*, I, 48–49; Guillemeau, *Childbirth*, "Introduction"; Witkowski, *Les accouchements*, 189.

10. Simon de Vallambert, *De la Manière de nourrir et gouverner les enfants dès leur naissance* (Poitiers, 1565), "Préface"; Guillemeau, *Childbirth*, "Introduction"; Héroard, *Journal*, 1–6; Bourgeois, "Récit véritable," 150; 164; Witkowski, *Les accouchements*, 188–194; Dionis, *Traité général*, 448–450.

11. Lévy-Valensi, *La médecine*, 378–379; Wickersheimer, *La médecine*, 188–190; Dionis, *Traité général*, 414–415; Bourgeois, "Récit véritable," 133.

12. Mauriceau, *Traité des maladies*, 243; du Tertre, *Instruction familière*, 89–94; Guillemeau, *Childbirth*, 88–94; Bourgeois, *Observations diverses*, I, 193; Paré, *Oeuvres*, II, 674–675; Héroard, *Journal*, 4; Dionis, *Traité général*, 208.

13. For pain remedies, Louise Bourgeois, *Recueil des secrets de Louyse Bourgeois* (Paris, 1635), 130; on position of the infant, chapters in Guillemeau, *Childbirth*; Bourgeois, *Observations diverses*; du Tertre, *Instruction familière*; instruments illustrated in Paré, *Oeuvres*, II, 704–706; recommending *clystères* are Guillemeau, *Childbirth*, 115; Bourgeois, *Recueil*, 125–130; for bleeding, du Tertre, *Instruction familière*, 89; with a dissent from Dionis, *Traité général*, 206.

14. Mauriceau. *Traité des maladies*, 348; Guillemeau, *Childbirth*, 185–188; Bourgeois, *Observations diverses*, I, 189.

15. On baptism, du Tertre, *Instruction familière*, 139–141. On premature births, *ibid.*, 81–83; Mauriceau, *Traité des maladies*, 194–201; Paré, *Oeuvres*, II, 672. Quote is from Guillemeau, *Childbirth*, "Introduction."

16. "Froissard-Broissia," 95; Héroard, *Journal*, 333; Bourgeois, *Observations diverses*, II, 13; *Livre de raison de la famille Dudrot de Capdebosc (1522–1675)*, Philippe Tamizey de Larroque, ed. (Paris, 1891), 24.

CHAPTER 5
PARENTS AND THEIR ALLIES:
KINFOLK, THE GOVERNESS,
AND THE NURSE

1. The most famous example is Bronislaw Malinowski, *Sex and Repression in Savage Society* (New York, 1966). For a summary of Malinowski's debate with psychoanalysis, and in particular with Ernest Jones, see Anne

Parsons, "Is the Oedipus Complex Universal: A South Italian 'Nuclear Complex,'" in *Personalities and Cultures: Readings in Psychological Anthropology*, Robert Hunt, ed., American Museum Sourcebooks in Anthropology (New York, 1967), 352–356.

2. The classic study of primitive kinship, stressing its systematic quality, is Raymond Firth, *We, the Tikopia: A Sociological Study of Kinship in Primitive Polynesia* (Boston, 1966). On France, see Pierre Maranda, "French Kinship: Structure and History" (unpublished dissertation, Harvard University, 1966).

3. On these marriages, Bonneau-Avenant, *La Duchesse d'Aiguillon*, 4; Tallement des Réaux, *Les Historiettes*, Georges Montgrédien, ed. (Paris, 1932), II, 5. On Henri and Du Pont-Courlay, BN, Fonds fr. 23201, folio 122, for example.

4. Castelnau, *Mémoires*, 298; BN, Fonds fr. 23201, folio 168.

5. Tallement, *Historiettes*, II, 122, 124; Castelnau, *Mémoires*, 298.

6. This practice could be carried to the second degree. Thus Etienne Bernard addressed his daughter's mother-in-law as *"ma soeur."* "Un père de famille," 172.

7. BN, Fonds fr. 23201, folio 172.

8. BN, Fonds fr. 23200, folios 86, 94.

9. Henri to Nicole, *ibid.*, 104; Nicole to Henri, BN, Fonds fr. 23201, folio 171.

10. BN, Fonds fr. 23200, folios 95, 100.

11. Alfred Franklin, *La vie privée d'autrefois. Arts et métiers, modes, moeurs, usages des parisiens du XIIe au XVIIIe siècle* (Paris, 1887–1902), XIX, 124–125.

12. Héroard, *Journal*, 4; Bourgeois, *Observations diverses*, II, 163.

13. Héroard, *Journal*, 208, 218, 228, 259, 373 n., 427; on the *gage*, see discussion between Henri IV and Louise Bourgeois in Bourgeois, "Récit véritable," 156.

14. Héroard, *Journal*, 11; on the character of Madame de Montglat, L'Estoile, *Journal . . . Henri IV*, II, 259.

15. Héroard, *Journal*, 7, 52, 275–276; see also L'Estoile, *Journal . . . Henri IV*, II, 48.

16. On Louis' attachment to Héroard, see incident described in Robert Arnauld d'Andilly, *Journal inédit* (Paris, 1857), 224. The doctor was appointed "à la faveur et recommandation de M. de Bouillon." L'Estoile, *Journal . . . Henri IV*, II, 41; for ties to Marie de Medicis, see Héroard, *Journal*, 347.

17. For a description of the profits Madame de Montglat derived from this and other charges, see Emile Magne, *La vie quotidienne au temps de Louis XIII* (Paris, 1942), 144–152.

18. "J'espère qu'un jour je serai à moi." The silver plate was among "the goods at the disposal of the prince" which eventually would belong to Madame de Montglat. Héroard, *Journal*, 373, 427.

19. Wickersheimer, *La médecine*, 519ff; Fagnier, *La femme*, 7; Jean-Jacques Rousseau, *Emile, ou de l'éducation* (Paris, 1906), 29, 31. See also Alice Ryerson, "Medical Advice on Child-Rearing Practices, 1550–1900" (unpublished dissertation, Harvard University, 1960), 60.

20. Dionis, *Traité général*, 457; Mauriceau, *Traité des maladies*, 443–444; Joubert, *Erreurs populaires*, 438.

21. On placement bureaus, Fagnier, *La femme*, 117–118; Franklin, *La vie privée*, XIX, 48–56. For specific instances of families and nurses, "Gay de Nexon," 597, 603, 610, 618–619; "Froissard-Broissia," 42, 44, 95; "Elie de Roffignac," 353, 369; "Feuillets de Garde: les Mairot (1535–1769)," Julien Feuvrier, ed., *Mémoires de la société d'émulation du Jura*, 7ème série, I (1901), 192–193; "Notes extraites de trois livres de raison de 1473 à 1550. Comptes d'une famille de gentilshommes compagnards normands," *Bulletin historique et philologique du comité des travaux historiques et scientifiques* (Paris, 1898), 452; "Journal de N . . . Vielbans, conseiller au présidial de Brive et consul de cette ville (1 août 1571–27 mai 1598)," *Bulletin de la société scientifique, historique et archéologique de la Corrèze*, XV (1893), 155; Louis Guibert, *Livres de raison, registres de famille et journaux individuels limousins et marchois* (Paris, 1888), 204–205.

22. Mauriceau, *Traité des maladies*, 496; Paré, *Oeuvres*, II, 684; Bourgeois, *Observations diverses*, II, 66; Scévole de Sainte-Marthe, *Paedotrophia; or the Art of Nursing and Rearing Children. A Poem in Three Books*, H. W. Tytler, trans. (London, 1797), 78–79 (II, 322ff). The law is discussed in Franklin, *La vie privée*, XIX, 48–54.

23. Joubert, *Erreurs populaires*, 406–409, 431; Paré, *Oeuvres*, II, 686; Bourgeois, *Observations diverses*, I, 163; II, 65; Pierre Coustel, *Les Règles de l'éducation des enfants . . .* (Paris, 1687), 66–67.

24. Joubert, *Erreurs populaires*, 402; Vallambert, *De la Manière*, 4.

25. Cases of the nurse's moving into the child's home in "Gay de Nexon," 603, 610, 618; Guibert, *Livres de raison*. 204; Elie de Roffignac," 353; "Journal de N . . . Vielbans," 155. Examples of the nurse returning to her own home in "Froissard-Broissia," 83; "Gentilshommes compagnards normands," 452; Guibert, *Livres de raison*, 318. Many historians seem to assume that this was the normal arrangement. As an example, Mercier, *L'enfant*, 32. See Montaigne's much-quoted defense of the practice of sending children *en compagne*, in *Essais*, III, xiii, 347–348.

26. Montaigne, *Essais*, II, viii, 26–27; couplet from Sainte-Marthe, *Paedotrophia*, 79 (II, 330–331).

27. Ariès, *Centuries*, 314.

28. Vallambert, *De la Manière*, 4.

29. Marguerite de Valois, *Mémoires*, Paul Bonnefon, ed. (Paris, 1920), 136. Other mothers nursing in "Froissard-Broissia," 34; Bougaud, *Sainte Chantal*, 121; Madame de La Guette, *Mémoires*, M. Moreau, ed. (Paris, 1856), 7–8. See also the cases cited in Chapter 6, note 4. On Suzanne, BN, Fonds fr. 23201, folio 200; also BN, Fonds fr. 23200, folio 185.

30. Quote from Vallambert, *De la Manière*, 4. On the role of the husband in hiring a nurse, Paré, *Oeuvres*, II, 684; Mauriceau, *Traité des maladies*, 496; Joubert, *Erreurs populaires*, 433; Rousseau, *Emile*, 12; Guillemeau, *The Nursing of Children . . .* (London, 1635), 1.

31. Vallambert, *De la Manière*, 28; Bourgeois, *Observations diverses*, I, 165; Sainte-Marthe, *Paedotrophia*, 82–83 (II, 36off); Paré, *Oeuvres*, II, 686. My argument here would fall to the ground if it could be shown that nurses were unmarried mothers—a not inconceivable conjecture. Doctors

always insisted that nurses be respectable, but we have had ample occasion to see how often their strictures went unheeded.

32. Dionis, *Traité général*, 464–465. The court was not always so strict about this rule. The husband of Louis XIII's nurse often appears in Héroard's *Journal*.

CHAPTER 6

THE FIRST STAGE:

FEEDING AND SWADDLING

1. Ryerson, "Medical Advice," 61; this interesting thesis helpfully discusses many of the issues raised in the present chapter.

2. Héroard, *Journal*, 7–9, 14–15, 18.

3. Guillemeau, *Nursing*, 45; Paré, *Oeuvres*, II, 678; Vallambert, *De la Manière*, 52; see also Bourgeois, *Observations diverses*, I, 156; Arnold van Gennep, *Manuel de folklore français contemporain* (Paris, 1943), I, i, 148.

4. On the royal children, Franklin, *La vie privée*, XIX, 95, 100. For individual cases, "Froissard-Broissia," 41, 42, 44, 46, 82, 95; "les Mairot," 192–193; "Journal de N . . . Vielbans," 153–155; "Gay de Nexon," 603.

5. Vallambert, *De la Manière*, 84–86, 135; Guillemeau, *Nursing*, 20; Sainte-Marthe, *Paedotrophia*, 88 (II, 449ff); Mauriceau, *Traité des maladies*, 445; Joubert, *Erreurs populaires*, 538–546.

6. Vallambert has the most complete discussion of *bouillie*, in *De la Manière*, 141–145; also, Dionis, *Traité général*, 408; Mauriceau, *Traité des maladies*, 446; see the engraving in Berthe Minne, "L'enfant," in *La vie populaire en France du moyen âge à nos jours* (Geneva, 1966), IV, 27.

7. Vallambert, *De la Manière*, 143; du Tertre, *Instruction familière*, 135; Paré, *Oeuvres*, II, 692; Mauriceau, *Traité des maladies*, 445.

8. Vallambert, *De la Manière*, 135; Héroard, *Journal*, 8.

9. On the use of farm animals to feed infants, Wickersheimer, *La médecine*, 520. On mortality rates, Goubert, *Beauvais*, I, 39–40; Roger Mols, *Les résultats*, vol. 2 of *Introduction à la démographie historique des villes d'Europe du XIVe au XVIIIe siècle* (Louvain, 1955), 295–315.

10. First stage of life discussed in Erikson, *Childhood*, 72–76, 247–251; *Identity*, 55–65; *Insight*, 115–117; Citations from *Identity*, 57; *Childhood*, 75, 77.

11. Erikson, *Identity*, 57.

12. *Ibid.*, 61.

13. *Ibid.*, 61–62.

14. Paré, *Oeuvres*, II, 664; Guillemeau, *Nursing*, 68; du Tertre, *Instruction familière*, 73; Sainte-Marthe, *Paedotrophia*, 92 (II, 509ff); Vallambert, *Da la Manière*, 84–86.

15. Du Tertre, *Instruction familière*, 25; Paré, *Oeuvres*, II, 688; Guillemeau, *Nursing*, "Preface"; Joubert, *Erreurs populaires*, 453; Sainte-

Marthe, *Paedotrophia*, 13 (I, 167ff). For dissenting views, Mauriceau, *Traité des maladies*, 423; Pasquier, *Oeuvres*, 582–583.

16. Bourgeois, *Observations diverses*, I, 222.

17. Guillemeau has the most thorough discussion of teething, in *Nursing*, 57–59; also, Paré, *Oeuvres*, II, 797–799; Dionis, *Traité général*, 394.

18. For purposes of comparison, see John Whiting and Irvin Child, *Child Training and Personality: A Cross-Cultural Study* (New Haven, 1964); *Six Cultures: Studies of Child Rearing*, Beatrice Whiting, ed. (New York, 1963).

19. Guillemeau, *Nursing*, 57; Héroard, *Journal*, 22–23; Dionis, *Traité général*, 396–397.

20. Montaigne, *Essais*, II, viii, 13; Fleury quoted in Ariès, *Centuries*, 131. For a thoughtful seventeenth-century observation of children playing, see La Bruyère, *Les caractères*, Robert Garadon, ed. (Paris, 1962), 316.

21. "... et presque jusques aux petis enfans." Jean Burel, *Mémoires de Jean Burel, bourgeois de Puy*, Augustin Chassaing, ed. (Le Puy-en-Velay, 1875), 241.

22. Rousseau, *Emile*, 11; Buffon, *Histoire naturelle de l'homme*, vol. 13 in *Oeuvres complètes de Buffon*, M. Lamouroux (Paris, 1824), 35.

23. Mauriceau, *Traité des maladies*, 441. Any consideration of the importance of this topic must begin with the controversy over Geoffrey Gorer's "swaddling hypothesis." See Gorer and John Rickman, *The People of Great Russia: A Psychological Study* (New York, 1962); also Margaret Mead, "The Swaddling Hypothesis: Its Reception," *American Anthropologist*, LVI (1954), 395–409; Erikson, *Childhood*, 388–392.

24. For the most detailed account of swaddling procedures, see Mauriceau, *Traité des maladies*, 441–442; Vallambert, *De la Manière*, 57, 113, 129; Guillemeau, *Nursing*, 22. See engravings in Ariès, *L'enfant*, 133; Witkowski, *Les accouchements*, 79.

25. Héroard, *Journal*, 17–30.

26. *Ibid.*, 32, 34, 44, 53; see Rousseau's comments on parental efforts to encourage children to walk, in *Emile*, 55.

27. Phyllis Greenacre, "Infant Reactions to Restraint: Problems in the Fate of Infantile Aggression," and David Levy, "On the Problem of Movement Restraint," both in *American Journal of Orthopsychiatry*, XIV (1944), 204–218, 644–671; Wayne Dennis, "Infant Reaction to Restraint: An Evaluation of Watson's Theory," *Transactions of the New York Academy of Science*, Series two, II (1948), 202–218; Orlansky, "Infant Care and Personality," 21–27.

28. Sainte-Marthe, *Paedotrophia*, 67 (11, 177ff); Héroard, *Journal*, 310; Vallambert, *De la Manière*, 113.

29. Mauriceau, *Traité des maladies*, 442; Rousseau, *Emile*, 11. See Ryerson on this subject, "Medical Advice," 105.

30. Mauriceau, *Traité des maladies*, 442.

31. Dionis, *Traité général*, 371; Sainte-Marthe, *Paedotrophia*, 67 n; van Gennep, *Folklore français*, I, i, 122.

32. Buffon, *L'homme*, 30–31.

33. On molding the child's skull, Vallambert, *De la Manière*, 38; Guillemeau, *Nursing*, 11; Bourgeois, *Observations diverses*, I, 157; Rousseau, *Emile*, 9. On the cradle, Rousseau, *Emile*, 33; also the translator's com-

ment in Sainte-Marthe, *Paedotrophia*, 54 n; Ryerson, "Medical Advice," 80. On the corsets, Wickersheimer, *La médecine*, 301–302; Buffon, *L'homme*, 31–32; Snyders, *La pédagogie*, 271.

CHAPTER 7
THE SECOND STAGE:
BREAKING IN THE CHILD

1. Héroard, *Journal*, 31–34, 55, 95ff.
2. On weaning, Vallambert, *De la Manière*, 133; Sainte-Marthe, *Paedotrophia*, 98; Paré, *Oeuvres*, II, 694; Joubert, *Erreurs populaires*, 562. For specific cases, "Froissard-Broissia," 34; "les Mairot," 192; "Gay de Nexon," 603. For references to the apparently much earlier weaning of the eighteenth century, Sainte-Marthe, *Paedotrophia*, 98 n; Rousseau, *Emile*, 46.
3. Charron, *De la Sagesse*, III, 81; Duval, *Vie admirable*, 3; Bougaud, *Sainte Chantal*, 332. On the schools, Ariès, *Centuries*, 257–261. For fighting among mothers, "Journal de N . . . Vielbans," 161; "Gay de Nexon," 613–614; see also G. d'Avenel, *La noblesse française sous Richelieu* (Paris, 1901), 74.
4. Henri IV, *Recueil des lettres missives de Henri IV*, Berger de Xivrey, ed. (Paris, 1843), VII, 385.
5. Héroard, *Journal*, 55, 62, 85, 93, 132–133, 299. On obstinacy and lying, Montaigne, *Essais*, I, ix, 61; Charron, *De la Sagesse*, III, 112–113.
6. Erikson, *Childhood*, 82. Discussion of this stage drawn from *Childhood*, 80–85; *Identity*, 65–74; *Insight*, 118–120.
7. Erikson, *Childhood*, 252.
8. *Ibid.*, 85.
9. Héroard, *Journal*, 93. This and the following incidents all occurred during Louis' third year.
10. *Ibid.*, 67, 68, 73, 85, 93.
11. On the governess as disciplinarian, *ibid.*, 85, for example. On Henri IV as a father, Nancy Roelker. *Queen of Navarre: Jeanne d'Albret, 1528–1572* (Cambridge, Mass., 1968), 397–398.
12. Guillemeau, *Childbirth*, "Introduction"; La Bruyère, *Les caractères*, 316.
13. Héroard, *Journal*, 68, 70; Duval, *Vie admirable*, 48; Fénelon, *De l'Education*, 19; also, Jacqueline Pascal, "Règlement pour les enfants de Port-Royale," in Victor Cousin, *Jacqueline Pascal. Premières études sur les femmes illustres et la société du XVIIe siècle* (Paris, 1856), 371.
14. Duval, *Vie admirable*, 40–42; Bougaud, *Sainte Chantal*, 330; also Fénelon, *De l'Education*, 19; Coustel, *Les Règles*, 66–67; Snyders, *La pédagogie*, 208.
15. Erikson, *Childhood*, 253–254.
16. Quoted in Franklin, *La vie privée*, VII, 45–49, 57, 138–143.

17. Mauriceau, *Traité des maladies,* 448; Vallambert, *De la Manière,* 103, 371; Guillemeau, *Nursing,* 80, 103; Joubert, *Erreurs populaires,* 550.

18. Héroard, *Journal,* 34, 204. Ariès, *Centuries,* 105.

19. Vallambert, *De la Manière,* 66–67; Sainte-Marthe, *Paedotrophia,* 68 (II, 187ff); Paré, *Oeuvres,* II, 682–683; Mauriceau, *Traité des maladies,* 439; Guillemeau, *Childbirth,* "Introduction."

20. Guillemeau, *Nursing,* 67, 76; Vallambert, *De la Manière,* 72, 204; Dionis, *Traité général,* 388; Sainte-Marthe *Paedotrophia,* 139–140 (III, 308ff).

21. Guillemeau, *Nursing,* 77; Joubert, *Erreurs populaires,* 473–474.

22. On purges, Paré, *Oeuvres,* II, 683; Mauriceau, *Traité des maladies,* 443; Vallambert, *De la Manière,* 72. On urine analysis, Lévy-Valensi, *La médecine,* 81–86.

23. For an interesting seventeenth-century discussion in this vein, see the remarks on the doctor Bourdelot and his treatment of the children of the Condé family, in Lévy-Valensi, *La médecine,* 599–600.

24. See the list of "remedies" in "Livre de raison et registre de famille des sieurs Pierre, autre Pierre et Michel Terrade, notaires à Chaumeil (1548–1685)," A. Leroux, ed., *Bulletin de la société scientifique, historique et archéologique de la Corrèze,* XIV (1892), 495. On the French reputation, Pilon, *La vie de famille,* 54.

25. L'Estoile, *Journal . . . Henri IV,* I, 169; Héroard, *Journal,* 77–78.

26. Bodin, *La République,* 22–23.

27. Héroard, *Journal,* 94–96.

28. *Ibid.,* 108, 123, 147.

29. *Ibid.,* 32, 42, 53.

30. *Ibid.,* 106–107.

31. *Ibid.,* 107.

32. Bodin, *La République,* 1, 8, 21.

33. Laslett, *World,* 187; Snyders, *La pédagogie,* 262–265. Declaration in Isambert, *Recueil général,* XVI, 520; Mousnier suggests that the legist who drafted this declaration was drawing on Bodin's text, in *Etat et société,* 155.

34. On parental power over children, Petot, "La famille," 13; du Plessis de Grenadan, *L'autorité paternelle,* 364; Bodin, *La République,* 24–25; Charron, *De la Sagesse,* I, 368. Coming-of-age ceremony cited in de Ribbe, *Les familles,* I, 245–246; Funck-Brentano, *L'ancien régime,* 28.

35. Pasquier cited in Funck-Brentano, *L'ancien régime,* 29, for example; original in Pasquier, *Oeuvres,* 420; other letters on children, *ibid.,* 171, 291–292, 417–418, 673–674.

36. Ariès, *Centuries,* 26; *L'enfant,* 15; see also Laslett, *World,* 2.

37. Erikson, *Identity,* 73.

38. Madame de Sévigné, *Lettres,* Gérard-Gailly, ed. (Paris, 1953), I, 366. See the discussion of friendship and equality in Antoine Courtin, *Nouveau traité de la civilité qui se pratique en France parmi les honnêtes gens* (Paris, 1682), 218.

39. On the differences between family relations and true friendship, Montaigne, *Essais,* I, xxviii, 226–228; see Snyders' interesting analysis of this question, in *La pédagogie,* 266.

40. Héroard, *Journal,* 260; Ariès, *Centuries,* 371–373; Montaigne, *Essais,* I, xxviii, 227; Corneille, *Rodogune,* I, iii.

41. Héroard, *Journal*, 105, 119. Fénelon deplored the tendency of parents to rely on vulgar stratagems—stories of devils and monsters—in their disciplining of children. *De l'Education*, 17–18.

42. Héroard, *Journal*, I, 26;, 272; II, 6, 13, 22, 57, 129–130.

43. Marcuse, *Eros*, 82–83.

CHAPTER 8

THE THIRD STAGE:
INFANTILE SEXUALITY

1. For this stage, Erikson, *Childhood*, 85–92, 255–258; *Identity*, 74–82; *Insight*, 120–122. On many of the issues raised in this chapter, see also Sigmund Freud, *The Sexual Enlightenment of Children*, Philip Rieff, ed. (New York, 1968).

2. Héroard, *Journal*, 5, 31, 35, 36, 42, 45.

3. *Ibid.*, 34, 50, 81, 317.

4. *Ibid.*, 117, 120, 123, 147, 197.

5. Ariès, *Centuries*, 103.

6. *Ibid.*, 105.

7. *Ibid.*, 103; Stone, *Crisis*, 664–668; many anecdotes in L'Estoile, *Journal . . . Henri III.*

8. Ariès, *Centuries*, 107–108; Fagnier, *La femme*, 178–179.

9. De Sales cited in Bougaud, *Sainte Chantal*, 261; Jean-Baptiste de la Salle, *Les règles de la bienséance et de la civilité chrétienne* (Rouen, 1819), 24–25. Moralists were not alone in demanding modesty from children. Ordinary parents joined in. See Souvigny, *Mémoires*, III, 87.

10. Héroard, *Journal*, 69, 117, 123, 152, 153, 195, 197, 199, 217.

11. *Ibid.*, 45, 53, 56, 69.

12. *Ibid.*, 76.

13. *Ibid.*, 117. For misjudgments of Héroard, Ariès, *Centuries*, 102–103; Franklin, *La vie privée*, XIX, 202.

14. Héroard, *Journal*, 194, 234, 250, 267.

15. He may, however, have been a Protestant; L'Estoile, *Journal . . . Henri IV*, II, 41–42.

16. Héroard, *Journal*, 315–316.

17. *Ibid.*, 164–165, 232, 251, 355–356.

18. *Ibid.*, 20, 29, 181, 327.

19. *Ibid.*, 253.

20. *Ibid.*, 193.

21. For examples of women-centered households, Maillefer, *Mémoires*, 9; Campion, *Mémoires*, 4–5; Du Val, *La Vie admirable*, 13; du Laurens, "Généalogie," 72–82. For father-centered cases, Souvigny, *Mémoires*, II, 92, 105–106; Arnauld d'Andilly, *Mémoires*, I, 27; Nicolas de Brichanteau, *Mémoires du Marquis de Beauvais-Nangis . . .*, Louis Jean Nicolas Monmerque and A. H. Taillandier, eds. (Paris, 1862), 154, 199.

22. Héroard, *Journal*, 108, 135–136, 150–151.

CHAPTER 9
OUT OF THE HANDS OF WOMEN

1. See discussion in Ariès, *Centuries,* 18–25.
2. Héroard, *Journal,* 203, 206, 252, 289, 343–344. See also Ariès, *Centuries,* 51.
3. Ariès, *Centuries,* 57.
4. Héroard, *Journal,* 114, 151, 253, 278, 318, 360.
5. Bettelheim is talking about puberty rites, but it seems to me that the principle he is formulating can also apply to earlier stages of childhood development. *Symbolic Wounds,* 113.
6. A favorite source for maxims and homilies was Pibrac's *Quatrains,* often used at court; Héroard, *Journal,* 173, 189, 205, etc.; on Louis' first confession, *ibid.,* 223.
7. *Ibid.,* 206, 386, 401.
8. *Ibid.,* 229, 283, 321, 346, 351, 391, 396.
9. *Ibid.,* 379, 386, 406–407.
10. Medical authorities agreed in locating puberty between the ages of twelve and sixteen: Paré, *Oeuvres,* II, 763, 770, 779; Mauriceau, *Traité des maladies,* 48; du Tertre, *Instruction familière,* 26; Buffon, *L'homme,* 75.
11. Quote from *Le Grand Proprietaire de toutes choses,* cited in Ariès, *Centuries,* 21. See also Jean Piaget, *The Language and Thought of the Child,* Marjorie and Ruth Gabain, trans. (London, 1959), 70–75, 124–126. For Ariès' discussion of age and school, *Centuries,* 189–240.
12. Erikson, *Childhood,* 259. On the difficulties of providing for dependent children, see Laslett, *World,* 105.
13. Campion, *Mémoires,* 246, 261–263.
14. Montaigne, *Essais,* II, viii, 13; Charron, *De la Sagesse,* III, 76; Bérulle cited in Snyders, *La pédagogie,* 194. See also Coustel, *Les Règles,* 173.
15. Cited in Ariès, *Centuries,* 132.

BIBLIOGRAPHY

For secondary works on childhood and family life in the old regime, consult the notes in the text.

For a catalogue of seventeenth-century materials on the subject, see Georges Snyders, *La pédagogie en France aux XVIIe et XVIIIe siècles* (Paris, 1965). Robert Mandrou provides an inventory of some of the less well-known published works of the period, especially the *livres de raison*, in *Introduction à la France moderne, 1500–1640. Essai de psychologie historique* (Paris, 1961). These bibliographies served as the foundations for the present work. The following list includes those sources which I have found most helpful in the course of the research.

Arnauld d'Andilly, Robert (1589–1674). *Mémoires.* Hamburg, 1734.

Bodin, Jean (1530–1596). *Les Six Livres de la République.* Paris, 1576.

Bourgeois, Louise (1563–1636). *Observations diverses sur la stérilité, perte de fruict, foecondité, accouchements et maladies des femmes et enfants nouveaux naiz. . . .* Rouen, 1626.

———. "Récit véritable de la naissance de messeigneurs et dames les enfans de France . . . ," In Gustave-Jules Witkowski. *Les accouchements à la cour.* Paris, 1922, 131–168. First edition, 1625.

———. *Recueil des secrets de Louyse Bourgeois. . . .* Paris, 1635.

Bougaud, Louis-Emile. *Histoire de sainte Chantal et des origines de la Visitation.* 2 vols. Paris, 1867. A nineteenth-century biography, relying heavily on original sources. My citations are all from volume one. Chantal's dates are 1572–1641.

Buffon (1707–1788). *Histoire naturelle de l'homme.* XIII–XV in *Oeuvres complètes de Buffon avec les descriptions anatomiques de Daubenton, son collaborateur.* M. Lamouroux, ed. 40 vols. Paris, 1824. First edition, 1749–1767. See "De l'enfance," in XIII, 1–119.

Campion, Henri de (1613–1663). *Mémoires.* M. C. Moreau, ed. Paris, 1857. First edition, 1807.

Les Caquets de l'accouchée. Paris, nineteenth century. First edition, 1622.

Charron, Pierre (1541–1603). *De la Sagesse.* 3 vols. VII–IX in *Collection de moralistes français. . . .* Amaury Duval, ed. Paris, 1820. First edition, 1601.

Cherel, Albert (ed.). *La famille française. Pages choisies de nos bons écrivains de 845 à 1924. Le moyen âge et le XVIe siècle.* Paris, 1924.

Coustel, Pierre (1624–1704). *Les Règles de l'éducation des enfants. . . .* 2 vols. Paris, 1687.

Dionis, Pierre (1658–1718). *Traité général des accouchemens, qui instruit ce tout ce qu'il faut faire pour être habile accoucheur.* Liège, 1721. First edition, 1718.

Du Laurens, Jeanne (1563–1635). "Généalogie de messieurs du Laurens . . . ," in Charles de Ribbe, *Une famille de XVIe siècle.* Tours, 1879, 35–99. First edition, 1867.

Du Tertre, Marguerite. *Instruction familière et très-facile, faite par questions et réponses, touchant toutes les choses principales qu'une sage-femme doit scavoir pour l'exercise de son art.* . . . Paris, 1677.

Du Val, André. *La Vie admirable de la bienheureuse soeur Marie de l'Incarnation.* . . . Paris, 1893. First edition, 1622. Marie's dates are 1566–1618.

Fénelon (1651–1715). *De l'Education des filles.* Paris, 1821. First edition, 1687.

"Feuillets de garde: les Mairot (1535–1769)." Julien Feuvrier, ed. *Mémoires de la société d'émulation du Jura.* 7ème série, I (1901), 161–208.

Grenaille, François de (1616–1680). *L'Honneste mariage.* Paris, 1640.

Guibert, Louis (ed.). *Livres de raison, registres de famille et journaux individuels limousins et marchois.* Paris, 1888.

Guillemeau, Jacques (1550–1613). *Child-Birth or, the Happy Delivery of Women. Wherein is Set Downe the Government of Women in the Time of their Breeding Children: of their Travaile, both Naturall and Contrary to Nature: and of their Lying in.* . . . London, 1635. Translated from *De l'Heureux accouchemen.* . . . Paris, 1609.

———. *The Nursing of Children, Wherein is Set Downe the Ordering and Government of them from their Birth.* . . . London, 1635. Translated from *De la Nourriture et gouvernement des enfants.* . . . Paris, 1609. In citations from these translations, I have not tampered with the old spellings.

Héroard, Jean (1551–1628). *Journal de Jean Héroard sur l'enfance et la jeunesse de Louis XIII (1601–1628).* Eud. Soulié et Ed. de Barthélemy, eds. 2 vols. Paris, 1868.

Isambert et al. (eds.). *Recueil général des anciennes lois françaises depuis l'an 420 jusqu'à la révolution de 1789.* 29 vols. Paris, 1821–1833. See index under "*mariage.*"

Joubert, Laurent (1529–1582). *Première et seconde partie des erreurs populaires et pensées vulgaires touchant la médecine et le régime de santé.* Lyon, 1608. First edition, 1578.

"Journal de N . . . Vielbans, conseiller au présidial de Brive et consul de cette ville (1 août 1571–27 mai 1598)," Louis Guibert, ed. *Bulletin de la société scientifique, historique et archéologique de la Corrèze.* XV (1893), 92–161.

"Journal domestique d'Elie de Roffignac (1588–1589)," Louis Guibert, ed. *Bulletin de la société scientifique, historique et archéologique de la Corrèze.* XV (1893), 337–391.

"Journal domestique de Martial de Gay de Nexon, lieutenant-général à Limoges (29 janvier 1591–4 mars 1603)," Louis Guibert, ed. *Bulletin de la société scientifique, historique et archéologique de la Corrèze.* XV (1893), 584–621.

La Bruyère, Jean de (1645–1696). *Les caractères ou les moeurs de ce siècle.* Robert Garadon, ed. Paris, 1962. First edition, 1688.

Bibliography

La Guette, Catherine Meurdrac, Madame de (1613–1680). *Mémoires.* M. Moreau, ed. Paris, 1856. First edition. 1681.
La Salle, Jean-Baptiste de (1651–1715). *Les Règles de la bienséance et de la civilité chrétienne.* Rouen, 1819. First edition, 1736.
L'Estoile, Pierre (1546–1611). *Journal de L'Estoile pour le règne de Henri III (1574–1589).* Louis-Raymond Lefèvre, ed. Paris, 1943. First edition, 1621.
———. *Journal de L'Estoile pour le règne de Henri IV (1589–1610).* Louis-Raymond Lefèvre and André Martin, eds. 3 vols. Paris, 1948–1960. First edition, 1732.
Livre de raison de la famille Dudrot de Capdebosc (1522–1675). Philippe Tamizey de Larroque, ed. Paris, 1891.
"Livre de raison de la famille Froissard-Broissia (1532–1701)," *Mémoires de la société d'émulation du Jura.* 4ème série, II (1886), 27–105.
"Livre de raison de noble Honoré du Tiel (1541–1586)," *Annales des Basses-Alpes.* VI (1893), 29–41, 76–88, 159–172.
"Livre de raison et registre de famille des sieurs Pierre, autre Pierre et Michel Terrade, notaires à Chaumeil (1548–1685)," *Bulletin de la société scientifique, historique et archéologique de la Corrèze,* XIV (1892), 488–500.
"Livre-Journal de Pierre de Bessot (1609–1652)." Philippe Tamizey de Larroque et al., eds. *Bulletin de la société historique et archéologique du Périgord.* XX (1893), 70–77, 148–195, 229–262.
Maillefer, Jean. *Mémoires de Jean Maillefer, marchand bourgeois de Reims (1611–1684)....* Henri Jadart, ed. Paris, 1890.
Mauriceau, François (1637–1709). *Traité des maladies des femmes grosses, et de celles qui sont nouvellement accouchées. . . .* Paris, 1675. First edition, 1668.
Montaigne, Michel de (1533–1592). *Essais,* Pierre Michel, ed. 3 vols. Paris, 1965. First edition, 1580.
"Notes extraites de trois livres de raison de 1473 à 1550. Comptes d'une famille de gentilshommes compagnards normands," *Bulletin historique et philologique de comité des travaux historiques et scientifiques.* (1898), 447–499.
Paré, Ambroise (1509–1590). *Oeuvres complètes.* Joseph-François Malgaigne, ed. 3 vols. Paris, 1840. First edition, 1579. See book XVIII: "De la génération de l'homme," II, 633–799.
Pascal, Jacqueline (1625–1661). "Règlement pour les enfants de Port Royale," in Victor Cousin, *Jacqueline Pascal. Premières études sur les femmes illustres et la société du XVIIe siècle.* Paris, 1856, 358–425.
Pasquier, Estienne (1529–1615). *Les Oeuvres d'Estienne Pasquier, contenant . . . ses lettres; ses oeuvres meslées et les lettres de Nicolas Pasquier, fils d'Estienne.* 2 vols. Amsterdam, 1723. First edition, 1583. The letters I consulted are in II.
"Un père de famille sous Henri IV. Lettres domestiques d'Etienne Bernard, 1598–1609." Henri Drouot, ed. *Annales de Bourgogne.* XXIV (1952), 161–175.
Rousseau, Jean-Jacques (1712–1778). *Emile, ou de l'éducation.* Paris, 1906. First edition, 1762.
Sainte-Marthe, Scévole de (1536–1623). *Paedotrophia; or the Art of Nurs-*

ing and Rearing Children. A Poem in Three Books. H. W. Tyler, trans. London, 1797. First edition (in Latin), 1584.

Sévigné, Madame de (1626–1696). *Lettres.* Gérard-Gailly, ed. 3 vols. Paris, 1953.

Souvigny, Jean de Gangnières (1597–1673). *Mémoires du Comte de Souvigny, lieutenant-général des armées du roi.* Le Baron Ludovic de Contenson, ed. Paris, 1906–1909.

Vallambert, Simon de. *De la Manière de nourrir et gouverner les enfants dès leur naissance.* Poitiers, 1565.

INDEX

Index